WINNING NOW, WINNING LATER

WINNING NOW, WINNING LATER

How Companies Can Succeed in the Short Term
While Investing for the Long Term

DAVID M. COTE

HarperCollins
Leadership

An Imprint of HarperCollins

Published by HarperCollins Leadership, an imprint of HarperCollins Focus LLC.

Any internet addresses, phone numbers, or company or product information printed in this book are offered as a resource and are not intended in any way to be or to imply an endorsement by HarperCollins Leadership, nor does HarperCollins Leadership vouch for the existence, content, or services of these sites, phone numbers, companies, or products beyond the life of this book.

ISBN 978-1-5995-1022-4 (eBook)
ISBN 978-1-5995-1021-7 (HC)

Library of Congress Control Number: 2020935961

Printed in the United States of America
20 21 22 23 24   LSC   10 9 8 7 6 5 4 3 2 1

To my big, raucous family with a variety of strong personalities, starting with my Momma (86 and going strong) and my Dad (deceased long ago). To my two sons, Ryan and John; their wives, Heather and Kristel; and eight grandkids— Hannah "Banana," Xavier "X Man," Samantha, Matthew, Robert "Skeeter," Adeline "Addie-Lion," Jacob, and Kaia "Kaia-Gator"—who make generation continuance so much fun. To my son, Ryan, in particular, for so scaring me with his pending birth that it provided the kick in the ass I needed to start a career. To my loving and wonderful wife, Maureen, who encouraged me for years to write a book and knows how to do everything. That's not a joke.

Contents

Introduction

If you run a team or an organization of any size, you face a seemingly intractable dilemma each day: Should you focus on making the numbers, often at the expense of the company's future health, or should you prioritize longer-term strategies, your quarterly or annual performance be damned?

Most corporate managers and executives choose the first option, running businesses quarter-to-quarter to the detriment of long-term performance. Leaders might value broader objectives like sustainability, competitiveness, and growth, and wax eloquent about their commitment to these long-term goals, but when called upon to allocate scarce resources, they focus on the current year's plan and do what it takes to meet their numbers. In their view, they have no choice: their job depends on pleasing bosses and shareholders *today*, not tomorrow.

The notion that there is no way to pursue long- and short-term goals at the same time, and therefore leaders have no choice but to embrace short-termism, is one of the most pernicious beliefs circulating in business today. A McKinsey study found that firms that followed long-term strategies amassed $7 billion more in market capitalization between 2001 and 2014, and generated 47 percent more revenue growth and 36 percent more earnings growth, on average, than companies that took a shorter-term approach.[1] Nevertheless, as one 2014 study found, two-thirds of executives and directors reported that "pressure for short-term results had increased over the previous five years."[2] Short-termism has become so rampant that influential leaders are speaking out against it, with some advocating that we relax the reporting requirements on public firms so that leaders don't feel such intense and constant pressure to make their numbers.

We can't regulate our way to long-termism—the problem is too complex and deeply entrenched. Instead, we need a comprehensive mind-set shift on the part of leaders and managers at every level. Somehow, we've convinced ourselves that we can only invest in the future if we let short-term performance tank. But that's not true. Strong short- and long-term performance only *seem* mutually exclusive. As a leader, you can and must pursue both at the same time. Unless you do, you and your team or organization will never reach your full potential.

MY BATTLE WITH SHORT-TERMISM

Early in my career, when I worked in various finance and general management positions at General Electric, my colleagues and I were hell-bent on hitting our numbers in the current quarter and year. We'd think about next year, but only when we had to. This obsessive focus on today at the expense of tomorrow didn't make a lot of sense to me. Our business would perform well for most of a given year, and we'd hire a thousand people to help us grow. Then in October and November, we'd create our plans for the coming year, only to realize we'd never make our numbers unless we laid off a thousand people. So we'd do that, disrupting our business and the lives of all those people. *Why*, I wondered, *hadn't we thought ahead and only hired, say, two hundred people instead of a thousand?* And yet, like most leaders, we didn't think we had a choice. We were working hard and doing the best we could, and we didn't see another way.

My opportunity to change as a leader began in February 2002, when I became CEO of the industrial conglomerate Honeywell, a $22 billion company with interests in aerospace, control systems, automotive, and chemicals. The company was underperforming, having struggled in recent years thanks to a botched merger with AlliedSignal in 1999, a couple of CEO transitions, and failed attempts to sell the company to United Technologies Corporation and then to General Electric. But from what recruiters, executives, and others had told me, and from what I could tell based on my own analysis, the company had some good businesses that had simply been poorly managed. Once someone stepped in, stabilized the organization, and focused on the future, Honeywell's performance would bounce right back.

During my first months on the job, as I began to probe into the company and its operations, I discovered the company didn't have good fundamentals—it was all a façade. Honeywell was a train wreck and on the verge of failure. We had billions in unresolved environmental and asbestos liabilities, a woefully underfunded pension, an entrenched "make the quarter" mindset, an organization beset by cultural warfare, depleted leadership ranks, no process initiatives in place to make us more efficient, no globalization initiatives to help us grow in the rest of the world, significant underinvestment in new products and services, and the list went on and on.

But it got worse. Strangely, the board and the outgoing CEO refused me any access to our financials until July 2002, when I became chairman. When I did gain access, I was hit almost immediately with a bombshell: our finance team informed me that we'd have to significantly reduce our earnings commitment for the year. We wound up lowering our second-half earnings projections twice by a cumulative 26 percent within a period of weeks, infuriating analysts and investors who already lacked confidence in me. Investors knew I hadn't been a finalist in the competition to succeed Jack Welch as CEO at GE, and I hadn't been the first choice to run Honeywell. By reducing our earnings estimates so early in my tenure, and by having to do so not once but twice, I reinforced the investor community's worst fears that I was a lightweight and didn't have it in me to run a big company like Honeywell.

Meanwhile, my own worst fears about Honeywell materialized as I probed why we had missed our numbers. It turned out that our accounting was unhealthy at best. No, we weren't doing anything illegal—everything fell within the parameters of permitted accounting practices—but the entire organization was gaming the system to try to make their numbers each quarter (during the previous decade, for every dollar in earnings, we only generated sixty-nine cents in cash, a fact that reflected aggressive book-keeping). As a result, our leaders lacked a clear and honest picture of their businesses. Accounting is your primary information system for making decisions, so if that information is bad, your decisions will be bad too. Our leaders were going through the motions, only pretending to run their businesses strategically or even competently. It was all a big mess—short-termism run horribly amuck.

PUTTING HONEYWELL ON A NEW PATH

I was flabbergasted, pissed, disgusted, and then some. But I wasn't defeated. One day, in the heat of our financial mess, I turned on CNBC and heard the commentators lambasting me, opining that I wasn't equipped to run Honeywell. I listened to them, shrugged my shoulders, and returned to what I had been doing. Someone in the room later told me how surprised they were that I didn't throw a hard object at the screen. But I wasn't angry. Rather, I was thinking to myself, *I'm going to show them. I'm going to figure out these problems and turn this company around.*

I was making a habit then of carving out time to sit by myself, put aside the daily pressures of my job, and just *think* about the company. During one of these "blue book" sessions, as I called them (on account of the blue-covered notebook I used), I challenged myself to identify steps I needed to take to put Honeywell on a better path. As I sat there pondering, it came to me that I would have to find a way to invest in new products, services, process improvement, geographical expansion, and so on. But given investors' low opinion of me, I also had to deliver something for them in the short term—otherwise, I wouldn't survive. I couldn't push investment off to some unspecified future date, and I also couldn't invest to such an extent that we once again fell short of shareholder expectations. We would have to do both at the same time—win today *and* set ourselves up to win tomorrow.

Further, I realized we *could* do both at the same time. Short- and long-term goals were more tightly intertwined than they appeared. By taking the right actions to improve operations now, we could position ourselves to improve performance later, while the reverse would also hold true: short-term results would validate that we were on the right long-term path. Beyond that, I theorized we would be able to win today and tomorrow if we followed the Three Principles of Short- and long-term Performance that I'd developed.

Three Principles of Short- and Long-Term Performance

1. Scrub accounting and business practices down to what is real.
2. Invest in the future, but not excessively.
3. Grow while keeping fixed costs constant.

First, we would address all of our unhealthy accounting and business practices, scrubbing the business down to what was real. Second, we would courageously sacrifice some earnings today to invest in our future, but not too many—we would still take care to do well enough in the short term. Third, and relatedly, we would become far more disciplined about our operations, challenging ourselves to run our businesses more efficiently and effectively so we could keep our fixed costs constant as we grew. Doing so would provide us with the flexibility to deliver returns to investors while investing in operational improvements and growth initiatives. As those improvements and initiatives began to bear fruit, a virtuous cycle would take hold: we'd improve our ability to perform, which would allow us to generate even more cash to invest, which would lead to further performance gains, and so on.

That was my basic approach, and it turned out to be correct. Over the next several years, we did the seemingly impossible, stabilizing the company and progressing on a number of fronts simultaneously. We tightened up our aggressive accounting, tackled environmental liabilities and other legacy issues, improved our processes and our culture, and invested in a range of growth initiatives, including customers, mergers and acquisitions (M&A), research and development (R&D), and globalization. In essence, by following these three principles, we forced ourselves to consider the long- and short-term implications in every decision we made, instilling cultural and operational norms that allowed our company to deliver more value at *all* times. We turned our company into a performance machine, one that satisfied shareholders' quarterly cravings while also becoming much nimbler, more efficient, more innovative, and more customer-centric over the long term.

By 2008, when the Great Recession hit, we were already on firmer ground, but because we continued to implement a dual short- and long-term approach, we made a number of unorthodox moves that positioned us to expand rapidly once the recession ended. And expand we did. By 2018, when I left the company, our market capitalization had soared from $20 billion to $120 billion, Honeywell had generated returns of about 800 percent (beating the S&P 500 by about two and a half times), and the company had won high-profile awards for financial and environmental stewardship. We had also created 2,500 401(k) millionaires because employees had invested in Honeywell, with 95 percent of them below the executive level and the lowest compensated earning an annual salary of only $43,000.

If our experience proves anything, it's that you don't have to be a genius to achieve remarkable short- and long-term performance (we certainly weren't). You also don't need to have some magic formula—we didn't, beyond the Three Principles of Short- and Long-Term Performance. What you do have to do is *believe* you can achieve two seemingly conflicting things at the same time—short-term performance and investment in the future. And then, on a daily operational level, you have to dedicate yourself to actually doing it, pushing yourself and others on your team and organization to go beyond what they think is possible, every small step of the way. Leadership matters—it really does. And the trick, as I like to say, is in the doing. Most leaders know what needs to happen operationally and strategically. They know they must do a good job for customers, come out with new products and services, pursue globalization, motivate their workforce, and so on. But most businesses don't execute all that well. To perform well today while investing in tomorrow, your business has to do what everyone else claims to be doing. And that will only happen if you as the leader demand it at the outset and accept no compromises.

ABOUT THIS BOOK

The chapters that follow show you how to turn your business or organization into a performance machine, in any season. I lay out ten key strategic and operational strategies we deployed in line with the Three Principles of Short- and Long-Term Performance. In part I, "Lay the Foundations," I explore the intellectual basis required for achieving strong long- and short-term results at the same time. As we'll see in chapter 1, you must first learn how to think about your business in a far more rigorous and demanding way, and how to help others around you do the same. That means challenging yourself and others to go beyond binary oppositions and do two conflicting things at the same time. In chapter 2, I'll argue that you must also translate that mind-set of intellectual discipline and curiosity into your strategic planning, committing yourself to honesty and transparency and to having *real* conversations about your business or organization, its challenges, and its future.

Part II of this book, "Optimize the Organization," discusses investments you must make to free yourself of challenges that might be dragging down your performance. In chapter 3, I detail how we swallowed hard and addressed Honeywell's longstanding pension, environmental, and asbestos liability issues. In chapters 4, 5, and 6, I describe how we invested in improving our inefficient and ineffective processes, ending the culture wars that were hobbling us, and rebuilding and enhancing our depleted corps of leaders. Each of these efforts, funded by keeping fixed costs constant while growing our company, dramatically improved our ability to perform over both the short and long term.

Part III, "Invest to Grow," deals with investment decisions you can make now to ensure your future expansion. In chapters 7 and 8, I explain how we invested in areas like customer experience, R&D, globalization, and M&A, getting the most value for our investment *without* compromising short-term performance. Part IV, "Protect Your Investments," explores how to sustain both a short- and long-term approach in challenging times. Chapter 9 reveals how we used this approach during the Great Recession to help us achieve explosive performance afterward, while chapter 10 examines how to think differently about leadership transitions, ensuring that superior long- and short-term performance can continue even after you're gone. I close the book with an epilogue that calls on all of us to challenge ourselves and others to go beyond what seems possible so we can achieve our fullest potential as leaders and help our teams and organizations outperform.

As you read this book, I invite you to expand your horizons and break free of diminished expectations. Don't assume you have to forego long-term investment to survive quarter-to-quarter, and don't fall back on that as an excuse for failing to invest. Organizations of all sizes and all kinds—businesses and nonprofits—have it in them to perform much better than they currently do, over *all* time horizons. Leaders just need to believe this—and then start executing. Nonprofits in particular seem to have a high tolerance for poor performance at the individual and organizational levels. If we at Honeywell could invest in the future while delivering short-term results at a failing company, think of what your team or organization could do.

Overcoming short-termism isn't just an imperative for individual businesses, but also for the broader economy. Capitalism has been the greatest force for good the world has ever seen, raising billions of people out of poverty as governments enabled individual businesses to thrive, as businesses drove productivity gains, and as standards of living (which are linked to productivity) rose. But there's no guarantee that economies will continue to thrive in the years ahead, or that American businesses will flourish. As China continues its rise to economic power, competition in global markets will intensify, and US firms will have to sustain new levels of productivity and innovation to remain on top, just as they did during the 1980s, when they were in competition with Japanese companies. Yet shareholders will only fund the significant investments companies must make in R&D, process improvement, and culture if they see adequate short-term returns on their investments.

It's incumbent on leaders to pursue growth *and* deliver quarterly results. Offering Honeywell as a case study, *Winning Now, Winning Later* shows how you can run organizations with a new kind of balance, discipline, rigor, and energy, investing in growth while performing well now. We can win against Chinese companies and turn our competition with those firms into a source of opportunity. We can take our own companies to new levels of performance. But only if we're ready to demand more of our organizations—and of ourselves. So what are you waiting for? Go ahead and take a chance. You can do it. Let's get started!

PART ONE

LAY THE FOUNDATION

CHAPTER ONE

Banish Intellectual Laziness

In 2003, about a year after becoming Honeywell's CEO, I traveled to the headquarters of our Aerospace division in Phoenix, Arizona, to conduct a review of the business. I was working hard at the time on implementing wide-ranging cultural change across Honeywell, and the Aerospace division seemed reluctant to buy in. No surprise: the executive leading it—I'll call him Rich—had interviewed unsuccessfully for my job, and likely harbored some resentment. In making the trip, I hoped to strengthen my relationship with Rich and his team, familiarize them with my desire to focus Honeywell on both short- and long-term goals, and offer up ideas for improving the division's performance.

My visit began smoothly enough. Shaking hands with members of Rich's team, I found them polite and seemingly happy to see me. We sat down in a conference room so that team members could present their strategic plan to me. A copy of the plan had been placed on the table facing each seat. Flipping through mine, I saw that it was thick—maybe 150 pages long, full of charts and tables. *Uh-oh*, I thought, *not good*. I had found so far at Honeywell that executives and managers often made presentations far longer than necessary, overwhelming audience members with facts, figures, and commentary in an effort to preempt sharp, critical questioning. "Looks like you guys have done a lot of thinking here," I said, pointing to the thickness of the binder. "I can't wait to hear it."

Rich nodded at a member of his team, who began running through the presentation. It started with a review of the market. So far, so good. But a few minutes later, when we were on page five, I stopped to inquire about the status of Primus Epic, a terrific new cockpit avionics system we were developing. The team assured me the project was proceeding on schedule and on budget. Then, a page or two later, I posed another question about maintaining our lead in another product line of ours, auxiliary power units, the engines that provide power to an aircraft when it is on the ground. Although Rich's team members answered my question and smiled politely at me, they seemed unhappy, exchanging glances with one another that seemed to say, "Can you believe this guy?" They continued with the presentation, but about five minutes later, when they were on page fourteen, I stopped them yet again, inquiring about overruns that had exceeded $800 million on our biggest programs.

Rich had had enough. "You know, Dave," he said, "if you don't mind, I'd really like the team to continue. We'll get to that point soon enough."

I glanced over at him. "I'd like to know about it now."

"Really, we cover it later. I can assure you, all of your questions will be answered."

"Okay," I said, "I believe you. What page is it on?"

He glanced at one of his team members, who flipped through his copy of the presentation. "Top of page thirty-six," this executive said.

I went to the top of page thirty-six and scanned the chart there. "Nope, that covers just Primus Epic overruns. I want to understand the root cause of our overrun problems. Is it bad estimating? Bad executing? Something else? I want to get us to the point where we can anticipate the *real* cost so that we can plan for it and execute."

Rich shot me a hard look. "Dave, before we go any further, I have to object to how you're running this meeting. We put a lot of time and effort into crafting this pitch for you. Please show us the courtesy of listening to it all the way through."

"I understand, Rich," I said, "but let's discuss the purpose of this presentation. If we're here for the team to put on a show for me, then you're right, I should sit back and listen. But if the point is for me to learn about your business and its issues, then we need to conduct the presentation in a way that facilitates my learning. I need to ask questions right away, get the answers I need, and then move on. Can we do that?"

Rich relented, and I was able to review their business in a rigorous and productive way that ultimately uncovered opportunities for better short- and long-term management. What I learned, to my chagrin, was that Aerospace had become adept at lying to itself, shoehorning costs here and there into a budget without acknowledging them openly. This put enormous strain on the organization, which then had to patch together significant short-term fixes throughout the year, including more aggressive bookkeeping and special deals with customers and others, to make its goals. A dysfunctional approach if I'd ever seen one.

Fundamentally, managing for both the short and long term isn't about changing specific processes, policies, or strategies, but rather about adopting a different, more intellectual mind-set. Planting seeds for the future while also achieving short-term results is much harder to pull off than just aiming for one of these goals exclusively. It's so hard, in fact, that many executives and managers throw up their hands. Absolving themselves of any responsibility to achieve both short- and long-term goals, they shrink from asking tough questions and actively shield themselves and others from probing too deeply. Instead of finding new ways to support innovation and investment while achieving short-term goals, they fall back on the same old strategies, policies, and procedures, relying on accounting sleight-of-hand to make it all work.

Don't let this be you. You *can* achieve short- and long-term goals simultaneously, but that means you will need to puzzle it out, quarter after quarter, year after year. Challenge yourself, your team, and your organization to think harder about customers, markets, and processes than you previously have. Cultivate a mind-set of analytic rigor and attention to detail. Ask challenging questions of yourself and others, and push hard until you've uncovered satisfying answers, even if that means acknowledging difficult truths. Decide right now to become a serious, engaged, and honest scholar of your business instead of a passive overseer of it.

ACCOMPLISHING TWO SEEMINGLY CONFLICTING THINGS AT THE SAME TIME

My own heightened appreciation for intellectual rigor dates from the early 1990s, when I served as CFO at General Electric's major appliance business. We were trying to reduce the amount of capital we deployed in operating our businesses, and in line with that goal, my boss had decided that our business unit needed to reduce the $1 billion in inventory we maintained. Guess whose job it was to lead the inventory reduction effort? The assignment caught me by surprise—I wasn't sure how to proceed. I had seen other businesses flounder when pursuing such initiatives. The boss would decree that henceforth the company would only keep a certain amount of inventory on hand to shrink the amount of cash it had locked up. Months later, inventory levels would creep back up, and the amount of cash locked up would increase as well—*again*.

I wanted to try a new approach, but I didn't know what that would be. We convened a cross-functional team and asked them: Why *did* inventory reduction initiatives usually fail? What can we do differently? "If we're going to fail," I said, "let's at least do it differently. The definition of insanity is doing the same thing over and over, always expecting a different result." A manufacturing leader identified dissatisfied customers as the reason why these initiatives usually failed. Once a business reduced inventory, customer delivery usually suffered because we didn't have the items we needed in stock. Customers complained, and the sales force applied pressure on the business to stock more product. Eventually inventory levels were right back where they had been. Inventory levels and customer satisfaction were directly related. You could have lower inventory levels or high customer satisfaction, but not both. You had to choose between two seemingly conflicting things.

That, at least, was the conventional wisdom. We wondered if we could find a way to reduce inventory levels *while also* keeping our products readily available and ready to ship so that customer satisfaction wouldn't plummet. My team and I spent an entire day puzzling over it. At some point, a team member urged us to take a step back and assess our entire process, from forecasting, to supply chain, to manufacturing, to transportation, to distribution. Running an analysis, we found that it took eighteen weeks end-to-end, from when a product was shipped out of the warehouse to the point when manufacturing was told to replace it. and then it was produced, shipped, and replaced in the warehouse. That seemed like an extraordinarily long time. What if we could render the whole process more efficient, shrinking our "cycle time," as we called it, down to a couple of days? We'd be able to reduce warehouse inventory while still providing great customer delivery because we'd be able to replenish our stock much more quickly. The dramatically improved efficiency would also help us reduce a lot of operational cost. The overall impact could be huge!

Our team began working on improving our processes to reduce cycle time in forecasting, supply chain, production, and distribution. We began providing immediate feedback to plants on what had shipped that day, shortening supplier lead times, dramatically reducing lot sizes (the quantity of a product model we made during a given production run), and reducing transportation time to warehouses. Over a four-year period, these ongoing efforts reduced cycle time to about two weeks. We were able to cut inventory levels in half, while also improving our on-time delivery rate from the low 80s to above 90 percent. By striving to achieve two seemingly conflicting goals at the same time, instead of just focusing on one goal, we had prompted ourselves to think far more carefully about our business as a whole, and to pose questions nobody had asked before. This fairly intense intellectual process led us to reengineer a significant part of our business so that it functioned better across a range of metrics, not just one. Because our subpar process had been the underlying problem, and because we'd improved that process, we could sustain these gains over time.

MY "ANY NINNY" THEORY

Coming away from this episode, it was clear to me: leadership was, at its core, an *intellectual* activity. Any ninny could improve a given metric—that didn't take much thought or creativity. The best leaders acknowledge the tensions that pop up all the time in organizations, and they get better results by probing deeper to resolve them. Conventional wisdom said that you could earn high margins on the goods or services you sold, but only at the expense of your sales volume. It said that you could empower frontline employees to make decisions, but only at the expense of your ability to maintain control and prevent mishaps from happening. It said that you could improve customer delivery, but only at the expense of your inventory reduction efforts. Great leaders, I came to believe, challenge themselves and others to understand their businesses better and rethink them so that they can achieve two seemingly conflicting things at the same time. That same intellectual discipline—that mind-set of rigor and curiosity—allows leaders to master what is arguably the most important conflict of all: attaining strong short-term results while also investing in the future to achieve great long-term results.

Even as I came to this realization, I was keenly aware that most executives and managers didn't challenge themselves to pursue conflicting priorities, nor did they appreciate the intellectual effort this took. During the early 1990s, leaders at General Electric were so pleased with our inventory reduction efforts that they asked us to speak with other GE businesses to share what we had learned. After hearing our presentation, audience members would raise their hands and ask, "So, what was the single big thing you did to achieve these great results?"

"Well," I said, "there was no single best practice. It was a mind-set of intellectual rigor we had adopted that made the difference. It's this mind-set that you should be striving to replicate in your own organization."

Audience members would nod their heads, but they didn't really get it. A few minutes later, someone would raise his or her hand and say, "Okay, yeah, it was a mind-set. But tell me: What was the *one thing* you did that really made a difference?" Audience members wanted an easy answer that would excuse them from having to think hard about their businesses, when in truth, thinking hard was the only real answer.

INTELLECTUAL LAZINESS RUN AMUCK

To my dismay, such intellectual laziness was endemic at Honeywell. When I arrived at the company a decade later, I stepped into an organization utterly unused to probing for root causes to problems and to advancing new and creative solutions. Executives and managers pursued goals along a single dimension, doing whatever it took to make their numbers in the current quarter without concern for their actions' broader consequences. "We'll worry about next quarter next quarter, and about next year next year," people said. Businesses went around in circles, struggling to achieve short-term results and stagnating over the long term. Leaders never pushed themselves to develop the kind of new and interesting solutions that would permanently change their businesses for the better and achieve multiple goals at once.

Inevitably, such intellectual laziness coarsened the level of discourse that existed day-to-day. Many businesses operated the way Rich and his crew at our Aerospace division did. Lacking any drive to think deeply about their businesses, and unchallenged by leadership to do so, teams held meetings that were essentially useless, their presentations clogged up with feel-good jargon, meaningless numbers, and analytic frameworks whose chief purpose was to hide faulty logic and make the business look good. When you did a bit of digging, you found that most executives and managers didn't understand their businesses very well, or even at all.

Certainly they didn't understand their customers. I'll never forget a trip I took early on in my tenure to an air show to visit with a customer of our Aerospace unit. The team had briefed me on the visit, and I had gone into the meeting, along with the leader of the business unit, his product manager, and the salesperson, thinking we would discuss a great new product we had. As is my practice, I kicked off the conversation by asking if Honeywell was meeting their expectations. "I'm glad you stopped by," the customer CEO said, "because we have just about finalized the lawsuit we are filing against you for nonperformance on our development project." What!? My colleagues looked at one another and at me in shock—none of them had known how angry this customer was. They had lacked the slightest bit of insight into how our customers were experiencing their relationship with us. I begged for time, and with a bit of scrambling on our part we were able to prevent the lawsuit from materializing.

But it wasn't just this team, and it wasn't just customers. Leaders at Honeywell hadn't studied their operational processes in any depth. They didn't understand the fundamentals of their technologies, their markets, or their business cycles. They didn't know their supply chains. They weren't in touch with how rank-and-file employees viewed the business. They didn't understand key liabilities, such as the environmental lawsuits we faced. And they didn't understand why their businesses were generating so little cash.

No wonder our company was performing so poorly.

MAKING SMARTER, MORE INFORMED DECISIONS

My first and most enduring challenge as CEO was to dramatically improve the quality of both our individual thinking and our group discussions. To convey how I did that, let me introduce a leadership framework I have long used. As I see it, leadership boils down to three distinct tasks. First, leaders must know how to mobilize a large group of people. Second, they must pick the right direction toward which their team or organization should move. And third, they must get the entire team or organization moving in that direction to execute against that designated goal. Most people associate leadership disproportionately with the first element: inspiring the group. They think of charismatic leaders like Steve Jobs delivering lofty speeches that blow people away and motivate them to perform. In truth, mobilizing people is only about 5 percent of the leader's job. The best leaders dedicate almost all their time to the latter two elements: making great decisions and executing consistently with those decisions.

Leaders at Honeywell wouldn't have known a good strategic decision if it bit them in the leg, because they weren't putting in the time to understand their businesses and to regard them critically. To remedy this problem,

I spent a great deal of time defining what it meant to make decisions in an honest, informed, deliberate way. The first and best way to do that, I realized, was to model the process of critical inquiry myself. I'd make it clear that, yes, we *were* going to push ourselves to achieve two conflicting goals at the same time. But rather than simply dictate these goals, I'd start team members down the path to making a sound decision, asking them critical questions about their businesses and prompting them to generate creative solutions.

The conversation I had with Rich in Aerospace was typical. Rather than listening passively to a presentation, I'd interrupt—firmly at times, but politely—with questions about the business. I would pose key questions to teams in advance of our meetings for them to ponder. Listening closely to their answers, I'd follow up with still more queries, and make it clear when I wasn't satisfied. Was I aggressive, demanding, maybe even a little (or more than a little) annoying? Absolutely. But, as the old saying goes, progress occurs because of the irrational demands of general management. I firmly believe that. Leaders must be demanding of their people, otherwise they'll achieve only marginal results. People and organizations are capable of far more than they think possible. At the same time, leaders don't have to be nasty about it. I always tried to pose my questions courteously, remembering how as an employee I responded better when leaders showed me respect rather than telling me that I was wrong or barking out an order.

Day after day, meeting after meeting, I'd politely but persistently inquire about key elements of the business. Sometimes people took my politeness as a sign of weakness. When they did, I corrected that impression. Others reacted negatively to all of my questions. Over time, they either developed more intellectual rigor or left the company. Good leaders enjoyed sparring with me, even if they found it taxing.

In 2006, I met several times over the course of a year with senior leaders in our Aerospace business tasked with improving the business unit's software development efforts. For weeks before these meetings, the team researched questions I posed to them. Tim Mahoney, then Aerospace's chief technology officer and now Honeywell's senior vice president of enterprise transformation, remembered how at our first session together I pummeled them with follow-up questions for five hours. We talked through the nuances of the technology the software developers were using, the financials, and the talent his team was deploying. "Yes, it was fatiguing," he said, "but it was also exhilarating." When he left the meeting, he remembered being "even more excited about what we were going to achieve" than he had been when the team had walked in.[1]

NO MORE FUZZY THINKING

In challenging other leaders intellectually, I strove specifically to push them beyond the incrementalism that usually exists inside organizations—the tendency to consider the short-term implications of a decision exclusively and to ignore the long term. When leaders were thinking of adding capacity to an existing high-cost plant, I would ask them why they hadn't considered establishing a new presence in a low-cost, high-quality location. "Well," they said, "it's less expensive to simply build on to our existing plant." Taking this particular short-term business situation in isolation, that might have been true. But when you considered how establishing a new presence elsewhere might pave the way for future expansion, it actually might have made more sense to pay a little more now and build in a potentially lucrative new market.

Likewise, when leaders assessed which parts of their business were core and which were susceptible to outsourcing, they tended at first to regard 95 percent of operations as core. When we dug into it, we found they defined some operational areas that way simply because they regarded it as too expensive for the company to outsource those areas. They failed to consider the broader, long-term picture: the cost of managing these parts of the business, the physical buildings required, the reduction in our ability to adapt to economic change, the cost of continuing to invest in these parts of the business, and so on. Factor in these hidden, long-term implications, and the cost equation often looked very different, making it far more desirable to outsource these supposedly core areas (in my experience, organizations can generally outsource between 30 and 70 percent of what they do).[1]

As CEO, I pushed leaders to think more deeply about the complex, long-term picture in every decision they faced. Further, I challenged them to think carefully about what might go wrong. It's so easy to discount low-probability events in decision-making, even though these events might prove disastrous if they do occur. By considering the downside more aggressively, our teams often illuminated important issues we might otherwise have missed.

You might wonder how much thinking is too much. It depends on the business and the type of decision. Long-cycle businesses have a tendency to turn even simple decisions into projects. Short-cycle businesses tend to move quickly, proceeding with only a superficial understanding of issues. In encouraging leaders to think more carefully before deciding, I sought to make them aware of their intellectual tendency as either a short- or long-term business. If the consequences of a decision were minimal or reversible, they might have spared some of the analysis and erred on the side of making a quick decision. Otherwise I asked them to take the time they needed to wallow in the details before deciding.

Take Your Three Minutes

While reading a book about the construction of the Panama Canal, I came across an anecdote about the project's chief engineer, whose math teacher used to say, "If you have five minutes to solve a problem, use the first three to figure out how you're going to do it." I repeated this story within Honeywell in an effort to get people to slow down and think about problems a bit more. On one occasion, leaders of our Aerospace business unit were considering

---

1   Even once we had properly distinguished core parts of our business from non-core, we had to ask our finance teams to break down capital expenditures (CAPEX) along those lines because our businesses were continuing to invest in operations they had identified as non-core. Talk about organizational inertia! We put the kibosh on any non-core CAPEX spending other than what was required for HSE (health, safety, and environmental) or essential maintenance.

whether to proceed with a possible acquisition. At the end of the meeting I asked the team if they really wanted to go ahead with the deal and if they could guarantee the results. Most of the team said yes right away, but the head of Aerospace at the time, Tim Mahoney, said, "I'd like to take my three minutes. Can I get back to you Monday?" I loved that response and readily agreed. Tim pored through the details of the deal yet again, taking the time to identify additional opportunities, and decided to proceed. We spent $600 million acquiring that company. About five months after the deal closed, Tim's team landed a $2.4 billion order we hadn't included when valuing the company. That extra three minutes really paid off!

PUSHING OTHERS MEANS PUSHING *YOURSELF*

Asking our leaders to make decisions in a more rigorous way meant that I, too, had to put in more work. Not only did I spend time in advance of meetings generating some key questions for teams, I also informed myself about the particular businesses involved, as well as broader trends affecting these businesses. During my fifteen years as CEO, I traveled to plants and customers in about a hundred countries to better understand our operations and the challenges they faced. Back at our headquarters, I read five newspapers a day as well as key business publications and books and magazines on a wide range of topics. I met with a variety of people—CEOs from outside our industry, financial types, investors, policy-makers—to understand how they were thinking about emerging trends. I also spent time during my blue book exercises sitting alone in my office thinking about our businesses. I posed questions to myself and tried to answer them, and I reflected on external trends affecting our markets, pondering how our businesses might have to adapt.

In keeping myself informed, I took it upon myself to develop a certain amount of functional expertise. Throughout my tenure at Honeywell, I would read up on diverse subjects, such as information technology (IT), law, and social media. I knew trends in these areas were affecting our businesses, so I wanted to be able to talk about them. I hardly became an expert, but the questions I asked prompted team members who were experts to think in new and creative ways. Because they knew I'd be asking hard-hitting questions, they had to be ready to explain their business ideas to me in simple ways that even a layperson could understand—an exercise that forced them to refine their thinking. Simplicity and concision are tough. The French philosopher Blaise Pascal famously noted that he'd written a long letter, having lacked the time required to write a shorter one.[2] As I believe, if you can't convey a thought clearly and in a few words, then your comprehension of it is probably lacking.

My efforts to inform myself in diverse fields also prompted nonexperts on our teams to read up on them. If the gray-haired CEO knew enough about the Internet of Things (IoT), say, to be dangerous, our senior executives in legal, human resources, or operations needed to as well. Otherwise they would risk looking uninformed during our conversations.

ALIGNING THE ORGANIZATION AROUND THE STRATEGY

Rigorous and informed decision-making is one thing, but it's not enough. Just because a leader makes a decision doesn't mean anything will happen. To achieve long- and short-term objectives at the same time—or any other two seemingly conflicting goals—leaders also have to take a rigorous and informed approach to execution. Too many leaders get lazy around execution because they feel it is beneath them. "That's why I hire good people," they say. "It's their job to keep track of the operational details." Leaders also believe they shouldn't try to micromanage the business. As they see it, people further down in the organization need a sense of autonomy in order to thrive, so leaders should delegate and get out of the way.

Delegation and trust are of course vital—you can't do everything yourself, and you shouldn't try. That said, you don't want delegation to verge into a total abdication of authority on your part. You must verify that employees and the organization are actually executing as they are supposed to. I learned this lesson the hard way when I served as vice president of General Electric's consumer service division, which fixed the company's appliances for customers. The business was sizable—about $500 million in revenues—but demand was decreasing because of improving product quality (people didn't need to repair their dishwashers or washing machines as often), and our labor costs were too high. To improve the business, I embarked on a restructuring plan (a decision I only made thanks to numerous field visits with customers, service technicians, and others). I also invested heavily in a big IT project to improve how we scheduled our service technicians. Once in place, this project would significantly boost customer service while reducing our costs.

Since I didn't know much about IT, I relied on our IT leader to keep me informed on how the project was going. Everything seemed fine—until one day, when the project blew up. It became clear that the system wasn't going to work and that we had wasted millions in developing it. What a disaster. Ever since, I made a practice of keeping far closer tabs on important projects.

The idea that as a leader you can focus on strategy and delegate its implementation to great people is a fallacy. You don't want to micromanage, and you do need to tailor the amount of oversight you give to the leader in question.[2] But time is limited, and faced with urgent priorities, even the most talented people will let difficult, longer-term projects slide. Leaders must get out in the field to confirm that these projects are actually happening. They also must make sure the "machinery" works everyday—that employees have the tools and processes they need to execute their decisions, and further, that they're working hard to improve these tools and processes.

Part of the intellectual discipline I instituted for leaders at Honeywell was remaining well-versed in the executional details. I made it my job to understand reality on the ground, in large part, as mentioned, by getting out there and talking to frontline staff, but also by talking to managers a

---

2   If you have a new leader, a leader who is weak in a particular area, or an average leader, then you'll need to verify more. If you have a leader who consistently accomplishes what they say in the short and long term, then verify less. I used to tell leaders that if they consistently met their commitments, they'd get a lot less help from me.

couple of layers down from me to get their opinions on key business issues, and by routinely querying my team members about how we were executing and how we might do things better.

THE LEADER AS PERFORMANCE COACH

Staying informed on execution isn't just about holding people accountable. By asking probing questions, I was also serving our leaders as a performance coach, keeping them focused on operations and giving them an intellectual framework they could use to solve specific problems. It's easy for a leader to say, "We need some new products. Here's some money. Go do it." But think of the benefit when a leader challenges people to think about *how* they're going to innovate so that they don't just fund a bunch of screwball projects. How will they set up ideation to ensure that lots of good ideas are generated? How will they determine which new product ideas to fund and which to jettison? Who will they assign to product development so that the organization takes it seriously? What will they do to ensure that technologists are interacting with the marketing team so that the market actually wants these new products? How will they understand the user, installer, and maintainer experience? Will a product manager own the product or service from the beginning to ensure that the introduction doesn't get bogged down?

In posing such questions, I was giving leaders the benefit of my experience, alerting them to the kinds of operational issues they would likely encounter when undertaking specific projects. During my career, I had learned firsthand why manufacturing processes went awry, or why organizations typically struggle with transformations, or why pricing increases didn't hold. Reflecting on my own successes and failures, I had developed a practice of asking questions in various situations as they arose so as to avoid my previous mistakes. By posing these questions to team members rather than providing easy answers, I helped them understand their business better and put them in a better position to execute, leaving it to them to come up with answers that would work in their specific situations. Hopefully, the time and effort I spent would increase the odds that team members would succeed.

TIGHTEN UP YOUR METRICS

As part of our intellectual discipline around execution, I insisted leaders apply a new scrutiny to metrics. When I arrived at Honeywell, every one of our plants had quality and delivery metrics that looked great. When we probed a bit, we learned every plant excluded harmful data that leaders didn't feel represented their performance very well. Consider, for instance, our measurement of on-time delivery of products to customers. If a certain percentage of customers placed their order outside of a plant's established lead time (how long it needed to deliver a product after an order was placed), or if their order hadn't been entered properly, these customers might not have received the product on time. And yet the plant in question still would have reported a 99-percent on-time delivery result. It would have excluded these orders from the measurement, reasoning that these weren't plant issues. Managers looking at this data in an attempt to understand our execution would have thought customers were entirely happy, even when a significant percentage weren't.

Problems such as these were endemic, so to fix them we audited measurement systems at every plant. I also prodded leaders to look closely at the metrics their teams were giving them and to ensure that they were building the right metrics into every operational plan they developed. I pushed them as well to look beyond the metrics in monitoring execution. Many people will say what gets measured gets done, but that's not necessarily true. If you measure something, the metric will get better, but the underlying performance might not improve at all. People will do whatever it takes to get the metric where it needs to be, losing sight of the business intent underlying the goal. It becomes "compliance with words," as I like to say, not "compliance with intent."

As leaders, we couldn't take performance as indicated by the metrics for granted. We had to review operations rigorously to make sure improvements in metrics reflected real improvements in the underlying processes. Often we looked to put balancing metrics in place to ensure that one metric didn't improve at the expense of other, critical parts of the business. In reducing the cost of functions like finance, IT, legal, or HR, we didn't want the support those functions provided across the organization to be compromised. So we conducted anonymous internal surveys to determine if customer service from those areas was improving.

Not infrequently, our insistence on rigorous metrics led to significant improvements. For years we had tried but failed to improve the diversity of our workforce. We had mobilized all of the "best practices" and had eked out short-term increases in the percentage of our employees from diverse backgrounds in a given year, only to see those gains vanish soon afterward. Part of the problem was that we were forging policy at headquarters with only a limited knowledge of our workforce in local facilities. To remedy the situation, we created a sophisticated tool that combined our own data with data from the Department of Labor. The tool allowed us to track the availability of talent in local areas by job code, broken down by ethnicity and gender. Using this tool, we could compare diversity levels in particular plants and even in particular teams to the diversity in local talent pools. That allowed us to challenge managers who claimed, for one reason or another, they didn't have access to well-qualified, diverse talent. We could hold local managers accountable in a whole new way, simply because we were tracking the data much more closely than we had been.

We also began to measure the opportunities a leader had to improve diversity by tracking what happened with new hires and with attrition. Were leaders doing enough to recruit and retain diverse talent who had come onboard? Every leader reported on his or her progress in this area twice annually to myself and my staff. As a result of these efforts, we made steady progress year after year, rather than simply maintaining the status quo, as we had previously.

As I reminded leaders at Honeywell, execution matters much more than it seems. "The trick is in the doing," I said. It was great to make smart, informed decisions, but the real substance of any decision was getting it done. Leaders everywhere had more or less the same knowledge. We read the same books and periodicals. We talked to the same people. We had access to the same consultants. To gain an advantage, we at Honeywell needed to execute better, and that meant understanding our operations better, looking for ways to improve, and putting those improvements in place. Leaders couldn't stand on the sidelines. That was the old way. They had to get out there in the field, immerse themselves in what their teams were doing, monitor progress, and hold people accountable. Then they had to use all of that executional knowledge they amassed to help inform their decision-making going forward.

THE BEAUTY OF "X" DAYS

You might find the prospect of modeling intellectual rigor for your team or organization daunting. How do you do it with so many demands on your time? For starters, I heartily recommend you dedicate time each month to learning about your businesses and engaging in unstructured thinking. It's hard to think, read, and learn when endless meetings clog up your day. I developed a practice of sitting down with my calendar at the beginning of each fiscal year and asking my assistants, Lois Brown and Debbie Mendillo, to designate two or three days each month as "X" days, during which they wouldn't schedule any meetings. I'd spend some of those days alone thinking about our businesses. On other X days I'd make impromptu trips to learn about our businesses or pay a surprise visit to a facility. I'd also designate twelve additional days as "growth days," holding intensive sessions with leadership teams to help them think through various growth or operations initiatives. My staff had to hold these growth days on their calendars as well so that we didn't have to reconcile our calendars in the event we wanted to schedule a meeting (team members got these days back to use as they pleased if we wound up not holding a meeting that included them). Sometimes I had to schedule meetings on an X day, but anticipating that this would happen, I set aside more of these days at the beginning of the year than needed.

On my regularly scheduled days, I made sure to free up as much time and mind-space as I could for thinking. If you haven't gotten serious about tightening up your calendar, now is the time to start. Do you really need all those meetings? Are there ways to minimize the length of essential meetings and still make progress? I am not against meetings—they are essential for leaders, not least because they help us bring facts to the surface and generate good decisions. At the same time, so many meetings are excessively long, unnecessary, and inconclusive. One of my favorite techniques is to require that teams provide me with a summary page at the beginning of the meeting or beforehand so that I could get the gist of the issue up front as well as the team's recommendations rather than waiting for the story to unfold.

"BRING-UP NOTES" AND BLUE NOTEBOOKS

To minimize the number of follow-up meetings required to resolve issues, and thus maximize the time on your calendar for thinking, I recommend ending every meeting by establishing the who, what, and when of any follow-up actions. Just because a team reaches consensus on an issue doesn't mean a decision will actually be implemented. Be clear what the follow-up action is, and when it comes to the "who," never accept "the team" as an answer. You want the name of someone who will stay awake nights to make sure the required work gets done. On "when," remember Parkinson's law, which says that work expands to fill the time allotted. Don't be afraid to create tight timelines, because sometimes the culture demands them. In one instance, I asked a finance person when they could perform a task for me. Clearly not used to being asked, the person responded, "Two weeks." Pointing to my watch, I said, "What time *today*?" The task was handed in by 5:00 P.M. that day. Sometimes organizations get used to telling time with calendars instead of watches, and it has to stop.

Also be sure to make the most of your unstructured hours between meetings. A great technique to try is what I call "bring-up notes." In their capacity as managers, most leaders keep track of all the deliverables people owe them and when. Rather than waste mental energy thinking about all that, I wrote down each deliverable and the due date on a separate piece of paper at the end of a meeting and had my assistant file it. Every day she handed me "bring-up notes" for items that had been due the day before. If I had already received the deliverable, I tore up the note. If I hadn't, I started inquiring about when I'd receive it. With bring-up notes, I was able to keep everyone accountable, allowing myself more time, energy, and mental space to read and think. Bear in mind, this began in an era before smartphones. These days productivity apps and other software can serve a similar function for you, especially if you don't have an assistant.

To help myself think independently, and to stay fresh in my job, I also got in the habit of keeping what I called my "blue notebook," a place to collect all of the new ideas and questions I came up with during the course of my free-thinking X days. Every six months or so, I'd take an X day and dedicate it to thinking about the company, investors, business trends, financials, people, and so on, jotting down my thoughts. Then I'd go back and review the notes I'd made on a previous X day. Did my new ideas on that day get implemented? If so, what had happened? Had others slipped through the cracks? If so, were they still valid and worth pursuing? As for the questions I'd posed myself, how would I answer them? Had any new evidence emerged in the interim? The process of working through my blue notebook—and my experience in general on X days—allowed me to break free of my daily context and look at our businesses from something approximating an outside perspective. On numerous occasions, ideas I'd written in my blue notebook led to new business initiatives that made a difference to our businesses. Most notably, our major process improvement initiatives, Honeywell Operating System and Functional Transformation (which I'll discuss at length in chapter 4), came out of questions I posed during a blue notebook session.

SEEK OUT INCONVENIENT TRUTHS

It's also important, especially as you rise in seniority, to make sure you're not just always thinking, but are constantly questioning your own decisions. In public, you have to convey confidence in the moves you've made because teams and organizations don't handle uncertainty very well. But that doesn't mean you can't question your decisions in private. It's vital to do that. It's also critical to avoid falling prey to your own confirmation bias. We all tend to pay more attention to evidence that supports what we already think and discount data that conflicts with it. The remedy is to systematically seek out evidence that negates your hypotheses or beliefs. Throughout my time at Honeywell, I would push my own thinking further by listening hard to people with opinions contrary to mine or who were bringing "inconvenient" data to a conversation. When I visited our facilities around the world, I would ask people open-ended questions about our operations, homing in on any evidence that conflicted with my presumptions. I would also ask trusted friends and colleagues what they thought about my decisions, knowing that if they saw flaws in my thinking, they wouldn't hesitate to let me know.

I wish I could say I was perfect at questioning my own beliefs, but I wasn't. One of my greatest regrets from my time at Honeywell concerns how we implemented Six Sigma, a well-known quality improvement methodology.[3] While we invested a great deal in the implementation, as I'll describe in a later chapter, it didn't work as well as it should have. From what I could tell at the time, the program was working fine. However, the signs of failure were there—I just didn't pay much attention to them. If I had been more disciplined in my thinking, I might have prodded myself to proactively run various analyses for the express purpose of testing my beliefs. For instance, I might have compared our quality levels for new products at various facilities with what those levels had been ten years earlier or compared quality forecasted at the design stage with what actually happened. But I didn't subject my ideas to this kind of scrutiny, and as a result, this initiative underperformed for years. Never rest on your laurels. Always challenge yourself, asking, "What if my hypotheses, assumptions, beliefs, or decisions are wrong?" If you really are right, you'll feel even more confident about it. And if you're wrong, you'll get the prodding you need to push your thinking—and your business—in a new direction.

---

3   Six Sigma is a very rigorous set of statistical tools businesses can use to create more robust processes and designs. The method was first championed by W. Edwards Deming and used to great effect by Japanese car makers to significantly improve quality.

If you set an example of rigor in your own thinking, you'll see a trickle-down effect, first among your direct reports and then among employees at lower levels. Because I demanded a lot of the teams that reported to me, those leaders became used to thinking harder and preparing more for meetings. "We knew we needed to do the work at a certain level of rigor," said Kate Adams, currently general counsel at Apple and formerly our general counsel, "because it was going to be subjected to a potentially very searching set of questions about its validity."[3] Sometimes people need a bit of prodding in order to think more broadly or deeply. At one point we hired a new tax leader who gave a presentation saying there wasn't much we could do to address a particular tax issue we faced. My response: "I could have paid someone a lot less to give me that answer." He got the message, challenged himself to offer more probing analyses, and became a star performer.

MIND YOUR MEETINGS

You can take additional steps to get your people thinking harder and to shift the level of intellectual discourse among teams. Pay more attention to how you run meetings. Do you tend to dominate the conversation and dictate answers to your team? If so, you're reducing the amount or quality of thinking that is taking place. The quality of your decision-making will decline, and you'll miss a valuable opportunity to enhance your team's critical thinking capacity. The same holds true if you reveal your own opinions on the issues before you too early: team members will come forward with ideas they think you'll like and will fail to share opinions they perceive as at odds with your own. As I like to say, it's important to be right at the end of a meeting, not at the beginning.[4] If you embrace that mind-set, you'll do a lot less talking in meetings, and focus instead on getting others to report facts and air their opinions. That of course means controlling your own ego.

---

4   I stumbled onto this approach when I first arrived at Honeywell. Realizing I couldn't trust my board or staff, I became a lot more careful about expressing my opinions up front. Then I realized I was making better decisions because I was allowing for a richer discussion. I proceeded to permanently change how I ran meetings.

If you struggle in this area, remember: as a leader you get measured on the quality of your decisions and the results they produce, not on whether an idea was originally yours.[5]

Controlling Your Ego: A Lesson from My Dad

My dad was a strong, tough guy—he had served in the US Navy in World War II, had seen a lot of action, and had been wounded. When I was a kid, I spent a lot of time working at the service station he ran. One day business was unusually slow, and we sat together on the curb waiting for something to happen. Sure enough, a car came screaming in. My dad went over and offered up his usual cheery greeting. The customer got out of the car, and for the next five minutes proceeded to berate my father for something he had done. I watched, incredulous and convinced my father would sock the man in the face. Dad was not the kind of guy to be pushed around. Instead, he became extremely apologetic, saying over and over again, "I'm sorry, I'll make it right." The customer drove off in a huff, and Dad came back to the curb. We sat there as he stared off into space—I sure wasn't going to say anything. Dejectedly, he said, "Dave, sometimes in life and in business, you have to put your pride in your back pocket."

That moment has always stuck with me. To be effective as leaders, we all have to put our egos to the side at times, no matter how tough or strong we might be.

At Honeywell, I would try to lead teams through an issue by posing a series of questions, seeking purposely to encourage a diversity of opinions (as the saying goes, if two people always agree, only one is thinking). When people made statements that ran counter to what I was thinking, I pushed them to develop those arguments to the fullest. When they articulated a

---

5   It's especially important to follow this approach when working with external advisors, bankers, or consultants of any kind. You're paying for their advice, not their endorsement. If you refrain at first from declaring your opinion and let them talk, you're more likely to get their unvarnished thoughts.

view that conformed to my thinking, I held my tongue and didn't rush to agree with them. I let the conversation run its course, making sure to really listen. Too often people tend to think about what they'll say next when someone else is speaking. I developed a practice of listening all the way through and waiting three seconds to respond—it's amazing how that small change allows you to really hear what someone is saying . . . or not saying. I also registered the body language and facial expressions of others around the table, seeking valuable clues on whose opinion to solicit next.

As conversations unfolded, I did my best to draw out everyone present, including introverts who might have been struggling to participate. In so doing, I tried to remain mindful of the specific situation I was confronting as a leader and tailored my questions or comments accordingly. Many leaders tend to evoke the same persona in every meeting, but that's a mistake. In one meeting you might need to come across as angry, in another pensive, in another friendly. It depends on what you're trying to accomplish. Also, if you do get angry, it's important not to let that frustration carry into the next meeting, as some leaders do, since the team there had nothing to do with the problem that upset you.

Once all the ideas were on the table, I went around and asked each participant what decision they would make if they were me. To avoid junior employees from echoing what their bosses said, I started with the most junior people and continued until I'd heard from the senior-most person. Then, and only then, did I share the decision to which I'd come. I'd explain my thinking in some detail. That way people would understand my thought process and would be better able to apply it to other decisions they might face.

To maintain the quality of our conversations, I made it clear we rewarded results, not effort. Too often individuals and teams want credit for working a hundred hours a week, irrespective of whether they actually accomplished anything. They confuse activity or effort with results, in the process distracting others from focusing on results and the actions required to achieve them. When people in my meetings tried to get credit for effort, I would always say something along the lines of, "That's interesting but irrelevant. If there is no result, there is no story." That might sound harsh, but it's how the world works. I needed our people to understand that reality if we were to make quality decisions and execute well on them.

I also required people to back up their arguments with data to the extent possible. In one memorable meeting, members of our HR Benefits team kept arguing against a proposed change, prefacing their opinions with the words "I feel." I ended the meeting by saying that if this decision came down to feelings, mine would win and we'd go with the proposed change. Not only did they bring supporting data to the next meeting (which, by the way, supported my feelings), but the leader of the group, Brian Marcotte, provided me with a CD containing ten songs about feelings. The message about data's importance reverberated throughout the HR organization, a welcome development in a function that often neglected it.

A final way I tightened up meetings was to discourage people from coming to my office afterward to tell me what they "couldn't say in the meeting" on account of who was in the room. What kind of leader would I be if I suddenly changed my opinion based on statements from the last person with whom I spoke? When people did come to me after meetings, I explained that because they lacked the guts to speak up, we had just wasted an hour of everyone's time and would now have to reconvene so that everyone could hear this new input. I only had to do that a couple of times before this baloney stopped.

Beyond the standard meetings I would hold, I sometimes found it necessary to lead teams through special exercises to spur their thinking around particular subjects. Even the best teams get stuck intellectually, and as CEO, I took it upon myself to perform some shock treatment and force a productive conversation. On one occasion I had asked the purchasing team in our Aerospace unit to provide me with a long list of ideas we could adopt over time to cut costs. Months passed, and after repeated requests on my part, they were "still working on it." Having had enough, I ordered team members to cancel all their meetings for the rest of the week. The next morning, they were going to go into their conference room at 8:00 A.M. and stay there all day until they had analyzed $1.5 billion in current costs and came up with ideas for aggressively saving money in these areas. If they hadn't generated these ideas by 5:00 P.M., they'd come in the next day to continue thinking on it. It wound up taking them two days, but they came up with the ideas. They just needed a little friendly encouragement from me.

When teams were struggling to envision a potentially different future, I would use a different technique, what I refer to as my "White Sheet of Paper" exercise. The name says it all: I asked teams to take a step back and reimagine their businesses from scratch. Often when teams have trouble creatively it's because their thinking is overly constricted by reality as they know it and they can only think of ideas that derive from the existing reality. To have a more productive discussion, they must become reanchored to a different position. I'd ask them to take a day and pretend they could build their business, process, or product from scratch. What would it look like? How would they design it? Usually suspending reality broke the logjam and allowed people to think of a future that was very different from the present.

In one instance, one of our union factories was struggling to redesign their inefficient work rules, all forty-three pages worth. Using the White Sheet of Paper exercise, they were able to pare their work rules down to only three pages, redesigning the work environment to be far more flexible and efficient. Once teams specify both their present position and desired destination, it becomes much easier to lay out the logical steps, the resources the team will need, and a realistic timeline for getting there.

INSTILL AN INTELLECTUAL MIND-SET

In organizations beset by short-termism, leaders often fail to invest sufficiently in R&D, process initiatives, and other growth programs. Spending there detracts from the quarterly numbers, and the returns don't show up until many quarters, or even years, later. When I arrived at Honeywell, our businesses had been shorting R&D spending and other potential growth initiatives for years. We needed to pump up that spending, but many leaders weren't certain how we could do that while still delivering the short-term results we needed.

As I'll describe in chapter 7, it turned out that we *could* deliver short-term results and plant seeds more productively for the future. In our Aerospace business, for instance, we had traditionally taken a mindless approach to R&D, developing new products for as many new aircraft models as we could, with little analysis of how lucrative these platforms would wind up being. Some of these investments paid off; some didn't. Now, for the first time, we began performing a marketing segmentation analysis, ranking potential R&D programs for their market potential. We focused our spending accordingly, investing only in products for the big platforms that were most likely to pay off for us. That represented a cost savings, so we took those extra dollars, as well as some extra income generated from better-than-expected sales, and directed them toward what we called "short-cycle" product introductions—smaller investments that would result not in a new product per se but in incremental enhancements to existing products and services that would generate more sales now.

Overall, we took the same R&D budget and allocated it more efficiently, in a way that would deliver both short- and long-term results. The big new product development projects would take years to show a return, but the short-cycle product introductions (along with salespeople to support them) would deliver returns more quickly. The strategy worked. Within a couple of years, short-cycle product development began generating revenue, and today it is a highly profitable, billion-dollar business. Over time, our long-term investments also delivered big for us. We won 75 percent of the new programs we went after, instead of just half of them, as we had previously.

The quality of thought in a team or organization matters. If you want a business that performs both today *and* tomorrow, you need to take apart your business and put it back together again so that it works more efficiently and effectively. That means instilling an intellectual mind-set, spurring your people to think harder about every business decision they face. Set the standard for intellectual engagement. Demand that your people pursue two seemingly conflicting things at the same time. Make it your mission to understand the nuances of your businesses so that you can shape and guide your teams' intellectual inquiry. Allocate your time thoughtfully; don't become a victim of your calendar. Carve out time to read, research, and *think*. Turn your meetings into vigorous, instructive debates. As you'll find, performing today *and* tomorrow is hard, but it's not impossible. You just need to put your mind to it. You need the right *mind-set*.

QUESTIONS TO ASK YOURSELF

1. What level of intellectual discourse prevails in your team or organization? Be honest! Do you have the discipline required to pursue short- and long-term goals simultaneously?

2. How much time do you *really* spend thinking? Do you organize your calendar to ensure that you have blocked out enough time, or are you a victim of your calendar?

3. Are you implementing the three aspects of leadership to the fullest, or do you spend a disproportionate amount of your time focusing on motivating or inspiring others, which should comprise just 5 percent of the job?

4. Do you engage intellectually during presentations, or are you taking in the proceedings as you would a Broadway show? Are you training your people to think critically and push hard to pursue conflicting goals?

5. Are you using meetings as opportunities to debate pressing issues in a rigorous way? Do you just bark an order, or do you take the time to run people through a series of questions to help structure their thinking? Do you push others to articulate their ideas and the logic behind them and reserve your opinions until the end?

6. Do you strive to understand the drawbacks of a proposed decision, asking, "What could go wrong?" Do you solicit input from every participant, even if it conflicts with your beliefs or the team's consensus? In deciding how extensively to debate an issue, do you differentiate between decisions that might have minimal consequences (thus potentially requiring less debate) and those that might produce extreme consequences (thus requiring more debate)?

7. Do you challenge yourself and others to think about execution, or are you content being a strategist? Are you delegating, or abdicating? Do you get out in the field enough to understand what's happening in operations, with your customers, and with other aspects of your business?

8. Can you spot opportunities to reanchor your people using the White Sheet of Paper exercise? Where might you profitably accelerate progress by "locking people in the room" and requiring that they produce a solution?

9. Are you as alert as you should be to evidence that conflicts with your own ideas or beliefs? What initiatives aren't working as well as you might think? Get out there and find out!

10. Are your metrics real, or are people massaging them in ways that yield a distorted picture?

11. Do you tend to listen to the last person with whom you've spoken, after they didn't take the opportunity to speak up during a meeting?

12. Do you focus on being right at the end of the meeting instead of at the beginning of the meeting?"

CHAPTER TWO

Plan for Today *and* Tomorrow

I f there's anything we expect a public company CEO to know, it's information about the organization's performance. And yet, for months after I became Honeywell's CEO in February 2002, I had no idea how we were doing. This might be hard to believe, but as I noted in the introduction, the board had restricted my access to the numbers until I formally became chairman four and a half months later. They wanted me to "learn the business," they said, and not "worry about our performance." The outgoing chairman, my predecessor as CEO, would monitor whether we were meeting our financial goals.

As I would soon learn, our company's performance was indeed troubling. Upon taking over as chairman on July 1, I asked the finance team for an updated estimate of sales and earnings per share (EPS) for the year (we had previously forecasted $2.36 EPS), informing them that I intended to take our numbers down to something we could feel absolutely confident about achieving. (Given Wall Street's negative views of me, I felt it was really important that I made my first commitments.) During the third week of July, our corporate finance team informed me that our results were rolling up to earnings of $2.27 to $2.32 per share. I chose to take guidance to an even lower number: $2.25 per share. The finance guys were irate, saying I would disappoint investors and destroy our stock price. But I wanted wiggle room in case we performed worse than expected. It turned out that these two extra cents per share weren't nearly enough. In mid-August, finance sheepishly advised me that our actual earnings for the year would be—get ready for this—only $2.05 per share. And that was with over half the year already booked. We basically had projected earnings for the second half to come in at $1.36 per share; now they would only be $1.05.

What!?

Despite my reputation for colorful language, I promised myself I wouldn't put cuss words in this book, or at least not too many, but you can imagine my reaction. How could our second-half performance decline by over 20 percent in just a few weeks? The finance team blamed me, saying I had "let our businesses off the hook" and wasn't demanding that they perform. That made zero sense. No action of mine could have possibly affected our sales or costs by 20 percent in just three weeks.

I needed answers, so I called the leaders of our four business divisions at the time: Aerospace, Automation and Control Solutions, Specialty Materials, and Transportation Systems. "What the hell is going on?" I asked. Their response: "Well, the financial goals we've been trying to meet were never realistic to begin with." Apparently, my predecessor and our finance team had generated these targets by some unknown process. The business leaders had complained that the goals were excessive, but finance had brushed off their concerns and demanded they formally adopt these numbers anyway. "Just get it done," finance had told them. "Do whatever you need to make the numbers."

I was angry, but not entirely surprised: I had seen signs of untrammeled short-termism and a compromised strategic planning process a couple weeks earlier while attending my first "make the quarter" meeting. This regular gathering with finance heads had existed under my predecessor and was replicated at lower levels throughout the organization. The purpose of this meeting was for leaders to approve a list of actions the company would have to take, in finance's view, to meet our quarterly goals. Perusing the list set before me, I saw that none of these actions strengthened the company by either increasing sales or reducing costs. Rather, the actions were one-time transactions designed to make Honeywell more profitable on paper. Finance wanted us to sell a business so that we could book a one-time gain. They wanted us to change how we accounted for certain items so as to book more income. They wanted us to approve deals with vendors that were specifically designed to pad our profits that quarter.

Such actions were perfectly legal under prevailing accounting rules, but decidedly unwise. While these transactions had allowed us to meet our short-term commitments, they hurt us in the long term. Every quarter we felt pressure to find additional, potentially destructive solutions not just to make comparable numbers but higher ones, because we needed to show increasing profits. As time passed and our businesses degraded, the pressure ratcheted up, and we'd become stuck in a destructive cycle of our own making.

To overcome an entrenched short-termism, it's not enough to inculcate a mind-set of intellectual inquiry and honesty into the organization. You also must embed this mind-set and a commitment to both short- and long-term goals deep into strategic planning. Unless leaders at every level and in every part of the business know they must take planning seriously as an intellectual exercise, and unless they are oriented toward planting seeds for the future even as they reap today's harvests, they'll give themselves a pass. They'll sign on to unrealistic long-term goals that make them look good to their superiors, then take ill-advised shortcuts to make short-term numbers. It's up to leaders at every level to define what a proper strategy looks like, and to give the organization the processes, funding, and analytic tools it needs to deliver results. This isn't easy or glamorous work, but as we'll see in this chapter, it must be done if you want your business to perform well years into the future while pleasing investors today.

CLEAR OUT THE UNDERBRUSH

The first step to improving the planning function is to eradicate the quick fixes that keep people stubbornly focused on today at tomorrow's expense.

A couple of weeks after my horrendous "August surprise," our finance team happened to be convening a hundred of our top finance people from around the world. I attended and used the opportunity to put a stake in the ground. I informed these executives that from then on, we wouldn't hold any more "make the quarter meetings," nor would we perform any more transactions designed to deliver one-time gains and an earnings boost. I couldn't yet identify all of these transactions across our businesses, but I let finance know I wanted all of this aggressive accounting off of our books, effective immediately, and I didn't care what it cost us in income.

After that meeting, executives began alerting me to specific financial transactions that served primarily to help us make the quarter. Some of these deals, I discovered, were especially widespread. There was distributor loading, in which we offered our product distributors special prices or payment terms during the last week of the quarter so that we could close transactions and book the revenue. The practice pumped up earnings, but at considerable cost. Distributors learned they could get better prices from us if they strategically timed their purchases. Instead of buying from us during the first weeks of a quarter, they piled all their purchases into the last week, receiving a discount or better payment terms. These large orders disrupted our businesses, because in order to fulfill them we had to inflate our inventories, hoping we had made products the market wanted, and then scramble to ship everything on time. In some businesses, 25 percent of the quarter's sales occurred in the last week. And because we had to replicate the performance in future quarters to grow earnings, the problem worsened over time.

Another practice that helped us make our short-term numbers was providing so-called ship sets to customers. When selling products like aircraft wheels and brakes, we would package free product into the deal as an incentive. We might offer to provide the first hundred ship sets or product units for free, accounting for those ship sets by capitalizing them, spreading out the cost over the next ten or twenty years. The cash would exit our business at the shipment, but we weren't recording any immediate expense for it. Today's earnings would look great, while future earnings would suffer. Executives regarded these ship sets as "free money" they could dispense to lure business. To them, it was free, even though the cash was going out the door. A few years later, their successor would have to work harder in order to make their numbers.

Similarly, businesses were capitalizing R&D expenses to bolster their current earnings. Since the brunt of these costs would be felt over years, leaders didn't scrutinize the spending to ensure they were getting the best possible value from it.

Still another way we boosted short-term profits without regard for our future was to structure contracts so that vendors front-loaded their costs. To obtain our business, vendors would agree to pay us a fee up front. Our businesses would book this payment as income now, looking good on paper, but saddling the business with higher costs years into the future. In many cases, these long-term contracts hurt our businesses—we were locking ourselves in, becoming overly dependent on a single supplier or overpaying for goods. And yet leaders would sign these deals because they helped them make the quarter.

We also sometimes sold off businesses not because doing so would help us develop and sell more products, but because our income statement would see a nice boost that quarter from the gain on the sale. In one instance, our Aerospace division sought to sell our Technology Solutions business, which provided services to government customers. When I examined the business, I found that it was in a decent position relative to some of our other businesses, and that with some investment on our part, we could grow it considerably over the next several years. We backed away from the sale, electing instead to operate and scale the company. Over a decade later, when we thought the business had peaked, we sold it and booked a much larger gain. By offsetting that gain with additional restructuring, we ensured that none of it fell through to income and could put it instead toward improving our long-term outlook.

At that initial meeting of global finance executives, I made myself clear: none of these common transactions were fair game any longer. No more distributor loading. No more capitalized ship sets or R&D. No more one-time business sales for the sake of booking gains. And while we were at it, no more stretching payments to suppliers beyond our agreed-upon terms at the end of the quarter. No more selling receivables at the end of the quarter just to make cash flow look better.

The outcry from corporate finance was swift: How could I do this? If we implemented all of these transactional reforms to discourage short-termism, our earnings would decline, investors would sell our stock, and its price would tank. But I wasn't backing down. We had to scrub our books and practices so that they reflected the reality of our underlying businesses. We also had to shake our executives out of their blinding fixation on quarterly results. Only then could we make planning decisions that supported long-term growth.

It took us eighteen months to do away with all of the aggressive and unhealthy accounting practices. On a number of occasions, leaders requested permission to complete a transaction that wasn't in our best long-term interests but that would help them make their numbers. We declined every one of these requests, reminding leaders that if we allowed them leeway this time, they would be digging a hole for themselves, and feel even greater pressure in the future to pad the numbers. These were tough conversations—some business leaders and members of our finance team couldn't stomach our rejection of short-termism. Ultimately, most came around, and those who didn't were ushered out of the company. In 2003, we hired Dave Anderson from ITT as our new CFO. He strongly reinforced our message, making it clear he wouldn't tolerate any end-of-quarter massaging of the numbers.

When communicating with investors, I acknowledged that our performance would lag over the next year or two as we straightened out our business, but asserted that we'd rebound after that. Some investors believed in us during the early 2000s, while others shunned our stock, depressing its price by about 25 percent. That hurt, but we had to stand up for what we believed was best for the company while delivering at least *some* short-term results so that our stock wouldn't go through the floor. Once we were running our businesses strategically rather than just pretending we were, our performance would track upward and shareholders would feel more bullish about our company. As we'll see elsewhere in this book, pursuing both short- and long-term performance requires a period of up-front investment, during which performance might lag for a little while. As a leader, you have to suck it up and make sure your investments pay off.

NO MORE LAME PRESENTATIONS

Given what I've revealed about short-termism at Honeywell, you might wonder if we had a formal strategic planning process in place. We certainly did. Each July our businesses made presentations to the CEO, with similar presentations taking place down through the ranks. These presentations were, in a word, bullshit. Leaders had no clue how they would run their businesses over the next five years, what big initiatives they would have to push to make their goals, or what changes in their industry they should anticipate, or better, lead. Rather than choosing goals thoughtfully, they picked ambitious targets they thought would please their bosses, without regard for whether the business could realistically achieve them. They might have factored in the benefit of downsizing, the introduction of new products or services, process improvement, or other cost-savings initiatives, but then didn't include as an expense the funds to bankroll these initiatives because it would depress the outlook. To cover themselves, they threw around lofty language and piled on hundreds of pages of charts and tables, hoping to look smart. Without much critical analysis, leaders gave their blessings, leaving the businesses to go execute whatever they wanted without follow-up or accountability. "Strategy," such as it was, had no relevance. Operational considerations and making the quarter became daily concerns, with strategy fading to the background.

Former Pittway president and longtime Honeywell executive Roger Fradin remembered that many business leaders failed to take planning seriously because they lacked basic knowledge about their market, customers, and competition. "General managers didn't think their job actually was to spend time in the market with customers and salespeople," he said in an interview. "They also were not in their jobs for very long," as it had become the norm to rotate general managers to new jobs every two years or so. In this context, "the plans were viewed as, 'I got a day in front of the CEO of the company. I'm going to tell a story that they're going to find attractive. Then I'll get back to delivering the same old lousy numbers I was planning to deliver. Or maybe I'll come up with some ideas for a one-time special.'" When the day of reckoning arrived, leaders felt confident they wouldn't be around to take responsibility.[1] "There was no integrity to our planning process back then," Fradin said. "It was total BS."

One of my top priorities as CEO was to eradicate the BS and reinvent planning. Every year, starting in 2003, I required teams presenting to me to write a three-to-four-page executive summary that highlighted the basic plan. That document would allow us to cut through the pages of obfuscating charts and bullet points. I scrutinized every word and phrase in these summaries and other key parts of these plans. As Fradin recalled, the plan for his business, which accounted for roughly $15 billion in revenue, was just under a hundred pages long. Even so, when he presented it to me, I spent our entire meeting analyzing the opening charts. The message was clear: If you say something, back it up with facts. If you don't know, don't bullshit. Just say you don't know.

When leaders tried to pretend they knew more than they did, I called them on it. A team would regale me with long lists of "competitive strengths"—an obvious red flag. A strong business is lucky to enjoy a couple of key advantages over its peers. These lists were just a bunch of words strung together. "Our competitive strength is our people," one executive told me. Oh really. Yes, having good people is a competitive advantage. But when we looked, for example, at our business supplying fluorines to customers, did our superior talent pool comprise our primary advantage, or was it the patents we held on certain fluorine molecules? Did we have data showing that our people were better than our competitors'? Confronted with questions like these, leaders often admitted that their supposed competitive strengths were traits their competitors also possessed, leaving us without a clear advantage in customers' eyes.

As I probed deeper into the realities of our businesses, I startled leaders at times by advocating radical change. In July 2004, the leader of our $3 billion chemicals business (our Performance Materials and Technologies business unit) argued that the organization couldn't possibly grow any further or become more profitable, as it was already placing in the top 10 percent of its peers. I asked how big the chemical industry was. The answer: $800 billion. Meanwhile, their business accounted for only $3 billion of that. Couldn't they find even a small piece of that $797 billion to claim for themselves? Of course they could.

In another instance, I asked leaders of our Specialty Materials business unit to create a chart that ranked each of the businesses they ran according to their profitability. Investors at the time were pressing us to sell this entire business. I disagreed. While Specialty Materials as a whole was underperforming, some of its component businesses were delivering well for us. Why should we sell them off, giving another company's investors the payoff for work we could accomplish ourselves? When I saw the chart our leaders had prepared, I drew a line through the middle of the page. I told the leaders: "All of these businesses to the right of the line, I want you to dispose of. All the ones to the left of the line, I want you to keep and build." The executive overseeing Specialty Materials protested, claiming they had been brought in to run a $3.5 billion business and double its size, and my cuts would shrink the business down to $2 billion. "I'm sorry about what you were told," I said, "but we're never going to grow with this existing portfolio. These business to the right of the line—they don't have any real competitive advantages. So get rid of them." Once this executive had a solid, albeit smaller, portfolio of businesses to run, we made real headway generating growth.

As more leaders began analyzing proposed strategic plans critically, our plans became much sharper, more realistic, and more successful. Our sensors business (part of our Automation and Control Solutions business unit) manufactured a range of products within two broad categories that generated roughly equal amounts of revenue: electromechanical sensors that employed both electronic circuits as well as switches or other mechanical parts, and sensors that used only electronic circuits. The latter was cutting-edge technology that the business leaders felt would take over the market. During the early 2000s, we were investing almost all of the business's R&D on developing electronic sensors, even though that category only accounted for half of the business unit's sales and none of its income. Meanwhile, we were investing almost nothing to refine and update our electromechanical sensors, sales of which were also growing and contributing half the revenue and all of the income. The strategy seemed to make sense—preparing for the future and to avoid being disrupted. But something didn't sit right to me, so we asked our business leaders several questions. How long had it been since we began forecasting the decline of electromechanical sensors? Was the electromechanical industry really in decline, or was the outlook more positive than we had thought? Finally, what would it take to make money in electronic sensors?

Leaders responded that we'd been forecasting the demise of electromechanical sensors for a long time, that they didn't know if that industry segment was still growing, and that they'd have to take a look to figure out what we'd need to do to make money in electronic sensors. Their analyses, presented during our next scheduled Growth Day, turned up two interesting findings. First, our legacy electromechanical sensors were hardly a dying business, as our leaders had presumed. Demand for these products continued to grow about 3 to 4 percent per year. And second, our R&D spending on electronic sensors was unfocused. We were throwing money at an array of potential end markets rather than thinking hard about which ones would most likely create value for us. We decided to reallocate a good chunk of R&D spending to creating innovative electromechanical devices, and to limit our spending on electronic sensors to just a few end markets, like the medical industry, where we could claim a true competitive advantage. Years later, this revised strategy helped make our sensors business extremely profitable, taking us from just a 5 percent margin to over 20 percent.

MAKE STRATEGY PART OF LEADERS' DAILY WORK

Beyond our uncompromising stance toward presentations, we took steps to make our planning process more regular and substantive. By setting aside growth and operations days for myself (see chapter 1), I created time in my schedule as well as in that of my staff to hold follow-up consultations with our business leaders. These were one-to-two-hour-long meetings on a variety of topics, held every six weeks, and organized around presentations that were short (no more than ten pages long) and that contained up-to-date data on the business's financial and operational performance. Our follow-up consultations forced leaders to gather and analyze data regularly throughout the year, since they now bore responsibility for reporting it to me. Strategy would no longer be a one-time annual event that everyone quickly forgot.

To further intensify this drumbeat of information, I asked the businesses to provide me with monthly reports on the Five Initiatives (which I'll cover in more detail in chapter 5) that defined our overall corporate strategy: growth, productivity, cash, people, and improvement initiatives such as Honeywell Operating System (what we called "enablers"). I wanted leaders at all levels in our businesses thinking about their strategies in some fashion almost every week.

As Roger Fradin recalled, such focus helped his organization because it prompted everyone to pay more attention to their markets. "We were all over what was going on with our competitors every day in the market," he said. "We were all over what was going on with our customers. I'm exaggerating by saying every day. But that was the culture. That was what the conversation was about."

By checking in more frequently, we could also focus better on challenging, longer-term goals. Take our fluorines business. During the 1990s, we had invented a fluorine molecule called hydrofluorocarbon (HFC) to replace the hydrochlorofluorocarbons (HCFC) and chlorofluorocarbons (CFCs) that had been degrading the ozone layer. Used in industrial contexts as refrigerants, HFCs served as an excellent substitute because they didn't deplete the ozone layer at all. Unfortunately, they were 1,300 times more potent than carbon dioxide in their contribution to global warming. To stay ahead in the industry, we needed to create and patent yet another replacement agent that wouldn't exacerbate climate change or deplete the ozone layer. That was a massive technical undertaking, requiring hundreds of millions of dollars in R&D spent over a number of years.

To assure that business leaders didn't cut R&D funding over that time and that they continued to assign their best people to the effort, we held regular strategic update meetings in which we discussed the team's efforts to date and any support the team needed. That oversight, along with an absolutely superb technology effort, made all the difference, allowing us to make slow but steady progress. After five years of dedicated effort, we invented a breakthrough molecule called a hydrofluoroolefin (HFO) that, according to independent studies, had a global warming effect 20 percent *lower* than carbon dioxide. As a result of that invention and the long-term contracts we were able to secure, our fluorines business today is thriving and highly profitable, with sales of over $1 billion.

The monthly reporting updates on the Five Initiatives we required of various businesses also helped, again because they allowed leaders to stay engaged and hold teams accountable. Our government services business provided a range of technology-based services to law enforcement, the military, and other government agencies to help them monitor data in the field, communicate securely, track conditions and local facilities, and so on. Around 2005, this business had adopted a strategic goal of seeking out bigger contracts (over $100 million) with government agencies. Since the business wanted to expand in size, it seemed to make sense to pursue bigger contracts, and leaders were convinced we could execute on them.

Month after month, I'd read updates sent along by leaders of this business. About eighteen months into the new strategy, it struck me that I hadn't seen us land any big new contracts lately, so I asked our leaders to analyze results over the period. It turned out that we had bid on eleven contracts but had landed only one, and on this one we were already the incumbent. That realization prompted us to reassess our strategy. We discovered that our customers didn't believe we could execute on the bigger contracts, and that in any case, they found it overly burdensome to transfer their business from their existing partner to us. We changed our strategy, pursuing smaller contracts in hopes of winning a higher percentage of them. Before long, our business started growing again.

As I like to say, modifying a famous statement of Thomas Edison's, "Business is 1 percent strategy and 99 percent execution." Take the time you need up front to get the strategy right so that you can then get the execution right. In particular, when leaders present executive summaries for their strategies, have them highlight what has changed in comparison with previous strategies. Organizations that shift their strategy every couple years become directionless and ineffectual. By taking extra time to ensure that your strategy makes sense and spending just a bit of time on a daily basis validating it, your organization can spend 99 percent of its time executing instead of flailing.

CONNECT OPERATIONS WITH LONG-TERM GOALS

In many companies, operations and strategy exist on different planes. Planning presentations take place in July, while operational budgets are formulated six months later, at year's end. Often, it turns out, businesses have less money than anticipated to spend because in the intervening six months costs ran higher and/or some sales didn't materialize. The business must then make short-term adjustments that can wreak havoc on long-term goals. As I recounted in the introduction, GE's appliance business sometimes laid off thousands of workers on an emergency basis in November of a given year, all because profit estimates for the following year came in lower than anticipated. We'd scramble to get corporate to allocate money for us to perform these layoffs and restructure the business, a disruption we might have avoided.

At Honeywell, we asked business leaders to think not just about the next five years when they presented strategic plans, as they traditionally did, but also to craft the following fiscal year's plan. We began consulting in depth with business leaders about the next fiscal year's strategy months before our July presentations. I did this casually, hopping on the phone with business leaders and sharing my strategic questions about their businesses, asking for their thoughts, and giving them my initial sense of what they should adopt as the following year's financial targets. Prompted to think about their goals for the next year earlier, leaders could mobilize others in their businesses to consider operational steps required during the current fiscal year, not just over the next five years, to deliver on the strategy—the specific initiatives they would have to fund, the workforce they would need (including whether they would need people with specific technical skills), the marketplace trends that would impact their business, and so on.

When July arrived, their operational plans for the following fiscal year were much more substantive, and their projected strategic goals and five-year financial performance forecast more realistic. This made the operational budget in November easier to adopt and allowed us to avoid last-minute, "emergency" situations related to that budget. Additionally, during the strategic plan presentation, leaders would show a comparison of their several previous five-year sales and earnings forecasts with their business's actual performance, gauging whether they had set and executed against the proper long-range strategic goals.

Business leaders initially disliked my focus on the next fiscal year. How could they possibly mire themselves in those details when they were still working hard to manage operations during the current fiscal year? I told them I assumed they would make their current year's numbers, because they had thought long and hard about them before committing to them. That usually stopped them cold. Then I got them to see that thinking about next year's operations now would help them succeed during the following year and on into the future. After all, the first priorities to lapse when a business falls into a crisis are long-term investments. When November arrived, and our leaders had to lock in their budgets, I wanted them to be able to make their short-term numbers while still planting seeds for the future. Ongoing operational planning guided by and infused with strategic thinking would prevent us from falling into a dynamic whereby emergency decision-making now made it harder in the future to achieve quarterly goals, leading to still more emergency decision-making and even fewer investments. By thinking ahead, we could pursue both long- and short-term goals simultaneously.

It took years for leaders throughout Honeywell to run their businesses at all times with long- and short-term perspectives in mind. I reinforced this approach constantly—at town halls, strategic planning meetings, annual operating meetings, training sessions, and other events. As I told people, succeeding in business often required them to do two seemingly conflicting things at the same time. We needed them to keep inventories low so we could save cash, but we also wanted to deliver for our customers. We needed to empower the people who worked for us, while also maintaining good controls. And in both our long-term planning and operational budgeting, we needed to obtain results today while laying the groundwork for our future success. Little by little, by dint of sheer repetition, the message sank in. I would hear people talking about "doing two seemingly conflicting things at the same time" and feel like cheering. As we'll see repeatedly throughout this book, driving change deeply into the organization requires consistency and relentless effort on leaders' part. When it came to managing for today *and* tomorrow, I wasn't giving in.

RESTRUCTURE LITTLE BY LITTLE

We've examined how to restructure the planning process, but what about the actual substance of strategic plans? The specifics will vary for businesses depending on their industry, size, market, and so on, yet one planning principle applies universally to businesses, helping them achieve strong or at least acceptable results now while cultivating future growth. I call this principle perpetual restructuring. Traditionally, companies restructure their businesses periodically to cut costs, primarily through mass layoffs and closures. Perpetual restructuring is a more gradual, moderate, and humbler approach. Instead of slashing costs dramatically all at once, keep your fixed costs steady while growing sales year over year. Operate more efficiently, doing just a bit more each year with roughly the same resources you used the previous year. To achieve those efficiency gains, deploy a variety of smaller restructuring programs that support ongoing process-improvement initiatives. Push to get a bit better—more efficient, more effective, more innovative—each year. Over time, as your business grows, deliver part of the added profits to investors, but set aside a portion to fund additional investments in R&D,

geographic expansion, process improvement, sales coverage, and strategic portfolio management (acquisitions, mergers, and divestitures). When you realize one-time gains from the sale of a business or some other asset, invest those as well instead of using them to artificially inflate short-term profits.

The Magic of Holding Fixed Costs Constant While Growing Sales

In most businesses, variable margins run somewhere between 30 to 80 percent. For every dollar of sales, between 30 and 80 cents goes to income, provided you hold fixed costs constant. If you allow fixed costs to increase, that margin gets chewed up. The chart below illustrates the impact. Just by holding fixed costs constant, we get 10 percent earnings growth instead of zero:

FIXED COSTS CONSTANT

	Year 1	Year 2
Sales	100	103
Variable Margin @40%	40	41
Fixed Costs	30	30
Operating Margin	10	11
		10% growth

FIXED COSTS GROW WITH SALES

	Year 1	Year 2
Sales	100	103
Variable Margin @40%	40	41
Fixed Costs	30	31
Operating Margin	10	10
		0% growth

In most businesses, labor comprises 70 to 80 percent of fixed costs. Every year wage and benefit increases alone could yield a 3-percent cost increase, assuming the headcount remains constant. That's why process improvement initiatives are so important, and why you should always put good reporting systems in place to track revenues and labor costs. Leaders and organizations always push for more people. They often don't examine what they could stop doing, do less of, or do better to make their existing staff more productive. Census constraints are, thus, vital to keeping fixed costs constant.

Perpetual restructuring won't allow you to maximize quarterly results, since you'll always be investing some percentage of profits back into the business. But as time passes and those investments come to fruition, you'll see additional and ever-increasing performance gains, which in turn enable additional investments. Growth becomes more robust, pleasing investors and allowing you to outperform competitors who haven't been steadily investing. Once the long-term investment flywheel is turning fast due to your increasing annual investments, you can stop increasing the rate of investment. At that point, investors' returns increase significantly because you can devote a greater portion of the income increases to them.

Most businesses don't move from good to great—or in Honeywell's case, from failing to great—all at once. They do it slowly, one year and one quarter at a time, in a disciplined fashion. Take our sensors business. By 2005, a series of acquisitions had left the business with thirty-seven relatively small-scale (about five hundred employees each) plants around the world. Coordinating that many plants was unproductive, and we couldn't deliver well for customers. Each plant also represented a considerable amount of fixed costs for us, including maintenance of the buildings, employee salaries, and the cost of running assembly lines.

I asked business leaders to imagine what their ideal production footprint would look like. After running through the White Sheet of Paper exercise described in chapter 1, they realized they could run the business quite well with only twelve plants. If we had taken a less thoughtful approach to planning, we might have decided to close all twenty-five plants all at once, swallowing a sizable restructuring charge in hopes of delivering short-term cost savings. We would have laid off thousands of workers simultaneously, unsettling the invisible processes at work that underpinned our operations (what is often called the "hidden factory"). We also would have temporarily disrupted customer service while transitioning to our new factory footprint.

Applying our perpetual restructuring philosophy, we spread our closure of these twenty-five plants over a decade, laying off just a few employees each year and gradually upgrading our production capacity. Along the way, our leaders improved a number of other areas, including R&D spending, as previously mentioned. All of this effort, managed while still delivering reasonably good quarterly returns, helped transform our sensors' business from good to great.

We applied perpetual restructuring to all of our businesses and saw dramatic improvements in all of them. Traditionally, Honeywell Transportation Systems had manufactured turbochargers for diesel engines, serving customers in the automobile industry. Leaders had resisted manufacturing turbochargers for gasoline engines, feeling our technology afforded no great competitive advantage. In 2007, when a new executive took over the business, we made a move into gasoline turbochargers, reasoning that gasoline engines comprise half of the total market, and would continue to do so for the foreseeable future. But rather than embark on a crash course to develop gasoline turbocharger products, we applied the perpetual restructuring philosophy and invested just a portion of our profits each year to R&D related to gasoline turbochargers. A decade later, we're a major player in both diesel and gasoline turbochargers, claiming about 30 percent of the gasoline turbocharger market and generating an additional billion dollars in revenues. The business has done so well that we recently spun it off to shareholders as an independent public enterprise.

Stories like this have added up to sustained success at the enterprise level. Perpetual restructuring allowed us to boost our self-funded investment in R&D from 3.3 percent of sales in 2003 to 5.5 percent in 2016. We also spent between $10 and $40 million each quarter on restructuring (in addition to any one-time gains) to improve our processes. Sell-side analysts initially wondered when this restructuring would end, and they didn't like our answer: never. One of Honeywell's biggest investors understood our approach, and good thing: over time we boosted our operating margins from about 8 percent in 2003 to about 16 percent in 2018, while almost doubling sales. Although Wall Street in 2002 had already thought of us as a "lean" company, we became far more efficient and profitable, all by devising strategies that worked in the short term while giving us the resources we needed to plant seeds for the future. Analysts who had formerly doubted perpetual restructuring became strong believers.

CHANGE HOW YOU PLAN

If your business hasn't planned for both today and tomorrow, start now. Clear out short-termism from your strategic thinking, banishing those easy, end-of-quarter fixes that might save you this quarter but compromise performance later. Make your planning process more rigorous and keep everyone focused on the strategy even as they go about making daily operational decisions. Avoid those overly ambitious plans and instead adopt a measured approach, balancing short-term profits with investment in future growth. You might believe it's too late to implement a specific long-term plan or strategy, and you might be right. But you probably aren't. I often quoted a popular Chinese proverb when addressing our leaders: "The best time to plant a tree is twenty years ago. The second best time is today."

Honeywell didn't learn all at once how to plan for today *and* tomorrow. In addition to the eighteen months we spent purging unhealthy accounting practices, it took us several more years before leaders internalized this new approach and adopted it as a cultural norm. You can expect a similar period of transition at your business. Ride it out by staying closely involved. When others ask you to authorize decisions whose only purpose seems to be "making the numbers," hold your ground. When others propose massive, one-time improvement projects, ask them to rethink it, breaking these projects into smaller pieces that you can execute more easily. Demand that your teams run their businesses better each year, growing while relying on the same fixed-cost budgets they used the year before, or at least growing costs much less than sales. Your stance won't be popular at first, but as results improve and the path to future growth becomes easier, people will see the wisdom of your approach. Strategic planning will shift from the pointless, burdensome exercise it might be today to your organization's lodestar.

You can plan for today and tomorrow at any level—whether you lead a business unit, a department, or a small team. If you run the payroll department at a company, ask yourself each year how you could handle an increasing volume of work while keeping fixed costs steady. How can you redesign your processes and systems so that you reduce errors, use fewer people, and are generally more effective? Generate some ideas (I'll focus on process improvement in greater depth in chapter 4), and then develop a strategic plan to implement them, as well as an operating budget. Find a way to reduce costs elsewhere within your organization to self-fund at least a portion of your ideas. Bring your ideas to your bosses and sell them, describing how you'll start slow, make sustainable progress, and see sizable performance gains over time.

This approach also works in small organizations and teams. Becoming more effective at planning and delivering both short- and long-term results gets you noticed by your superiors as someone who can think independently and make a difference. If that doesn't happen, and if your bosses persist in holding you to unrealistic goals, then perhaps you should move to an organization that is more honest with itself and committed to high performance. (Before reaching that conclusion, make certain that these goals really are misguided, and that your bosses aren't just pushing you to think more broadly.)

WATCH YOURSELF

As you pursue perpetual restructuring, you might feel tempted to depart from the philosophy and allow businesses to boost profits occasionally by booking a juicy one-time gain. Don't do it! Even occasional padding of profits can instill organizational laziness. The next year you'll set unrealistic goals, and people will insist on taking similarly desperate measures to reach them. The craving for fiscal shortcuts is rather like alcoholism: when you stop, you need to do it cold turkey and permanently. If you take another drink, even years later, you risk relapsing. As a leader, adopt a posture of constant vigilance. Don't ever assume that others have fully bought into perpetual restructuring and responsible planning. Keep pounding away, pointing out at every opportunity that organizations really can—and must—plan carefully for short- and long-term goals simultaneously.

If you lead a public company, pay special attention to investors. Like executives in your organization, many investors won't get perpetual restructuring at first, and they probably won't see the important steps you're taking internally to reform strategic planning. Resist the urge to meet their earnings expectations to the letter. Alert shareholders and analysts to the growth investments you're making, explain their worth to the business, and give shareholders and analysts some sense of how long it will take for investments to mature. Quarter by quarter, make your life easier by setting earnings goals conservatively. Adopt goals that run just under what you reasonably think your business can achieve but that are high enough so that investors won't flee. If your business outperforms those goals, great—channel part of those earnings into additional restructuring. If your business runs into unanticipated challenges, you'll have wiggle room and won't feel tempted to resort to the sort of last-minute deals and accounting tricks that used to damage our business.

PLANTING TREES INSTEAD OF CUTTING THEM DOWN

In 2002, after I eradicated our "make the quarter" meetings and banned the last-minute deals our people made to beef up their numbers, I wondered if these measures were changing reality on the ground. Using one of my X days, I paid a surprise visit to a chemical plant of ours in Louisiana to inspect the facility and talk to leaders and employees.

When I arrived, the plant manager greeted me and showed me around the inside of one of the facility's buildings. As we walked, he explained how the plant operated, what it produced, and what difficulties it had been experiencing. After perhaps fifteen minutes, I asked if he had noticed any operational changes since we had eliminated our "make the quarter" meetings. "Definitely," he told me. "I used to spend hours every week putting together special deals so that we'd make our numbers. I'd waste time figuring out other accounting ideas. I don't have to do that anymore, so I can actually run the plant."

We cracked open a door and walked outside to tour some of the plant's extensive grounds. Glancing around, I saw great expanses of flat, open land extending to the horizon, all belonging to the plant. "Hey," I said, turning back to him. "Do you have any examples of things you did to make the numbers? What are you doing differently now that you weren't before?"

"Yeah, I can be more specific," he said. He pointed straight ahead. "See those fields out there?"

I nodded.

"Those all used to be trees—hundreds of acres worth. One time, to make the quarter, I had all those trees cut down and sold for timber. For most of the quarter, I spent my time on that transaction, as opposed to running the plant, because financially it was the biggest deal we had going. When that sale closed, it helped us reach our goals for the quarter. Would you believe, I actually got an award for creativity for coming up with the idea of selling the timber, and they started looking at all the other plants to see if they could do the same thing."

I shook my head in disbelief. "Wow."

"Yeah. But thanks to the changes we've implemented, I don't have to spend my time doing that stuff anymore. I can focus on real issues, like getting our customers the product they need in the most efficient way possible."

Planning for today *and* tomorrow takes work. I spent a sizable chunk of my time as CEO following up with general managers on their strategic plans, analyzing them, and promoting our philosophy of perpetual restructuring. Other leaders did this too. But all that effort paid off. Instead of looking for quick fixes, jerry-rigging our businesses together quarter by quarter, we changed the way work got done and improved how our businesses ran. Instead of cutting down trees, we planted them.

QUESTIONS TO ASK YOURSELF

1. What kind of short-term, "make the quarter" activities do you see in your organization? Are they hurting long-term effectiveness?
2. What can you do to generate funding for long-term initiatives while still generating adequate short-term results? Have you considered ways to hold fixed costs flat, or at least to have them grow at a rate far below that of sales growth?
3. Is your planning process more of an annual event rather than a rigorous, ongoing examination of your strategy?
4. Is your CFO conservative in his or her outlook? If your CFO is an optimist, you're in trouble!
5. How might you encourage people to reflect upon next year's results at the beginning of this year rather than at the end?
6. Instead of always trying for a "big bang" of growth, have you considered areas where perpetual restructuring might help you?
7. In your day-to-day interactions, do you spark people to think about business basics like doing a great job for customers, generating real sales, cutting costs, and investing wisely for the future?
8. Do certain long-term initiatives never seem to generate short-term results? What can you do to fix them?

PART TWO

OPTIMIZE THE ORGANIZATION

CHAPTER THREE

Resolve Serious Threats to the Business

In 2003, about a year after I became CEO, an employee was killed while working at our chemical plant in Baton Rouge, Louisiana. I immediately sent in a team of environmental specialists to determine what had caused this tragedy. Touring the plant's grounds, they found a number of old chemical cylinders lying around. Labels affixed to these cylinders indicated which substances they contained, but nobody knew for sure if the labels were correct. The deceased employee had died because he had opened a one-ton cylinder filled with chemicals and had been overcome by the powerful fumes. As we discovered, the cylinder he had opened had been incorrectly labeled, and he had opened it in violation of our safety protocol.

I wanted to know why the employee hadn't followed protocol. And why were there old, mislabeled cylinders lying around? To get some answers, I flew down to the facility, paying leaders there a surprise visit. When I arrived, the receptionist didn't know who I was—that's how much of a surprise it was. The plant manager gave me a tour of the plant and showed me the spot where the fatal incident had occurred. Afterward, I met with plant leaders in a small conference room and asked them to explain what was going on at the plant. "You have to understand, Dave," one of these leaders said, "this accident could have occurred anywhere. Chemical plants are dangerous places. We were just unlucky that it happened to us."

Unlucky. Did he just say that?

I asked additional questions and got more lame answers: "Everyone runs plants like this." "Failing to follow safety instructions is human nature." "Accidents like this can happen at any facility at any time, and there's nothing you can do about it." After ten or fifteen minutes of this, I'd had enough. Raising my voice, I berated the leaders seated next to me. "Do you understand that a man *died* in this facility and that it could have been prevented if we had handled these cylinders out there properly, and if he had followed the protocol he had learned in his trainings? You've got an abysmal safety culture here—I mean, *abysmal*. Rather than make excuses for yourselves, you've got to get your butts in gear and fix it!"

Subsequent investigation revealed that safety issues comprised an important threat not just at this plant but firm wide. An untold number of incidents like this were waiting to happen at our facilities around the world. To prevent them, we would have to invest heavily in training and process improvement.

Safety was hardly the only serious issue I inherited as CEO. During the first year of my tenure, I was chagrined to discover that Honeywell's legal and environmental liabilities were far greater than I realized. I had known we were fighting a significant number of lawsuits related to asbestos, but I hadn't realized that we faced billions in liabilities, or that we'd need billions more to clean up chemical contamination at our facilities. And then there was our underfunded pension fund to deal with, and the aggressive accounting practices described in the last chapter. Holy cow! These issues loomed darkly over our business—time bombs just waiting to go off. They also bothered me personally. As a child of the 1960s, I didn't feel comfortable leading an organization that didn't take its social responsibilities seriously.

A conversation I had with Kate Adams, a new litigation lawyer we hired, offered a fairly stark indication of just how big of a challenge these legacy issues posed. About six months after Kate started, I happened to run into her in the hallway. "So," I said, "now that you've settled into our company, are you having buyer's remorse?"

Her face brightened. "No, not at all. We have such a tremendous portfolio. It's so exciting to be here."

"Wonderful," I said. "Yes, we do have a great portfolio of businesses here, and it will be exciting to see how we can build on them in the years ahead."

"Well, that too," she said. "But I was really talking about the portfolio of lawsuits we have. We get sued for everything! All kinds of stuff, all around the world. It's really interesting."

Now, I'm all about enthusiasm on the job, but this is *not* what any CEO wants to hear.

As important as it is to balance the short and long term in strategic planning generally, some historic liabilities are so potentially damaging that you have to take a greater short-term hit than you might like—and sometimes an ongoing hit—in order to mitigate them. Otherwise you won't be nearly as successful down the road with *either* short- or long-term objectives, and you won't succeed in setting up a virtuous cycle, in which short-term gains set the stage for longer-term achievements, and vice versa. Overcoming short-termism means finally tackling those legacy issues that have been pushed off onto the next leader's shoulders for too long. As I told my team again and again, you can't build a good house unless you have a strong foundation. If your organization or team lacks such a foundation, now is the time to set money and other resources aside and start building.

THE SCOURGE OF SHORT-TERM THINKING, REVISITED

Most companies that have been in business for decades—or in Honeywell's case, over a century—will have legacy issues of some kind. Laws and social expectations about safety and health change over time, as do our knowledge of the consequences of technologies and production processes. Activity that seemed reasonable and safe decades ago caused harm, for which the law rightly or wrongly holds companies responsible. Although settling these liabilities can hamper growth, it's by no means necessary for liabilities to pile up to such an extent that they threaten an organization's capacity to compete and grow. That they do at many companies is owed to a common scourge: short-termism.

At Honeywell, previous leaders had exposed us unnecessarily to liability because of their failure at key moments to consider the company's long-term health. In the case of asbestos, we had two big sources of legal exposure: from our Bendix brake business (brake linings we'd manufactured over the years contained asbestos), and from a small business called NARCO we had owned decades earlier that manufactured the special, heat-tolerant bricks used in the construction of industrial smokestacks. We had sold NARCO during the 1980s for about $60 million but were still liable for its asbestos problems. That's because our leaders back then, eager to seal the deal, had agreed to a clause in the final agreement that said we would retain liability for future claims in perpetuity. By the early 2000s, our legal liability from this one company amounted to—get ready for it—$1 billion. If you needed proof that short-termism can have drastic consequences for a business, there you go.

Even more significantly, short-termism had caused these and other liabilities we faced to pile up and worsen over time. Issues like safety concerns, environmental and asbestos liabilities, and our pension shortfall had also been ignored in large part because no one would sacrifice quarterly earnings in order to resolve them. Instead of cleaning up a polluted site or biting the bullet and resolving an asbestos issue, leaders had opted to fight lawsuits in court as far as they possibly could, paying out only when a jury decision or a judge left us no choice. Because the vast majority of these cases weren't getting resolved, we faced the possibility of even greater liabilities in the years to come.

All our legacy issues—not just environmental and asbestos but pension and accounting too—hurt our relationship with Wall Street. At every meeting during the first several years of my tenure, I'd try to kick off the proceedings by talking about our businesses and the growth opportunities we saw, but I couldn't because analysts would pound me with questions about our legacy liabilities. In 2006, JP Morgan downgraded our stock rating specifically because of the uncertainty created by our environmental challenges. As their research report on us noted, "Environmental related costs have been . . . a key drag that continues to mask otherwise favorable end market leverage in core operating units. . . ."[1] Wall Street couldn't get excited about our businesses when they saw so much potential risk.

Many members of the public didn't like us very much either. Honeywell should have been seen not merely as an environmentally friendly company but as a world leader in sustainability. After all, the products and services we sold (and still sell) helped the world reduce emissions, generate green energy, defend the country, and protect the ozone layer. Because of our handling of legacy issues, however, our brand image was terrible. At around the time when I became CEO, we were facing several criminal and near-criminal investigations. In 2003, the District Court of New Jersey rendered a decision sharply criticizing our handling of environmental issues and ordered us to conduct a massive cleanup at a site in Jersey City. "I find that Honeywell was less than cooperative and embarked on a dilatory, foot-dragging scheme for 20 years," the judge wrote.[2]

In other communities around the country, environmental and asbestos lawsuits yielded vast amounts of bad press for us. A 2003 op-ed in the local Syracuse, New York, newspaper warned of "lakeside toxic tombs" at Honeywell-owned sites, while a 2004 article in the *Arizona Republic* carried the headline "Honeywell Sued on Toxic Fuel."[3] In the latter article, the state's attorney general was quoted as saying that "Honeywell seemed to think they could tell the regulators anything they wanted with impunity and not be bound by the truth." Not terribly flattering. And as you can imagine, such stories didn't win us plaudits from employees either. It's hard to feel proud about where you work when your employer is constantly being sued and acting like a bad guy in court.

You might wonder whether previous generations of leaders had experienced pangs of conscience about failing to deal with legacy issues like pollution or asbestos. If they did, I didn't hear about it. As I've said, it was inevitable that we would have legacy issues, but from the perspective of leaders, it was best to ignore or downplay them, minimizing their short-term financial impact on our businesses. Lawsuits and public outcry were unpleasant byproducts of doing business. Maybe someday these issues would be permanently resolved, but that wasn't our problem. We needed to focus on performing *now*.

If you're running a team or organization with legacy issues, don't think like this. Younger generations of employees and consumers expect transparency from companies, and they have less tolerance than ever for leaders and organizations that shirk their social responsibility. Companies that step up to repair the harm they've caused and prevent new harm from occurring have a much easier time attracting top talent to their doors. It's probably going to be cheaper for your organization to resolve your legacy issues now than it will be a decade from now, when the harm will have mounted even more. But if none of this convinces you to take action, think about your legacy. What kind of leader do you want to be? Do you want to be known as the leader who passed the buck and feigned ignorance? Or do you want to be known as the one who had the courage to do what others wouldn't, even if it bit into short-term results?

RESOLVE LEGACY ISSUES STRATEGICALLY

When I became CEO, I was determined to fix these issues *now*, even if it depressed our earnings in the short term, because as I saw it, our future depended on it, and I didn't want my successor to deal with these time bombs. In 2002, we set aside $1.5 billion in a reserve fund to settle our thousands of asbestos-related lawsuits. We also boosted the amount of money we set aside each year to handle our many dozens of outstanding environmental issues, raising it from $80 million a year to $250 million. Subsequently, we allocated almost $900 million to properly fund our pension, pouring another $4.5 billion into it during the Great Recession. We invested in better safety training not just in our Baton Rouge plant but across Honeywell, and we spent two years getting our financials on a much sounder footing.

We couldn't just throw money at legacy problems—short-term performance still mattered. To make the hit on our business as manageable as possible, we invested strategically to resolve environmental issues over time. To enable us to resolve our legacy issues as efficiently and effectively as possible, I built a new team dedicated to the purpose. I had hoped I'd be able to find existing leaders within Honeywell, but it turned out that our people in Health, Safety, and Environmental (HSE), the function that oversaw our efforts in these areas, didn't have the vision or determination. Also, regulators knew and, in some cases, hated these leaders, a reality that would make it difficult for us to develop more collaborative and productive relationships going forward. We needed leaders whom regulators trusted, but also leaders who could help drive creative and collaborative solutions that could accomplish two seemingly conflicting things at the same time: save us money *and* remedy environmental issues correctly.

During the first few years of my tenure, we rebuilt our HSE function from top to bottom. To oversee our litigation efforts, we brought in Kate Adams, an extraordinarily capable attorney whose father, John Adams, had founded the National Resource Defense Council, one of the nation's most prominent environmental activist groups. Hiring her sent a message to regulators that we wanted a new kind of relationship—with her pedigree, people knew she wouldn't take actions on our behalf that compromised environmental health. Another key leader we hired was Evan van Hook, a former regulator and environmental attorney who commanded trust on both sides of regulatory issues. These two leaders began replacing the HSE leaders assigned to our main business units, and those executives, in turn, built out their own teams. Soon, the HSE function throughout our organization was peopled with leaders and managers who were committed to solving problems smartly, not ignoring them, passing the buck, or doing the bare minimum.

As our team coalesced, we began taking a markedly different approach to our environmental litigation. Rather than tying up environmental legislation with painful and expensive legal maneuvers, we began approaching regulators and communities and negotiating with them to come up with more creative, long-term solutions. Regulators often seek to obtain the most money they can from environmental polluters, irrespective of whether the particular remediation method under discussion is the best one. When we engaged with affected communities, we wanted to see if we could find solutions that got the job done right, but that did so in innovative, cost-effective ways. We wanted everyone to win—the environment, local communities, *and* our shareholders. And we wanted to partner with communities over the long term, sharing the cost and responsibility in situations where it made sense to do that.

In the spirit of cooperation, we went above and beyond our legal responsibilities to clean up polluted sites, investing to develop new uses for these sites that created jobs, recreational opportunities, and other benefits for communities. At Baltimore, Maryland's inner harbor, we undertook a $100 million cleanup overseen by the Environmental Protection Agency. Partnering with the City of Baltimore, we helped redevelop the site as Harbor Point, an "integrated and sustainable waterfront neighborhood." To date, several modern office buildings have been erected on the site, and plans call for the creation of parks, residential units, and other amenities. As a prominent local politician said, "Harbor Point promises to be a vibrant and new transit-oriented and sustainable mixed-use development that provides a diversified mix of office, residential, and retail options for all city residents."[4] At another Baltimore site, Dundalk Marine Terminal, we've partnered under a consent decree negotiated in 2006 to clean up a site heavily contaminated with chromium. Cleanup costs have run to over $100 million, with Honeywell paying the largest share of the costs and the Maryland Port Commission also chipping in.[5] "Throughout all the years that we've known Honeywell, we've developed trust and friendship," said Edythe Brooks, a neighborhood community leader. "Honeywell has done everything they said they were going to do, and more."[6]

THE BUSINESS CASE FOR RESOLVING LEGACY ISSUES

As good as projects like these have been for local communities, they've benefited us immensely by building up goodwill. In one instance, arsenic from one of our old industrial sites was found leaking in a Baltimore playground. We hadn't even known the arsenic was there, but now that we did, we didn't wait around for someone to sue us to clean it up. Although it cost us millions, we got out our checkbook. Sometime later I happened to run into a US senator at a social event. Pulling me aside, she expressed her satisfaction at what we had done, telling me, "I just want you to know how much all of us in

Maryland appreciate how you handled that situation." Because of our more proactive and collaborative approach, we now had a community that thought more highly of our company, including an influential political leader.

Our new approach saved us money too. It's impossible to say how much, since in any particular case we don't know what a court or a jury would have eventually ordered us to pay had we taken our old, adversarial approach. But one situation that unfolded in 2005 gives us some indication. Although we had moved to reach negotiated settlements in many pending lawsuits, we had chosen to fight one claim concerning a chromium-contaminated property in Jersey City, New Jersey. Our legal department assured me that we didn't bear legal responsibility and were highly likely to win our case in court. We wound up losing it, to the tune of $400 million dollars. As a result of the loss, we had to restate our earnings, a step that on a personal level hurt like hell. We had just started building credibility with investors, and now we had taken a big step backward. I can't say for sure, but if we had negotiated a settlement, we might well have found a way to resolve the situation to everyone's satisfaction for $100–$200 million, and not had to restate our earnings.

A key part of our proactive approach to handling legacy issues while minimizing the short-term hit entailed managing our relationship with Wall Street. Although we made sure to disclose everything the law required, we didn't do much to tout all of the progress we were making because I didn't want to mobilize all those people who feel large companies are never doing enough, and I also didn't want to focus investors' attention on our liabilities more than absolutely necessary. I saw pretty quickly that any progress we were making on legacy issues wouldn't register immediately with Wall Street. After we set aside about $1.5 billion for asbestos claims, CNBC's Jim Cramer applauded the move and spoke positively about our stock. But other investors felt differently, asking again and again how much more I thought we'd need in the future. When I told them this was it, and between our reserve and ongoing changes to operations we were all set on asbestos, they didn't believe me. "Everyone always underestimates their liabilities," they said to me. I assured them we had been very careful and conservative in our estimates, but it didn't matter—they still felt nervous.

I tried to win investors over by pointing out that if we set aside money up front and made other short-term sacrifices, our costs would remain fixed over time. As the company grew, these charges would *decrease* as a percentage of sales, allowing our earnings to soar. Furthermore, as I've suggested, we'd be able to tackle our legacy issues more cheaply if we addressed them immediately rather than wait for new disasters to strike (more employee deaths in our plants, for instance, or huge jury verdicts in environmental suits) and then react. Over time, investors did see the wisdom of this approach. Costs related to our liabilities decreased over time as a percentage of profits, even if some of those costs—specifically, those related to resolving our environmental liabilities—turned out to be significantly greater than expected in absolute terms.[1] Whereas JP Morgan had downgraded our stock in 2006, it upgraded us two years later, noting that environmental issues were "still a risk, but being managed well."[7] Investors might not love you at first for resolving legacy issues, even if they claim to like long-term thinking. But they don't need to love you. Do your best to address their concerns, be consistent in your messaging, and have faith they'll come around eventually. If you move seriously to resolve these issues, and if you do it in a smart, disciplined fashion, they'll eventually notice.

BUILD A MORE RESPONSIBLE ORGANIZATION

Beyond resolving harms that had already taken place, we saw a tremendous opportunity to prevent new issues from cropping up going forward. A good example concerns our manufacturing facilities in developing countries.

---

1   We set aside as much as possible to resolve our environmental issues under applicable accounting rules. Most of these issues can't be reserved on a company's books (in other words, formally considered a liability) until leaders can ascertain a reliable, potential range of costs. Before that range is established, these issues remain a contingent liability. They are not officially on the books as a reserve, but the investment community recognizes them as a potential liability of some magnitude. Although we didn't know what our environmental liabilities would cost us, I embarked on a process to address them, guessing that it would eventually cost us $2 billion over ten years. The real cost amounted to $3.5 billion over fifteen years.

As we expanded our global footprint (a topic discussed in chapter 7), we had insisted that any new facilities we built in these countries be safe and clean for workers. I didn't want to risk a situation where safety or health problems at a plant one day harmed employees or others, creating a real crisis for us. I also didn't want to be a leader who allowed people to work in conditions I wouldn't have wanted to endure myself. Leaders had always assured me that our facilities were top-notch, and I had believed them. In 2012, we did a complete audit of our facilities in developing regions, making sure the cafeterias, bathrooms, dormitories, and other facilities were places we ourselves would want to use. It turned out that some of our facilities were subpar. In addition to making the necessary fixes, members of my team began traveling the world to see facilities for themselves, rigorously holding plant managers accountable. We included a review of our facilities in the regular safety and HR audits we did, implementing new standards such as the requirement that cafeterias be good enough that facility managers wanted to eat there.

An even bigger way we aligned our people proactively behind the prevention of HSE problems was through the Honeywell Operating System (HOS), a major process improvement initiative we undertook across the entire organization. HOS is a system for organizing work that mobilizes other well-known process improvement tools like Lean methodologies and Six Sigma, galvanizing leaders and frontline workers to improve operations in their facilities. I'll offer a detailed look at HOS in chapter 4, but for now I'll note that as we rolled out the program around the world, thanks to the leadership of Evan van Hook, our vice president of Health, Safety, Environment, Product Stewardship & Sustainability, we presented it explicitly as a means not merely to achieve efficiencies and reduce costs, but to also improve our health, safety, and environmental performance, involving HSE leaders intimately in the rollout and building HSE into daily work processes.

As part of HOS, we mandated that each facility conduct an audit of its operations every year to identify projects for increasing energy efficiency. We also required the rigorous reporting of all safety incidents when they occurred, a measure that caused our numbers of reported incidences to rise but afforded us a far more accurate picture of conditions at our plants.

Employees received ongoing training on best practices in sustainability and on related technology. Just as important, workers in our local plants drove ongoing improvement in HSE by conducting daily meetings to monitor conditions and identify problems as they occurred. As Evan recalled, every single HOS-related meeting started with a conversation about safety or sustainability issues: "From the plant floor workers all the way up to plant leadership, you're starting with, 'Okay, what's going on in environmental and safety? What are the key things we need to deal with? Are there any major issues?'"[8]

As part of these discussions, employees or managers at every level were empowered to make suggestions for *kaizens*, or improvement events, that bore on HSE concerns (these events, which convened relevant parties, including hourly workers, to solve process issues in real-time, were fundamental to HOS). In 2010, to focus our businesses even more on care for the environment in particular, we mandated that each business adopt annual budgets for energy and water usage and greenhouse gas emissions alongside their standard financial budgets. Spurred by this new accountability, our businesses unleashed HOS to drive huge additional sustainability gains. Instead of bringing in outside consultants to generate recommendations for improvements, our people did all of this work themselves. As van Hook noted, in particular plants "it was literally a matter of people saying, 'Okay, guys, the next two weeks we're going to have our kaizen focused on identifying places where we're using too much energy.' The number of projects and savings generated were just amazing." And because employees were developing the solutions themselves, they became far more personally engaged in sustainability and determined to see the solutions through.

At a plant in Singapore, workers noticed we were using an electrode during our manufacturing process that contained a mildly radioactive material. It wasn't a huge safety risk, but mildly radioactive particles were being released into the air at points on the electrode that were subject to grinding. Workers came up with an idea to substitute electrodes made of a different material that wasn't radioactive and didn't pose a potential health hazard. The change improved safety while also saving the plant money. Under

Singaporean law, the plant was paying a small fee each year to dispose of the radioactive material. Now disposal cost nothing.[2]

At our plant in Olomouc, Czech Republic, workers noticed that certain steps in our use of cleaning chemicals were redundant. In particular, we were cleaning parts multiple times when they were already clean. This increased how much toxic degreasing solution we used. By redesigning the process, workers eliminated the production of thirty tons of chemical waste and reduced our consumption of natural gas by 6.5 percent—a boon for the environment. Workers were safer, since they didn't have to handle as many chemicals, and production time was shortened. The plant also saved money—about $15,000 a year.

Some Typical Process Improvements Undertaken as Part of HOS

- In Shanghai, China, workers designed a new cutting tool that reduced worker exposure to sharp blades, decreasing the risk of hand and eye injuries and improving productivity.
- In Nantong, China, workers built a new storage tank and pump system that allowed for reuse of water during the production process, lowering consumption and saving $30,000 each year.
- In Groveport, Ohio, workers installed a new barrier at our dock doors, reducing the risks that employees would inadvertently fall off the docks.
- In Chennai, India, the plant implemented an energy conservation program. The process changes they implemented saved 5,000 kilowatt-hours a month of energy, and almost $900,000 a year.
- In Pune, India, our plant installed solar panels on the facility's roof, a measure that will generate 18 percent of the plant's power needs and save an estimated $70,000 each year.

---

2   This paragraph and the next, as well as the accompanying text box, draw on internal Honeywell documents.

SUSTAINED INCREMENTAL IMPROVEMENTS ADD UP

Leaders often think of improving safety and reducing their environmental footprint as inherently costly, and it's true that making gains in these areas usually does require some up-front investment. But as we've found, process improvement can reduce costs while also proactively reducing harm to employees and the environment. Why wait for environmental and safety lapses to pile up? Attack them *before* a lawsuit, injury, or public outcry forces you to.

It took fifteen years, but thanks to HOS and the massive investments we've made in resolving our historical liabilities, we've gotten these challenges under control. We continue to litigate many asbestos cases, but we managed to contain our NARCO-related liability by creating a trust that uses revenues from that company's operations to help pay back plaintiffs, with Honeywell responsible for the difference. Regarding our environmental lawsuits, it cost us more than I imagined—$3.5 billion over fifteen years versus the $2 billion over ten years I had originally projected—but we have resolved all of our big environmental liabilities. Our annual spending on our asbestos-related and environmental liabilities has remained constant, even as our revenues have nearly doubled. Whereas initially we spent 2 percent of revenues each year on these liabilities, today it's significantly less than that, meaning we have additional resources freed up to invest in actually *growing* our business. At the same time, we've reduced risk to our business, eliminating all of those potential time bombs.

Thanks to our organizational improvements, we're now a much safer, more environmentally responsible company than we used to be. The frequency of environmental incidents at Honeywell has declined by 93 percent between 2005 and 2018. As of 2018, we were about 70 percent more energy efficient than we had been in 2004, and our safety record has dramatically improved—we're currently 80 percent better than the industry average. Meanwhile, we've received dozens of awards for our financial and environmental performance, won plaudits from investors, and had a pension fund that was *over*funded by 10 percent—huge changes compared to where we had been, and changes that would benefit the company well into the future. Instead of a company under siege, we're in control of our destiny, all because we were willing to own our problems and make the necessary short-term investments.

CHANGING HOW YOU APPROACH LEGACY ISSUES

You can put your business on a surer footing too. Suck it up and deal with the skeletons in your closet—not next year, or in three years, but *now*. And for heaven's sake, don't do it halfway. Be *honest* with yourself, your investors, and your bosses about the situation your business is in and set aside all the funds required to resolve legacy issues. Underestimating the size of these issues might improve your short-term results, but they'll create new headaches later on. In general, when you have a problem to address, it pays to over-resource the solution up front, since it always costs less to resolve problems earlier rather than later, even if the short-term cost seems high at the time. I often used the following simple chart to describe what happens to problems and the resources required to address them over time:

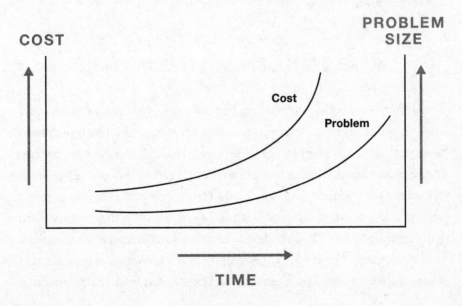

The last thing you want to do is go back to bosses or investors for more money later once your investments have proven insufficient. You'll lose credibility, leaving the impression that you don't understand the depth of the problems before you. On the other hand, if you wind up overestimating the costs, you'll look even better later on. You'll have resolved the issues, while also presenting bosses and investors with a pleasant surprise: it hasn't cost as much as you thought.

Don't just put money behind the resolution of legacy issues; put the right talent too. Look for people who have the respect of plaintiffs and regulators, understand how they think and can work with them and you, and who are smart and creative enough to address lingering issues in new ways. More generally, take an "inside out" approach to legacy issues, improving the entire organization so that it behaves more responsibly toward workers, local communities, and the environment. If you're paying to resolve harm done decades ago, and you're still polluting the environment or subjecting workers to unsafe conditions, then you haven't fully put your organization on a growth footing. Future leaders will still have a mess to clean up, one that was created on *your* watch. And to the outside world, your efforts to clean up polluted areas and settle outstanding lawsuits will seem half-hearted at best.

ADDRESSING LEGACY ISSUES FROM THE MIDDLE

Some mid-level managers reading this might doubt whether they have enough power to resolve legacy issues. Actually, you might have more power than you think. Not every legacy issue rises to the level of corporate strategy. If you manage a particular facility, and a broken process you inherited is causing a safety hazard, you can change the process and give your employees the safety training they need. If you have a site on your property filled with potentially hazardous materials or other junk lying around, you can take money out of your budget to clean it up. If a broken sales organization seems poised to cause problems in the years ahead, you can reform that organization now. If specific work processes in your facility are subjecting workers to repetitive stress injuries, rework the processes.

On one occasion when I was running General Electric's silicones business, I visited a plant that was a mess and told the leadership team there to clean up the place. I directed everyone's attention to the drums of chemicals that were lying around, machines that were broken and posing safety hazards, and so on. One employee raised her hand and said, "Hey, if you really want to solve these issues, why don't you take a look at the big trash pile that's located right outside my workspace? It's probably loaded with toxic materials, and it's been there for years." I asked to see this spot and was appalled by what I saw: a large space full of buckets, chemical drums, and random junk. There we were, talking about safety and health, and this facility has a garbage dump right out in the open, in close proximity to employees.

The plant manager, whom I had recently installed, told me it would take time to dispose of all of this material properly, but he would chip away at it, working with the HSE people on-site to make sure the work was done properly. He was true to his word, and within a few months the entire garbage heap was cleared out. I didn't ask my boss if I could have my plant manager spend the money to clean up the plant, nor did I coordinate it with our corporate health and safety folks. I just did it. And you can too. Don't sit there like a victim and say, "I don't have a choice." By stepping up now and taking the hit to profits, you lower the risks to your business and position yourself for success later.

Now, I'm not suggesting that you should turn the issues you find into a holy crusade. Clearly you need to be thoughtful about it. Try to consider your boss's perspective. Your boss isn't going to be happy to learn of a safety or environmental issue that requires fixing—he or she has numbers to make too. So take the time to explain the problem fully, and to think through and suggest a number of alternatives. Don't just say, "The only way to solve this problem is to hire consultants and buy a $3 million piece of equipment." Instead, offer a low cost (but possibly less effective) solution, a middle-range solution, and a more expensive solution that would allow you to go all in and solve the problem to the greatest degree of certainty. Be prepared to argue for the solution you believe best, but give your boss some leeway in deciding how to proceed.

If your boss denies the problem and refuses to address it, then your situation becomes a bit more difficult. If you see serious environmental or safety issues cropping up, you might need to go above your boss's head, even if this will potentially damage your career. Would you want someone to die or become seriously injured because you failed to take action? Before you do that, though, see if there might be another way to address the problem. If you face an environmental issue, reach out to the environmental officer assigned to your facility, or to someone from legal, and ask for any ideas they might have as to how you should proceed. They might decide to address the issue themselves, which will take some of the career risk off your shoulders. At the very least, they might have suggestions for how to explain the problem to your boss so that he or she understands the situation and takes action. If you have concerns about those approaches, you might consider reporting the problem anonymously to someone in the organization (many large companies maintain 1-800 numbers for this purpose). Do your best to see that the problem gets addressed, only taking on career risk to the extent it's ethically warranted given the nature and seriousness of the problem. If the problem won't cause imminent harm but is instead a longer-term threat, you want to be more careful and allow for the possibility that your judgement about it is incorrect.

CLEANING UP "AMERICA'S MOST POLLUTED LAKE"

A century ago, Onondaga Lake, a roughly four-and-a-half-mile-long lake adjacent to the city of Syracuse, New York, was an entertainment and leisure destination, with hotels, beaches, dance halls, and restaurants lining its shores.[9] It was the "Coney Island of Central New York."[10] For hundreds of years before that, the Haudenosaunee Indians had regarded the lake as sacred, relying on it for food and water. Then along came industrialization, and everything changed. The lake was used as a dumping ground by companies, including Allied Chemical, now owned by Honeywell. During the mid to late twentieth century, Allied Chemical's operations allegedly released some "165,000 pounds of mercury into the lake."[11] Other industrial contaminants in the lake included "polychlorinated biphenyls (PCBs); pesticides; creosotes; heavy metals, including lead, cobalt, [and] cadmium . . . ; polycyclic aromatic hydrocarbons; and volatile organic compounds such and chlorobenzene, benzene, and toluene."[12]

For decades, the City of Syracuse had also deposited untreated sewage directly into the lake, leading to an array of environmental issues.[13] By the 1940s, the lake was off-limits to swimming, and fishing was banned during the 1970s. One local woman told a reporter she was told as a child that her skin would slough off if she stepped into the lake, while another remembered his family rolling their car windows up during the 1950s while driving past the lake because the smell was so bad.[14] The lake became known as America's most polluted lake.[15]

Since the 1970s, efforts had been made to clean up Onondaga Lake. In 1994, following a lawsuit filed by New York State, the site became listed as a Superfund site by the Environmental Protection Agency.[16] In 2006, after many years of study and extensive discussion with government officials, Honeywell agreed to completing a remedy for the lake that the agencies estimated at $451 million, including the removal of millions of cubic yards of contaminated sediment, the covering off of contaminated areas of the lake bed with layers of material, and the rehabilitation of shorelines and wetland areas.[17] Local authorities agreed to spend another $500 million to address the sewage pollution problem.

As this work has proceeded, the lake's recovery has been palpable. Levels of contaminants measured in the water have plummeted, fish species have returned to the lake, and bird life has also flourished.[18] As the New York State Department of Environmental Conservation reported, "Many years of research and remediation has made Onondaga Lake the cleanest it has been in over a century." Although some advocates contend that the cleanup hasn't gone far enough, a milestone was reached in 2015, when people could once again swim in the lake. At an event covered by local media, several dozen people, including our own health and safety leaders, jumped into the water to celebrate the lake's return. Cornelius B. Murphy Jr., a former president of the State University of New York's College of Environmental Science and Forestry, exulted in the progress: "The lake now is joyful. It lifts our spirits. It's an extraordinary asset."[19] Joanie Mahoney, the county executive of Onondaga County, remarked that "Honeywell's willingness to meet and exceed its obligations is the reason that we're standing here today. I'm very proud to be partnering with them in this cleanup."[20]

In 2017, Honeywell completed its work on the lake, although smaller projects were still ongoing, including the construction of trails and wildlife habitats.[21] As of this writing in 2018, residents were continuing to rediscover the lake as a place for swimming, fishing, boating, and other leisure pursuits. Local authorities were even exploring whether to construct a new beach. As the State Departments of Health and of Environmental Conservation said, "A beach on Onondaga Lake is now a real possibility, thanks to the significant improvements in lake water quality evident for more than a decade, and the recent completion of the Onondaga Lake remediation."[22]

The recovery of Onondaga Lake stands as one of our proudest accomplishments in recent years. If we had continued to pass the buck to future leaders, the lake would likely be much dirtier than it currently is, and Honeywell would probably be paying an even bigger bill down the road to clean it up while seeing our image deteriorate further. Because we sat down to negotiate with local communities, we contained the risk to our business while also doing the right thing and building our brand. It wasn't easy at the time coming up with that $451 million. Few people applauded our endeavors, least of all investors. But thankfully, we stayed the course, and today I take great satisfaction in knowing that we helped make the planet a better place while putting future Honeywell leaders in a stronger position to pursue the company's fortunes. Our workforce feels great about what we've done too.

I want something similar for you. If your business has long labored under the shadow of legacy issues, do something different. Get real about your business and its challenges. While senior leaders should look to tackle big, corporate-level issues, managers elsewhere in the organization can address an array of longstanding problems at the team, facility, or regional level, such as outdated sales force organizations, legacy manufacturing processes that might harm people or the environment, or bad engineering practices that yield poor designs. Whatever your area of responsibility, resolve the outstanding liabilities that threaten to drag down future growth, even if it means taking a short-term hit. Show some courage—be the leader *you* want to be. Without legacy issues hanging over your head, you'll be able to focus on building up your business to compete better and win, and you'll channel the money you save by resolving issues proactively back into the business. You won't reap all of the financial benefits—your successors will inherit them as well. What you will reap is a legacy; a reputation as a strong, transformational leader. And from where I sit, that feels pretty good.

QUESTIONS TO ASK YOURSELF

1. Have previous leaders of your business been putting off handling historic issues? How big are your liabilities really?
2. When is the last time you paid surprise visits to check up on conditions in your facilities? If problems are arising, don't be shy—get out there!
3. When you make big decisions, are you thinking about minimizing risks to your business years, even decades down the road? Are you ignoring any potential time bombs?
4. Is your business really living up to the lofty ideals enshrined in your mission or vision statements? Are employees or others noting the contradictions?
5. How do you react when employees or others bring potential liabilities to your attention? Do you investigate them fully and remedy them if necessary, or do you let them slide and focus on other priorities?
6. Do you tend to over-resource the resolution of problems at the beginning so that you can close them out more effectively, or do you let problems linger?

7. Do you have the right people in your organization to drive meaningful progress on legacy issues? If not, go get some, even if it means making unexpected hires.

8. Are you honestly communicating to investors and other interested parties the full extent of your liabilities?

9. Are you constantly improving your operations to minimize the risk of creating new liabilities that future leaders will have to deal with?

10. If you're a mid-level manager, are you responding appropriately to issues you uncover? You might have more power than you think to make a difference.

CHAPTER FOUR

Focus on Process

There's an invisible hero at Honeywell's industrial plants: compressed air. We use it to perform mechanical functions in our production processes—moving parts from one place to another, cleaning them, spray-painting them, attaching other components to them. In 2012, as part of our efforts to standardize and improve operations across all of our facilities, we decided to review how efficiently we were using compressed air. Although air was cheap, compressing it to high pressure required quite a bit of energy and expense. We surveyed conditions at twenty-six facilities, uncovering over 1,600 leaks in our compressed air systems. Fixing those leaks—and importantly, keeping them fixed—saved us over $800,000 in energy costs. We also took the opportunity to survey how we were using industrial gases like nitrogen, argon, and helium, and realized an additional savings of about $120,000.

These numbers were small for a company of our size, but these were just two process improvement projects among countless others we were undertaking. In 2005, we had embarked on a company-wide quest to improve operations at our facilities worldwide, rolling out a new approach to organizing how we worked called the Honeywell Operating System (HOS). HOS was—and is—a comprehensive system for operating our plants that brought managers and employees together to continuously improve processes. Whereas companies often struggle to make process improvements stick, we designed HOS to help us make changes permanent so we wouldn't have to go back a few years later and implement them again. Although HOS incorporated tools from the widely adopted Six Sigma and Lean process improvement approaches, it was broader, addressing not just specific processes and workflows but the complex relationships between the many processes in a given facility. Involving everyone associated with a given process, HOS fit specific tools within an overall culture and management system that determined how a given plant would operate in its entirety, and that allowed us to standardize our approach to process change across Honeywell's operations.

With HOS in place, individual plants had both the mind-set and the tools to scrutinize their existing operations and improve them on an ongoing basis. The result was a constant stream of projects large and small that permanently improved quality, customer satisfaction, and safety while reducing cost, inventory, and our environmental footprint. Our plants performed better financially because they *were* better. One plant of ours in Illinois used to require forty-two days to make gas detection equipment and get it to customers' doors once an order was received. After HOS, it took ten days—and we needed only a quarter of the factory floor space for production.[1]

In addition to massive productivity gains across our company, HOS delivered the staggering improvements in safety and environmental performance described in the previous chapter. It's hard to quantify the overall financial impact on Honeywell, but it was profound. A 2012 article in the *Economist* credited HOS with helping to make Honeywell "one of America's most successful companies."[2] *Fortune* observed that the "rewards" of the Honeywell Operating System "have been spectacular."[3]

Constant, sustained process improvement is vital for any company seeking to win today *and* tomorrow. Earlier in this book, I described our strategy of perpetually restructuring our businesses in order to keep fixed costs constant as our businesses grew, thus increasing profits over time as well as the funds available for growth initiatives. Such restructuring won't help you if it isn't linked to ongoing, permanent improvement of underlying operational processes. Businesses of all kinds are little more than collections of processes, and in most businesses, all processes are highly inefficient. As a leader you should *assume* you can render any process in your organization more efficient and effective, thus accomplishing two seemingly conflicting things at the same time (improve delivery *and* lower cost, for instance).

By improving processes on an ongoing, permanent basis, companies can realize big-company efficiency with small-company speed. They do this by increasing output without adding to one of their biggest costs: people. Companies focused on process improvement realize other efficiencies too. If processes on an assembly line work better, you can keep less inventory on hand, operate fewer warehouses, and maintain fewer IT systems to control those warehouses, for instance, while also improving employee morale because the work is more fulfilling. Over time, you do wind up hiring more people because you become more competitive and grow sales, not because you're working inefficiently. Process improvement thus represents another area in which initial investments, properly calibrated to maintain sufficient short-term shareholder returns, can pay dividends later on, setting a company up for better short-term performance, as well as an ever-increasing ability to invest in its future.

BRING INTELLECTUAL ENGAGEMENT TO THE FACTORY FLOOR

Our introduction of HOS originated in one of those X days I described in chapter 1, where I took time out to sit alone in my office, think freely about our company and its stakeholders, and jot down my musings in a blue notebook. In 2003, about a year after I'd arrived at Honeywell, I was scanning through a report on our employee headcount across our facilities, looking for ideas for improving our business, and I found myself wondering what our workforce did exactly. I noticed about half of our 115,000 employees at the time worked in manufacturing. If we could improve these employees' productivity, I thought, we could dramatically improve our profitability.

One strategy that occurred to me was to enlist employees' help in improving processes at our plants. As I knew from my days as an hourly factory worker, the vast majority of workers want to do a great job and use their minds to improve weak or wasteful processes. But in traditional manufacturing environments, they lack formal processes and procedures for doing so. I had operated a machine that punched out little pieces of metal. What were these pieces for? Where did they go after they left my station? Damned if I knew. Managers expected me to do my job, but I didn't receive much instruction, nor did I get a sense of the broader picture of my plant. Managers didn't expect me to actually *think* about what I was doing, and they didn't give me a voice in improving my job or the plant's overall operations. I would notice a particular procedure and ask managers, "Why do we do it this way?" but I never got much of an answer. All managers cared about was that those little pieces of metal got punched out at a fast enough clip. As a result, I hadn't been engaged at all in helping improve plant processes.

At Honeywell, involving frontline staff in process improvement would allow us to achieve multiple objectives at the same time: we could weed out inefficiencies and improve performance across a number of dimensions while also giving workers a voice and engaging their minds to the fullest. But as I saw it, there was a catch: any process improvement effort we undertook would have to be a company-wide initiative, not something we devolved on individual businesses or plants to pursue as they wished. There was no consistency to how work was done at Honeywell, and no officially sanctioned model for how to operate a plant. Local plant leaders all thought their way was best, if they thought about it at all. As a result, many of our plants were highly inefficient and ineffective. Some plants had been trying to improve processes, but their efforts had gone nowhere because they weren't part of a comprehensive system consistently applied over an extended period.

Joe DeSarla, manufacturing head for our Automation and Control Solutions business unit, used to joke that he lived in terror of one of his plant managers reading a book over the weekend and coming in Monday morning saying, "I've got the answer to what we've been doing wrong." Managers had a habit of throwing out previous improvements efforts on a whim and bringing in some new idea. A year or two later, they would leave, and a new manager would bring in their supposedly genius ideas. "We'd never make progress because we just kept churning," DeSarla said.[4]

If we could implement a uniform system for continuously improving operations in all of our plants, and if we could design that system to engage the brainpower of thousands of people in process change rather than relying on the weekend reading habits of individual managers, we could make sustained progress and over a period of years shift the entire company's fortunes. But how, I asked myself, should we go about devising such a system?

I thought immediately of the Toyota Production System (TPS), the automaker's legendary system for improving processes at its plants to reduce waste and improve efficiency and effectiveness.[5] I'd been reading about it for years, and from what I knew, this system wasn't just about running plants better; rather, it was a way of structuring the workdays of managers and employees so that they would interact regularly. When issues arose, employees could immediately bring them to managers' attention and be assured that managers would take those issues seriously and work to resolve them. Workers had a chance to participate in kaizen events that helped them understand the larger processes to which their jobs contributed and that allowed them to provide input as to how those processes might be run differently or better. TPS also emphasized making sure that plants were clean and orderly, and that work was standardized to the extent possible.

I wondered if we might connect with Toyota to see if we could learn more about TPS and incorporate elements of it into a new operating system for Honeywell. Later that year, I asked DeSarla to lead a visit of sixty of our high-level leaders in manufacturing, purchasing, and logistics to Toyota's training facility in Georgetown, Kentucky. What these leaders saw impressed them. As DeSarla remembered, the Toyota teams he observed "knew what to do when crises hit, and you didn't have a bunch of people yelling at each other or pointing fingers, because everything was done through a process." The plant was clean and clearly marked, with teams tracking performance on work boards and via quality checks within production lines. Most importantly, the people were "engaged in the process. It wasn't all top-down . . . These were fully engaged employees, fully engaged management." Because the work was standardized, people "knew what they were supposed to do, and they took ownership."[6] These were all elements we sought to bring back to Honeywell.

RAMP UP PROCESS CHANGE SLOWLY

Our people returned from Toyota and from some best-practices visits to other companies eager to introduce TPS everywhere and all at once. They wanted it to cover every one of our plants and every function within those plants, as well as our corporate functions. "Whoa," I said. "Slow down." Toyota had rolled out process improvement methodology in new plants with newly hired employees who had been chosen based on their predisposition to work according to TPS. Some of our factories had been around for eighty years and had workers and managers who had been on the job for decades. We couldn't pop in on these people and tell them, "On Monday everything's going to work differently around here, so come prepared with a new mind-set." Workers and managers would just ignore TPS, regarding it as a bunch of corporate bullshit, another "program of the month" that wouldn't last. Also, many workers and managers felt they were already busy with their jobs. In unveiling a new initiative, in their minds, corporate would be asking them to do something additional. Why should they make the effort?

Before we could succeed with TPS, we would need to help our workforce see the system not as something added on to their jobs but as a better way to do their jobs, and in fact as a defining and permanent feature of work at Honeywell. That mind-set shift would take time. It would only work if we unrolled TPS slowly, carefully, and relentlessly, building understanding and support among the workforce (salaried and hourly) plant by plant. We had to allow for a period of acculturation if our workforce was to accept and use TPS as we envisioned.

We had seen previous change efforts underperform precisely because we had failed to change mind-sets and galvanize our workforce. In 2002, we had begun to comprehensively train our workforce in the Six Sigma methodology for both design and manufacturing, hoping to improve the quality of our production processes. Previous Six Sigma training had touched only a small percentage of manufacturing people and products, and no engineers. But I rolled out the program too quickly and hadn't refined how we presented it to workers and managers so that their mind-set would change, and they'd view it as more than just a training exercise. Plants that had trained in Six Sigma didn't see appreciable improvements in quality because they hadn't changed how they did their work. We were a mile wide, so to speak, in how much training we had delivered, but only an inch deep in terms of how people were using the tools. Company-wide, we improved in quality, but not nearly as much as we might have.

My failure to prepare the company and implement changes in a way that would stick would hit me some time later, when I visited our Aerospace facility in Malaysia. The plant manager proudly showed me charts documenting how teams had improved producibility (the percentage of parts that emerge from production perfect the first time around) from 72 percent to 85 percent. That represented progress, but I couldn't help but wonder why, after years of Six Sigma, we weren't at 99-plus percent. Digging into it, I learned that the business had recently shifted production of a number of its poorly designed products to a new facility in Malaysia rather than fix the designs. In other words, they decided to manufacture poor designs in a lower-cost factory rather than fix the designs. Not very "Six Sigma" at all.

We went back and implemented Six Sigma again more rigorously. Our Aerospace leader put in place quantifiable, trackable producibility metrics to govern every new design. The engineers protested, claiming this would slow down their design schedules, but we insisted that they do two seemingly conflicting things at the same time: deliver producible designs and do it on time. Our leader also allocated full-time staff to fix one thousand previously existing designs so that they were more producible. We called it D-Day, and then Normandy. By fixing old designs and making sure that new ones were producible, we were both draining the swamp, so to speak, and stopping inflow to that same swamp, two actions that are always required when addressing an issue. In this way, we finally got Six Sigma to stick, and it has paid off enormously.

TAKE A PHASED APPROACH

To avoid such problems with TPS, we implemented it differently, phasing it in stages so that we could analyze our initial experience and refine our approach. We piloted the methodology in ten plants for six months, tracking whether safety, quality, delivery, cost, and inventory improved. Afterward, we determined what had worked and why, and then revamped how we implemented TPS. For example, we learned how critical it was to have a plant manager who recognized the magnitude of the change we were seeking and truly bought into it, adding this to the checklist we ran through before implementing TPS in a given plant. We unrolled the revised methodology in five more plants to see what happened. Analyzing this round of implementation, we made some further tweaks, like adding experts trained in TPS to plants on a full-time basis, and then tested TPS in another two plants.

With our implementation plan now fully refined, we rolled out our version of TPS in 30 plants out of 250 or so, investing heavily in the right people and support to ensure the methodology really worked, and making leadership changes in factories as needed. About 80 percent of this new methodology owed to TPS, while the remainder consisted of tools or processes that we borrowed from other companies or developed ourselves. Despite the obvious debt we owed to Toyota, we branded the methodology the Honeywell Operating System (HOS), since we wanted people to think of this new methodology as a true operating system, and something to which Honeywell was deeply committed. HOS wasn't just flavor of the month. It was the way we would run our company.

These initial implementations took place over about three years. We then asked each of our business units to identify the next group of factories where we could introduce HOS. After we had implemented HOS in this cohort, and as we continued to add subsequent cohorts, we began to incorporate HOS into our M&A strategy (chapter 8). When we integrated new acquisitions into our own company, we wanted to ensure that their manufacturing facilities were inculcated in the HOS mind-set and tools, recognizing that we would realize tremendous cost synergies. We also implemented a rule that leaders within Honeywell couldn't restructure or combine manufacturing plants unless those plants were already certified at a certain level of competency in HOS. A system like HOS allows you to uncover hidden processes that exist in factories—all those workarounds that accumulate over time as people try to deal with bad, official processes in place. As we found, you could restructure or consolidate manufacturing a whole lot more effectively if you had already surfaced and dealt with the "hidden factory." For instance, our acquisitions in gas detection benefited greatly from HOS. We significantly improved money-losing operations, making them highly profitable and improving quality and delivery.

Despite our more careful approach, the implementation of HOS wasn't without its bumps. During the early implementations especially, plant managers and their staff members sometimes resisted HOS, disliking change. In a few cases, we had to let these leaders go in order for HOS to take root. Resistance in these plants died down considerably, and implementation became easier.

As we spread HOS across the company, we managed to cut the time it took to fully implement HOS in a facility from three years to eighteen months. During our early implementations, factories saw almost immediate efficiency and productivity gains. In 2006, our plant in Atessa, Italy, lowered defects in its products by 80 percent and saw a seven percentage point increase in its on-time customer delivery rate after implementing HOS.[7] Managers at other plants heard about such successes and became more eager to roll it out as well. Meanwhile, our manufacturing leaders did a good job of alerting plants that change was coming so that they could begin preparing for it.

Another significant source of resistance came from our finance organization. About six months after we had begun piloting HOS, our CFO told me that in his view HOS was a monumental waste of time and money—it simply wouldn't deliver benefits for us. I could have just shut him down, but instead, in line with the philosophy of testing my own beliefs and assumptions, I asked him to analyze the project closely, understand what it cost and the effects it was having on our businesses, and then come back to me with a conclusion. He and his team spent three months studying HOS and afterward reported that he had changed his mind—the program would work, and he was getting behind it. This was a huge win. An entire organization within Honeywell that might have opposed HOS and impeded its implementation were now true believers and supporters. Meanwhile, I received valuable reassurance that we were indeed on the right track. If after reading chapter 1 you needed more proof of how important it is to encourage dissenting opinions within an organization, now you have it.

PROCESS CHANGE PAYS OFF

All told, we spent a decade relentlessly implementing HOS across the company. In a typical plant, HOS empowered employees to propose hundreds of ideas to improve processes. Costs dropped by 15 to 20 percent, while safety, inventory, delivery, and quality all improved by similar margins. In previously crowded factories, we could suddenly do more with fewer people and 20 to 30 percent less floor space thanks to the more efficient and effective processes HOS engendered. And because HOS enabled ongoing process improvement, our gains continued to mount over time. If a given plant became 3 percent more efficient each year thanks to HOS as opposed to only 1 percent more efficient without it, that translated into an incredible performance gain over a decade or more thanks to the miracle of compounding. HOS was taking us to new heights in performance, while also increasing how fast our performance was improving.

HOS boosted worker engagement in our factories as well, including at union facilities that often resisted corporate initiatives like these. Employees appreciated the chance to improve their work via kaizens, as well as management's new responsiveness to issues workers raised. Every day, first thing in the morning, they had an opportunity to bring up concerns they encountered, and this information would dart up and down the chain of command in subsequent meetings held every day. Someone would be assigned to fix the problem and report on it the next day. (See the figure below for a more detailed summary of how improvement or kaizen events transpired).

Although rendering processes more efficient would frequently eliminate the need for some workers, employees didn't see that as a threat. We were becoming a better company, which meant we were growing. As a result, we would usually find new jobs for anyone who had been displaced, and we were also in a position to raise salaries as productivity increased. Most people hate to work with inefficient, ineffective processes—they want to go home each night to their families and proudly talk about what they had accomplished. By giving employees the chance to engage mentally with their work and to be part of a team that worked *better* together, HOS improved both retention and morale.

While visiting Honeywell plants, DeSarla remembered listening to a presentation about process improvement ideas delivered by a number of unionized hourly employees. One employee stood before a white board and described a complex map of a new, more efficient production process, noting the improvement had reduced the workforce required by two people. "I thought that was incredible," DeSarla said. "It's not what you usually hear. The enthusiasm of a unionized hourly work force just reinforced the idea that we were on the right track." DeSarla further noted that this excitement wasn't limited to particular geographies. He recalled, "The enthusiasm in Eastern Europe, China, India, the UK, Western Europe—it didn't matter where we were applying [HOS] principles, you could watch that spark get lit. It was very exciting to participate in that growth around the world."[8]

"Go slow to go fast" became our mantra when it came to process change. Early on in an improvement initiative, excitement can overwhelm judgement, and while change happens, it usually doesn't stick. You simply must go more slowly than you might want. Doing so at Honeywell required quite a bit of discussion with analysts and investors, who wanted to know how many basis points our margins would grow each year as we implemented HOS. In the short term, they weren't satisfied with my truthful answer that we didn't know, nor did they like it when I told them that we wouldn't see much visible impact in the beginning, and that the impact would build over time. Over the long term, as our margin rates did grow, they were of course quite pleased.

IMPROVE YOUR BUSINESS FUNCTIONS

Process improvement isn't just for production lines. You can also use it to improve back-office or administrative functions as well. I first got the idea of applying something like HOS to our functions in 2004 while performing—you guessed it—another blue book exercise. I was looking at our financial statements, and when I reached the line for SG&A (Sales, General, and Administrative, which includes functions like IT, legal, finance, and HR), I thought, *Hey, we aren't really doing anything to improve operations in these areas.* We didn't feel much pressure here to operate more efficiently. When I became CEO, Wall Street already credited us for having relatively little administrative overhead. Our finance, IT, legal, and HR functions also believed themselves incredibly lean and under-resourced. But were they really?

I came up with a financial goal for our functions, asking them to reduce their costs by 50 percent as a percent of sales. And in keeping with my philosophy of doing two conflicting things at the same time, I wanted them to cut those costs while also enhancing the services they delivered. Rather than reduce the size of these departments and force them to do the same work with less, I informed everyone that budgets for these departments would remain flat forever, and that we would expect these departments to better their services even as our company grew and demands on these departments increased.

To achieve this seemingly impossible goal, we asked our functions to enhance work processes, implementing metrics (usually via anonymous surveys of their internal customers) to ensure that they delivered better service to their internal customers even as they reduced costs. We referred to this initiative as Functional Transformation, and as part of this effort, we asked our functional leaders to begin submitting five-year strategic plans every year, just like our business units did. Business leaders would participate in their strategic reviews, contributing their opinions about how well our functional teams were performing for them and identifying areas for improvement. In my experience, corporate staff usually get to comment on what business managers are doing, but business heads seldom have an avenue for letting the staff functions know how well their people are serving them. That had to change. I wanted our functional departments to commit to providing great customer service, recognizing that our businesses brought in the revenue that supported everyone at Honeywell. As we told corporate functional leaders, it was no longer enough for them to be smart in their functional area. They had to make sure that work got done more efficiently *and* effectively.

Four Steps to Better Functional Organizations

1. Create a financial goal for each business function.
2. Demand that functions hold costs flat (no inflation adjustments) or even cut costs as the organization grows while also improving service.
3. Have functions develop annual strategic plans that accomplish both.
4. Establish service metrics and goals, then use surveys to confirm that service is getting better over time.

Some functional leaders pushed back, doubting we could ever reduce costs as a percent of sales by 50 percent. Our IT department ran a study, benchmarking four of our functions against peer companies. It turned out we weren't quite as lean as we thought. On average, our functions were twice as expensive as a percentage of sales as those at other companies that were then considered world class. Our finance team still didn't believe it, so they ran their own study—and came to similar conclusions. With leaders finally on board, our functions overhauled numerous processes. Our IT department consolidated servers, revamped its purchasing, and adopted new technologies to become more efficient and effective. Our HR department performed a wide-ranging analysis of their work in the field, discovering that they employed too many generalists. By adjusting roles within the department and consolidating and automating some of their activities, they were able to provide better service at much lower cost. Our legal team performed a preventive analysis of all existing lawsuits, implementing numerous changes that reduced the number of lawsuits filed against us.

Over time, a mind-set of continuous improvement in our functions took hold. HR and finance actually began a friendly competition over which department would show the biggest service improvement gains. One year, when our HR team came out ahead, they put up a big poster on one of our windows that faced the area where the finance team sat. The finance team still had higher overall levels of service quality, so they put up a poster of their own that helpfully pointed that out.

Our Functional Transformation efforts paid off handsomely. Between 2004 and 2006 alone, we saved over $170 million thanks to this initiative.[9] Over the next ten years, Honeywell doubled in size, yet our budgets for these functions *declined* by about $1 billion (about 30 percent in real time dollars, 44 percent as a percent of sales), or about $1 per share, while service quality improved. Now we really were running leaner, putting real money into investors' pockets while improving our performance.

GO DEEP ON PROCESS

If you wish to improve operations in your organization, proceed deliberately. Focus on changing underlying mind-sets, transforming the culture so process change becomes permanent. It's so important to do process improvement right. If you don't, you don't merely waste resources and stagnate as an organization— you stand a strong chance of moving backward. Bad process improvement is devastating. As people discover they haven't made progress, they become even more dispirited, unmotivated, disillusioned, and unengaged than they had been. Customers suffer, forced to navigate processes that have become even more inef-fective. As some of these customers leave, business results slide. Meanwhile, companies find that they need to re-implement process change again after a few years because it didn't stick the first time. Such failures cost money and reinforce the notion that process change is merely a passing fancy among management.

Rather than implementing your initiative the way organizations commonly do, first immerse yourself in the details to discover what works for *your* organization. As tempting as it might be to rush, test and refine how you're rolling out major operational changes, and build a track record of success that can get others in your organization excited about the change. Also, put resources behind it. We dedicated dozens of full-time people across the company to implementing HOS, placing a full-time HOS expert on every plant manager's staff. That was important, because it showed our workforce that we were committed to HOS success, and it also gave our plant managers the ability to run their plants while still ensuring that change was taking place. As the old saying goes, if you make a change initiative everyone's part-time job, you get part-time results. We wanted full-time results, so we put the necessary people and money behind it . . . full time.

With a strong implementation plan in place, keep a close eye on how your process improvement initiative is progressing. Never take change for granted. Facilities have no problem generating nice-sounding stories about the changes they're making. But what do the numbers say? Is the change as profound as plant leaders think? And is it persisting? Entropy is the rule in organizations, as it is in the physical universe. Over time, all organized systems evolve toward chaos. Unless you pursue change relentlessly, your efforts will eventually wither away.

The metrics we used to evaluate our HOS introduction at individual plants allowed us to confirm that the changes we wanted were real, and that the plant was sustaining them. We also defined multiple levels of proficiency in HOS, awarding bronze, silver, and gold certifications to individual facilities based on their improvement numbers. This allowed individual facilities to chart their progress and to feel inspired to continue. Because we audited the results facilities reported, we knew that when a facility achieved a certain designation, the change we wanted had really happened.

Our certifications also allowed us to prevent our plants from backsliding once they'd achieved a certain level of competence. We always told managers and employees that achieving bronze was the beginning of HOS at their facility, not the end. Still, we found that many plant managers became complacent after their facility had achieved bronze. In response, we instituted a procedure for removing the bronze certification from plants that began to lag. That got people's attention. Similarly, we made a practice of publicizing internally the top ten and bottom ten[1] performers on HOS. Leaders and teams liked placing in the top ten, but they absolutely detested being publicly identified as a bottom-ten performer. This tactic helped generate a sense of urgency around HOS, raising performance across the entire organization. In fact, I recommend using this tactic whenever you're trying to change anything in an organization. It helped us accelerate improvement in quality, delivery, and a number of other change initiatives.

HOS Overview – Implementation Framework

ONGOING

Phase 1	LAUNCH	Phase 2	Phase 3	Phase 4	Phase 5	BRONZE	SILVER	SILVER EXCELLENCE	GOLD
Organizational Readiness (Pre-Launch)		Baseline and Planning	Learning Through Observation	Work Process Improvement	Pursuing Excellence				

1   Getting ready. Leadership is ready to embark and sustain the journey

2   Baseline analysis and prioritize opportunities. Establish your deployment

3   Begin to execute your changes to create future state organization

4   Implement future state to achieve targeted results

5   Site management operating system in place to drive continuous improvement culture

B   Integrating leadership beyond facility walls across all functions with all employees

S   Leverage and improve operating system supporting enterprise

G   Bringing all best practices/processes into a single focus to grow faster than competition

Structured Approach to Deployment

Our graduated framework for implementing HOS, as it had evolved by 2016

---

1   Top 10/Bottom 10 is a great way to move any organization forward. Interestingly, while being in the Top 10 is rewarding, the real effect is that no one wants to be in the Bottom 10. The scramble to not be in the Bottom 10 moves everyone upwards. It is very powerful over time.

When both introducing and sustaining change, leadership matters. The organization needs to see that you, personally, are taking this seriously. As we rolled out HOS, I talked about its importance for our business at every opportunity. I held regular meetings to make sure we were actually implementing it and that we were getting the results—something I didn't do for Six Sigma, and a reason it underdelivered. When one of our plants was performing poorly, I would send a little note to the leadership there— "Not a fun experience" for them to receive it, DeSarla remembered. Process improvement will require more of your time and other resources than you think it should. It takes time to get people past their concerns about how they will do their jobs while implementing a new improvement initiative. But the effort is well worth it.

Change Management Checklist

When pursuing any improvement effort, be sure to do the following:

- Understand the significance of mind-set and culture. If the mind-set doesn't change, operations won't change either. In particular, be sure to get people past the mentality of "I have to do my job and this too?"
- Pilot/test an idea before full rollout.
- Roll out an initiative thoughtfully. Do it slowly enough to ensure the change sticks, but fast enough to build momentum and get as much benefit as possible.
- Make sure you have the right leaders in place to effect change. As a fellow CEO once said, "Sometimes the best course to change management is to change management."
- Resource the initiative well with people and money. All change efforts require an injection of bureaucracy.
- Make the change or initiative visible to people by implementing a reporting structure, and by personally conducting reviews and field visits.
- Have your staff attend the training program that teaches the change and

attend it yourself. If you don't, leaders below you will find a reason not to attend as well.

- Look for falsification bias instead of confirmation bias to make sure the change initiative is really working.
- Create real, auditable metrics to confirm that change is happening.
- Keep at your change effort relentlessly. Just because an initiative seems to be working doesn't mean it has become part of the fabric of the organization.

PROCESS CHANGE IS FOR EVERYONE

Back in the 1980s, when I served as CFO of General Electric's Production and Engineering division in Lynn, Massachusetts, I'd gather together a group of trainees—young people from various functions a couple of years out of school—and assign them to work on a project of importance to the business. One year, some of our engineers told me it was taking us an inordinately long time—seven months—to make design changes on specific products when they were requested. When I asked engineering leaders about our design-change process, they said, "We've looked at the process fifty times already. There's no way we can do it any quicker." I wasn't convinced, so I assigned our trainees to look at the process and got an engineering leader to serve as a senior advisor. I asked trainees to take fifty specific design change requests and trace back what had happened step-by-step as those changes were processed and implemented. What exactly was going on? How could we be doing it better?

When our trainees dug into the assignment, they discovered that nobody had ever rigorously mapped out the steps in the design-change process. It did in fact take us seven months to make a design change to a product. Three of those months were spent photocopying the designs and sending those designs in snail mail back and forth between the team members involved in the design change. If you're old enough, you might remember how long it took for administrative processes to run their course in an era before email and other digital technologies. In our case, all photocopying took place at a central facility, and teams had to wait for the center to process their order for a hundred or more copies of their designs before they could be sent to relevant parties.

The trainees recommended two process changes. Instead of sending a new design to the photocopy center to have a large number of copies made, engineers should quickly get two copies made for the key decision-makers so that other steps in the process could proceed. Similarly, instead of waiting for our extremely slow internal mail system to do its work, they should walk those two copies over to the key decision-makers themselves.

These two simple changes cut *three months* out of that seven-month design-change process. Our engineers couldn't believe it. They thought they had understood how their process worked, but in fact they hadn't. All along they had considered each core step individually and thought about how to make that step more efficient. But they hadn't thought about the *whole* process, which included connections between the core steps, as well as the external players (the mail and photocopy services) that performed those steps. A sizable part of the inefficiency lay precisely in those connections.

I relate this story for two reasons. First, process change is for teams of any size and doesn't have to roll out at the organizational level. Any group of operators can improve short- and long-term performance by investing in process improvement. If you lack the budget to develop a full-blown operating system for your team or organization, then inventory the major processes that define your work, and focus people on constantly reviewing these processes and adjusting them so that they work more efficiently and effectively. Recognizing that most processes reach across other functions, ensure that you understand the process from one end to the other. Confirm that your processes are changing by looking at simple metrics. Let's say you're seeking to enhance your four-member payroll department. If after process improvement you still need those same four people to process the same number of checks, and nobody else in the organization or company has seen any extra benefit, then your improvement effort hasn't done much good, even if the process might have marginally improved in some respects.

When analyzing processes, I've always found process maps helpful—and if you are the leader of a small team, you don't need to hire fancy consultants to create them. When I worked as an auditor for General Electric, I would create my own, informal process maps all the time to understand the operations I was trying to audit. I would begin with the person who performed the first step in the process and ask them what they did and to whom they sent their work for the next step. I jotted the information down in a notebook and went on to the next person, proceeding until I had mapped out every step in the process. All along I asked people to tell me what would happen if a problem arose with their step. Quite often the people I interviewed would tell me about actions they would take when the process didn't work as it was supposed to, so I would map out those "exception" steps (which, by the way, are another example of what's called the "hidden factory"). By methodically creating a map in this way, I uncovered all kinds of inefficiencies teams could remedy. Bear in mind, I had zero training in process improvement at that point. But I didn't need any; it's just not that complicated.[2]

Finding and Fixing the "Hidden Factory"

1. Map out your existing process step by step from beginning to end.
2. Map common workarounds in case of problems.
3. Optimize your process and involve end users.
4. Confirm that the new processes are more efficient *and* improve results for end users.

It's hard to believe, but many companies don't fully understand how their processes work. If you map out each step, you'll understand the "hidden factory" that has been operating all along in your facility but that your

---

2   In addition to creating a map, try taking a group of sample transactions and trace them through the process to see what actually happened. At each step, ask what happens when this part of the process doesn't work as planned. It's amazing how many error reports you can discover that will highlight what happens when a process step doesn't work as intended.

leaders and managers have overlooked. Optimize these processes and process steps, and you'll improve your short- and long-term performance. Be sure to involve end users, as we did with Functional Transformation. It's so easy for people to comply with words rather than intent—to satisfy a directive to make processes less costly, but to do so in a way that compromises on the value the process is intended to deliver. True process improvement must accomplish two seemingly conflicting things at the same time: it must make processes more efficient, but it must also make them more effective so that they deliver more value to end users, whether these are paying customers or internal ones. Our HOS-compliant plants not only were cheaper to operate, they produced goods more quickly and of higher quality, allowing us to deliver better for customers.

As you go, keep in mind the following figure. It has been around for a while, but it serves as a tremendously instructive reminder about what processes truly are versus what we might think they are or wish they were. That difference is the "hidden factory."

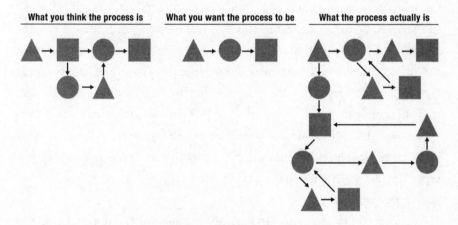

| What you think the process is | What you want the process to be | What the process actually is |

MUNDANE BUT MAGICAL

The second reason I relate the story about how we improved our design-change process is to emphasize the mundane but magical nature of process improvement. Improving how we implemented design changes wasn't going to boost General Electric's quarterly performance by a meaningful amount, any more than cutting back on the compressed gas we wasted would at Honeywell. But such changes didn't need to affect our financials in a significant way in order to make a difference. It's the *habit* of process change—the undertaking of numerous, sustained changes over time—that counts. So often leaders try to change a business overnight by taking a single, bold action. Process improvement is less dramatic and glamorous than that. It's a change in mind-set and operational norms that takes months or even years to establish, and that yields incremental, accumulated gains years into the future (remember that the compounding effect of 3 percent versus 1 percent annual productivity is huge over time). Process improvement is also about yielding some of your authority as a leader and empowering others closest to the action to improve the real work, incrementally, day after day. *Their* insights, judgments, and decisions large and small, compounded over a period of years, move the organization forward.

The true magic of process improvement is that it enables an organization to evolve and stay flexible over time. When people think of Charles Darwin, they always associate him with the mantra of "survival of the fittest." In my view, Darwin's key point was survival of the most *flexible*. Over the history of life on earth, many species have existed that were well-adapted or "fit" to survive in a particular environment. When their environment changed, these species couldn't adapt—they weren't flexible enough—and they ultimately died out. In introducing HOS to our company, I wanted the entire organization—from the hourly employee on the shop floor, to managers at the plant level, to leaders in every function and business—to become more flexible so that we could adapt to changing business conditions and lead our competition.

Revolutionary change sounds good, but it's not the optimal route to strong short- and long-term performance. If you go with revolutionary change, you're taking a huge risk, because you can never be exactly sure what the future holds. Revolutions can move in unintended directions. An organization that is adept at constantly evolving usually won't need to take enormous risks to bring about revolutionary change, because it'll have been changing all along. Think of it this way: If various dimensions of your market are changing, say, 4 percent a year, that might not sound like a lot. However, if you don't change with it, or better yet, stay slightly ahead of the change, then these changes will compound year after year. A decade down the line, you'll be looking at an enormous gap between where you are and where your market is. Then revolutionary change, and all the risk and disruption it entails, really will be necessary just to catch up. Sometimes a revolution is required depending on the state of your business or organization, but it's far better to keep pace with change as it occurs or to stay ahead of it, and to develop an organization that is committed to and capable of constant, incremental evolution.

When I took over at Honeywell, some people thought the company might well go extinct before too long. We managed to grow and flourish because we challenged ourselves through HOS, process change, and cultural transformation to constantly improve what we did, and to get better at improving over time. Enhancing our processes incrementally and sustainably became part of our culture at Honeywell, informing how we ran everything about the company. If you work at it, you can make it part of your culture too.

QUESTIONS TO ASK YOURSELF

1. Are processes in your team or organization as efficient as they might be? Do you understand them fully—not just the core steps, but the links between those steps? If employee engagement isn't as high as you'd like, might inefficient processes be playing a role?
2. Do you have a system in place for constantly improving processes? How well does it work? Do you empower frontline workers to improve how work gets done?
3. Aside from your core business operations, have you worked on rendering your back-office, administrative functions more efficient? How efficient and effective are these functions really?
4. Are change initiatives "sticking" in your organization? If not, why not?

5. How much attention have you paid to pushing process improvement forward? Are you driving it daily, or are you abdicating responsibility? Are you pushing your organization to achieve small-company speed with big-company efficiency?

6. Have you structured your process improvement initiative in such a way to sustain improvement over time? Are you personally verifying that it is working?

7. Is your team or organization adept at constantly evolving, or do you cling too closely to the operational status quo?

8. Are there situations in which you might use the top ten/bottom ten technique to improve performance?

9. Are you resourcing your improvement initiatives well enough? Remember, all change efforts require an injection of bureaucracy.

CHAPTER FIVE

Build a High-Performance Culture

W hen I took over as CEO, I wanted to acquaint myself with Honeywell and its culture, so I spent the first few months visiting our facilities around the world and conducting town hall events. During one such event, held at our sprawling aerospace facility in Phoenix, Arizona, a woman stood up and posed what at first seemed a rather odd question. "Dave," she said, "are you blue or red?"

"Excuse me?" I asked. I had recently moved to the New York City area from Kentucky, where a red versus blue rivalry—the University of Louisville versus the University of Kentucky—was a big deal.

"Are you blue or red?" she said again. "AlliedSignal or Honeywell?"

Oh man, I thought, *so that's what she meant.*

During the early 2000s, Honeywell's company culture was not merely in sorry shape—it was nonexistent. AlliedSignal, an industrial firm with interests in aerospace, chemicals, and automotive products, had acquired Honeywell in 1999, with the combined company using Honeywell's name and AlliedSignal's corporate headquarters. In 2000, this "new" Honeywell had acquired a third company, fire alarm and security system manufacturer Pittway. Employees who had worked for Honeywell legacy businesses saw themselves as focused on technology and something called "customer delight," which was ironic because their performance was so poor they weren't satisfying their customers very well, much less "delighting" them.

Legacy AlliedSignal employees maintained a separate but equally dysfunctional culture focused on making quarterly commitments at all costs. I would joke that I could see Allied employees strolling into their boss's office at the end of the quarter to say, "We can make the quarter but we have to screw the customer," and the boss saying, "What's your point? Make the quarter." Honeywell's employees were known as "red" within the company, and legacy AlliedSignal employees were "blue," reflecting the colors with which the two organizations were branded before the merger. Legacy Pittway employees didn't participate in the color wars, as it was called. Believing that the rest of the organization possessed a "big company" mentality, they ignored everyone else and ran their business as they always had.

All this division was taking a tremendous toll on our business. Mark James, Honeywell's senior vice president of HR, Security, and Communications, first arrived at the company in 2000 as an HR director in our Aerospace division. As he recalled, the environment was "total chaos," with "everybody doing their own thing," and with no standard ways of operating. "The best way to describe it was if you just went and hired a bunch of people and didn't have them talk to each other. Everyone's in it for themselves, that's what it felt like to me. There was no one giving guidance, no one ever did a review with me of any sort or showed up to do a business review."[1] Not surprisingly, the company had trouble retaining top talent. Young managers came in knowing our culture was disorganized and unsupportive. They assumed they'd grin and bear it for a few years, obtain some good experience, and move on to build meaningful careers elsewhere.

When I arrived as CEO, ending the color wars and building a unified culture became one of my top priorities. Some of our executives wondered why should we spend so much time fixing our culture, given all the other strategic issues we had to deal with. If we were going to do anything, they said, we should invest in a short-term initiative to build morale. No way, I said. If morale was a problem, the best way to fix it was to build a winning, high-performance company. And that meant we needed to have a winning, high-performance *culture*. We could make all kinds of strategic decisions, but if nobody in the company acted on them, we wouldn't make any progress.

A strong culture—one in which people feel intrinsically motivated to do well, and in which they comply with the *intent* of policies and procedures, not merely with words but with actions—is important for any organization to perform at its best. But if you're aiming for the higher bar of achieving short-term results even as you secure longer-term growth, such a culture becomes central. Unless everyone feels driven to execute, organizations might achieve one of these goals or the other, but they stand little chance of accomplishing both at the same time.

Skeptics might contend that aiming for a desired culture is pretty standard for companies today. I agree—there's nothing revolutionary about knowing a company needs a defined culture. And determining the key factors of a culture isn't rocket science. We defined our culture as underpinned by twelve key behaviors, including growth and customer focus, getting results, fostering teamwork, taking intelligent risks, being self-aware, and having a global mind-set. I used to tell my team all the time that these behaviors were not revolutionary. Nobody at Harvard would ever come down to our head-quarters and exclaim, "Wow, how did you come up with *that*?" The trick was in the doing. Honeywell committed itself over many years to getting all of our people to live these behaviors (as well as five key strategic initiatives that we also defined), and we followed through on that commitment relentlessly. Our culture changed in due course, as did our performance. If you want to achieve short- and long-term growth, you have to be equally relentless. Don't just talk about culture—get busy *doing*, and never stop.

DEFINE THE CULTURE IN DETAIL

As obvious as it sounds, you should start your culture-building efforts by defining the culture you want. I had understood culture's importance dur-ing my time at General Electric and had developed a pretty clear sense of what constituted a high-performance culture. During my second month at Honeywell, I came up with the *five key strategic initiatives* I wanted Honeywell to focus on: growth, productivity, cash, people, and operational enablers (like Six Sigma, and later, the Honeywell Operating System). I also generated a list of ten behaviors I wanted to define our culture and held a full-day meeting with my team to discuss them. We wound up adding two more behaviors—for twelve total—while modifying some of my original ones. As some of us joked, the Lord only needed ten commandments, but trying to end the color wars and get a large organization to become a performance machine required a couple more.

The Five Initiatives

1. Growth (via customer service, globalization, and technology)
2. Productivity (went hand-in-hand with growth)
3. Cash (improve working capital and have high-quality earnings)
4. People (keep the best talent, organized the right way and motivated)
5. Organizational enablers (including Six Sigma, Honeywell Operating System, and Functional Transformation)

The Twelve Behaviors

1. Focus on customers and growth (serve customers well and aggressively pursue growth).
2. Lead impactfully (think like a leader and serve as a role model).
3. Get results (consistently meet any commitments that you make).
4. Make people better (encourage excellence in peers, subordinates, and/or managers).
5. Champion change (drive continuous improvement in our operations).
6. Foster teamwork and diversity (define success in terms of the entire team).
7. Adopt a global mind-set (view the business from all relevant perspectives, and see the world in terms of integrated value chains).
8. Take risks intelligently (recognize that we must take greater but smarter risks to generate better returns).

9. Be self-aware (recognize your behavior and how it affects those around you).

10. Communicate effectively (provide information to others in a timely, concise, and thoughtful way).

11. Think in an integrative fashion (make more holistic decisions beyond your own bailiwick by applying intuition, experience, and judgment to the available data).

12. Develop technical or functional excellence (be capable and effective in your particular area of expertise).

We didn't simply name these Twelve Behaviors—we fleshed them out in detail. It's one thing to say, "We want teamwork." But as I've often seen, people sometimes use teamwork as an excuse for suppressing dissenting opinions. The result: a pernicious groupthink. In defining teamwork, we made it clear that everyone on the team had to speak up freely when they had opinions; that team leaders had to ensure that everyone on the team had a chance to contribute; and that leaders ultimately had to make decisions—consensus was not the goal. In addition, team leaders had to explain their decisions so that everyone understood their rationales. Too often, people assume that if leaders don't agree with what employees said, they weren't listening. That's not true. Team leaders could listen and understand, but not agree. In these cases, people needed to know their opinions mattered, even if they didn't get their way, and leaders could ensure their people knew by explaining decisions and their underlying logic to the group. As the final step, team members then needed to support and implement the decision, even when they didn't agree. When these dynamics played out in group settings, that was teamwork as we wanted to see it.

Or consider how we defined another of our behaviors, adopting a learning mind-set. If our people wanted to advance, they had to be constantly learning. That meant reading, talking to others, listening well, and staying updated on markets, customers, and so on. But it also meant becoming more self-aware. We wanted everyone to understand their own strengths and weaknesses better, recognizing that we all have our own issues we need to work on. Our leaders especially needed to understand how they were impacting others so that they could bolster their weak areas. I know, for instance, that I can be defensive and at times overly decisive. It's just who I am. But I needed to mitigate those reactions in order to lead people the most effectively. Others needed to uncover their own weaknesses and correct for them. If all or most people inside Honeywell did that, we'd have a much stronger, higher-performing organization.[1]

Once my team and I aligned around all Twelve Behaviors and their precise definitions, we branded our desired culture as One Honeywell. It wasn't an especially original name, but in our case, it was quite appropriate. We had been multiple companies at war with one another, but from now on we would be unified. One Honeywell would be the glue that would keep everyone working together and our company thriving. To further strengthen this sense of togetherness, we linked One Honeywell to a company objective everyone could hold in common: a focus on serving customers. We needed to define a common objective around which people could unite. Instead of arguing about which subculture was right, One Honeywell focused all of us on doing right by our customers, and in the process, building our business.

SPREAD THE CULTURE—AND SPREAD IT SOME MORE

With our desired culture in hand, we started spreading it throughout the organization. And I mean *spreading* it. Over the next couple of years, we incorporated the behaviors into our training programs and performance evaluations, and we based compensation decisions in part on whether leaders demonstrated the culture we were seeking to build. Our appraisal forms came printed with the Twelve Behaviors, and bosses had to specify

---

1   I would share my personal efforts at self-awareness with training classes to get attend-ees to think more about their own issues and how to mitigate them. We also helped employees develop more self-awareness through performance appraisals, and through 360 reviews performed when leaders attended training classes. We didn't implement 360 reviews across the company because from what I had seen elsewhere, those efforts tended to die from their own weight, becoming cumbersome, time-consuming, and ineffective.

how well each of their team members was delivering on those behaviors. Likewise, during our annual management resource reviews (MRR), when we evaluated the quality and capacities of managers down in the ranks, we specifically evaluated how well they were living the Twelve Behaviors. If we uncovered managers who weren't adopting the behaviors, and who weren't changing even after we had pointed this out to them, we let them go.

During hiring, we also started assessing candidates for whether they tended to behave according to the Twelve Behaviors. I'll talk more about how we hired and compensated leaders in the next chapter—for now, just know that cultural considerations played a big role. In my first three years as CEO, we wound up changing out about half of my staff members, replacing them with leaders who bought in strongly to One Honeywell. We also wound up hiring more leaders from inside Honeywell for key jobs. Previously, most of our leadership hires—65 percent—came from outside the company, and many within Honeywell felt this made for a more mercenary culture. It would be hard to make One Honeywell stick if we were constantly turning to newcomers for key jobs. By the time I stepped down as CEO, we were hiring about 85 percent of our leaders from inside the company. A certain number of external hires will inject new thinking into the organization, but hiring internally the vast majority of the time is vital for ensuring cultural consistency.

We attended to our culture as well when it came to personnel decisions regarding our tens of thousands of hourly employees. To succeed with the Honeywell Operating System (chapter 4), we needed factory employees who would bring a higher level of intellectual and personal engagement to their jobs. We developed a special questionnaire managers could use during hiring to ensure that incoming employees were "HOS-ready." These questions would confront employees with theoretical situations and ask them to tell us how they would likely respond. On this basis, we obtained at least some insight into whether they would fit in with the culture we were trying to build, since the Twelve Behaviors and HOS were very closely aligned.

In retooling people processes to support the culture, we didn't just focus on the Twelve Behaviors per se, but more broadly on instilling the spirit of unity and One Honeywell. Consider MRRs. Although most companies perform them, we took our process much more seriously than the typical company does. In addition to holding MRRs for individual businesses, I gathered my staff together each year to do a single, comprehensive MRR covering all the top management in the company across businesses and disciplines—around four hundred people in total. We discussed each of these leaders one by one. During this conversation, our functional leaders had an opportunity to comment on the performance of leaders in the business units, while our business leaders could comment on how well executives within the functional organizations were doing. This exchange broke down the silos between businesses and corporate functions that usually exist inside organizations, reinforcing the idea that we all needed to work together and were all responsible to one another. No longer could a functional leader say, "Just leave me alone to control my own organization." Others across the organization would have a chance to weigh in—and they would take it.

We took a similar approach when designing other key events inside Honeywell. When planning our IT systems, we didn't just include IT professionals but also representatives from our business units. When I was reviewing a strategy during one of my growth days, I invited relevant functional players (HR, legal, and so on) as well as business leaders. Or take our annual technology symposium, which brings together Honeywell engineers and scientists from around the world to showcase their newest, "gee-whiz" innovations. We also invited marketers from throughout Honeywell to attend. As we recognized, technological innovations don't become commercially valuable without the injection of marketing expertise. By developing the technology symposium as an opportunity to bring both kinds of experts together, we hoped to get intellectual engagement between them happening earlier in the research and design process.

More generally, we tried at every turn to eradicate a tribal mind-set and get groups of all kinds inside our company working together. This kind of collaboration wasn't happening under our old culture. But it was now—a critically important expression of One Honeywell. You can never organize perfectly to ensure that all potential interactions happen across functions, product lines, processes, geographies, and so on. But you can work hard to ensure that as many people as possible get to know one another. Distrust kills cooperation, and it prevails when people are sequestered from one another. The more trust you build and the more widespread your desired culture becomes, the greater the chances that the thousands of decisions people make every day will break the way you'd like them to.

MAKE CULTURE YOUR PERSONAL MISSION

As important as it is to enmesh your desired culture into processes and structures, you also have to communicate it personally. Many leaders know this, but they don't always work as intensely as they should to highlight the culture for employees and managers. Given how dysfunctional our existing culture was, we knew we couldn't just make a few process changes and call it a day. We had to stick with the culture and relentlessly drive it into people's brains, month after month. Throughout my tenure, I probably devoted about a quarter of my time to our culture and to ensuring that we hired and retained people who would bring One Honeywell to life. I talked about our culture constantly across Honeywell and attended every training session at headquarters I could to reinforce our culture—probably two or three a month.

Recognizing how important it was to get other leaders on board, we turned to our annual senior leadership meeting as an opportunity to talk about high performance and the culture that would deliver it. Previously, our leadership meeting was a one-day event, held in the cafeteria of our headquarters building to keep costs down. Not terribly inspiring, and as a result nobody really cared all that much about attending. Beginning in 2003, we revamped the meeting, holding it in a desirable location, making it a three-day event, and inviting only three hundred carefully selected leaders. It became a privilege to attend, a perk we could dangle to reward leaders for strong performance. In line with our One Honeywell mentality, we made attendees at the event as diverse as possible, inviting leaders from around the world and from all of our business units, and also paying attention to racial and gender representation. We designed gatherings at the event so that leaders had a chance to meet people in different geographies or parts of the business (through random seating, for instance) with whom they might otherwise not interact. Only on the last day did leaders meet with others in their specific business, but even then we had corporate leaders attend, allowing us to forge deeper connections between our businesses and headquarters. Everybody needed to understand that they were in it together, and as the years passed, our annual leadership meeting emerged as an important catalyst to grow that understanding.

Formal events like these set the tone, but the real work of instilling the culture takes place on a daily basis. At every turn, and in a multitude of ways, my leadership team and I underlined that the Twelve Behaviors were not only mandatory but critical to our success. Sometimes, such as at our training programs, we talked explicitly about these behaviors. More often we let our own behavior do the talking. Acculturation doesn't occur because people rationally imbibe information that's thrown at them. They do it because they see principles or ideas in action. Our job as leaders, then, was to remain ever mindful of our behavior and whether it accorded with the Twelve Behaviors. We also had to stay on the lookout for occasions in which our people were making decisions inconsistent with our culture and take steps to correct them.

THE DAY OUR CULTURE SAVED US $25 MILLION

Remember our learning mind-set behavior and its emphasis on self-awareness? In 2014, we had an opportunity to sell an underperforming business of ours called Friction Materials. Although we would be selling at a $50 million loss, the business had consistently operated at a loss, so it would be worth it to get it off of our books. We held a long meeting in which we reviewed the potential deal in great detail. At the end, I gave the deal my blessing, emphasizing it was only a preliminary decision, since we didn't need to deliver a final decision to the buyer for a few days.

Ordinarily, I might have left the decision at that. But mindful of my own tendency to come to decisions too quickly, I wanted to use those remaining few days to continue to think through the deal. I organized another meeting of our group on the day the decision was due. Because I was in China, we had to hold this meeting via conference call late at night my time. Others on the team didn't like it. We'd been through the deal exhaustively once. Why did we have to do it again? But we did—and good thing, because I learned about some nuances in the numbers that hadn't been explained before. As a result, the deal we were about to sign was significantly worse for us than it had seemed just three days earlier—we would be losing about $75 million, not $50 million. I wound up deciding to back out of the deal, to the great consternation of many on the phone who thought we'd never get another chance to sell the business.

It turns out we did. Just a few months later, we sold Friction Materials to the same buyers at a loss of $50 million. Because I had been mindful of my weaknesses, I had been able to correct for them and save $25 million. Because other leaders had witnessed me behaving in a self-aware manner, even at the risk of making an unpopular decision, I'd like to think they were more inclined to do so as well, thus reinforcing our culture. In the aftermath of the deal, I was able to use it as an example in our trainings and in informal conversations to help employees and managers better understand our desired behavior of adopting a learning mind-set.

SUPPORTING OUR OWN BUSINESSES

In many other instances, we made decisions with an eye toward spreading a general respect for One Honeywell. At the outset of our cultural transformation, a number of our businesses would buy goods from other companies, even when other Honeywell businesses made the exact same goods with competitive prices and quality. When I confronted leaders about this and asked them to buy Honeywell goods, they would brush me off, saying, "Well, our stuff doesn't work as well." I would push them for the specifics. When we dug into it, we usually found that leaders had no good reason for buying from competitors. As I would observe, people would rather fight with their brother or sister than with the family next door. I made it clear: If Honeywell made a competing product, our businesses needed to look seriously at it to see if they could use it. If our product wasn't suitable, they needed to speak to the Honeywell business that manufactured it to explore what they could do to the product so that it was competitive. Chances were, that conversation would lead to changes rendering the Honeywell product more competitive with external customers as well as internal ones.

Seeing a real opportunity here to improve both our culture and our businesses, we audited our businesses to track down situations in which we could be buying goods internally but weren't. We found many instances, some of them small (we were buying safety equipment from competitors instead of using our own), others quite large (our chemical plants weren't using our own world-class technology in process controls to manage processes). I put Mark James, who was running our sourcing in addition to HR, in charge of ensuring more internal commerce between Honeywell businesses. To overcome internal resistance, I intervened in extreme situations, sending the organization an unequivocal message: One Honeywell mattered. It was simply the way we did business.

In one memorable episode, Mark came to me and told me how our Performance Materials and Technologies business was building a big plant and didn't want to use a gas flare manufactured by Callidus, a business within Honeywell that made environmental- and combustion-related technologies. I called a meeting with the business and manufacturing leaders of Performance Materials and asked them to explain the problem to me. They claimed Callidus gas flares didn't meet their needs all that well, and in any case, they had signed a contract with one of our competitors that prevented them from using Callidus gas flares. That sounded odd, so I asked them to double-check that this was true. They got angry with me, accusing me of meddling too much with details that were their purview.

Undeterred, I called the member of our legal team who had been advising them and asked him if Performance Materials had a contract that prohibited them from using our product. "Well, not really," he said.

"What?"

"Yeah, the business manager came over to me and said, 'We don't want to use Honeywell equipment; we want to use an outside vendor.' Can you give us an excuse or a reason so we don't have to? So that's what I did."

Oh man.

After calling the Performance Materials business leaders back in, I told them their general management and project management folks as well as representatives from Callidus were going to come in first thing in the morning and huddle together in a conference room to pore through every aspect of the situation, exploring if there was any way Performance Materials could use the Callidus product in their new plant. Using the technique described in chapter 1, we'd get everyone together at one time to sort out an issue, not leaving until it was resolved. If what Callidus made simply wasn't adequate, we needed to understand exactly why. Our general counsel would assign an attorney to the meeting who understood our agreement with the competitor and could ensure that we didn't make a decision or disclose information that violated our contractual obligations. I would kick off the meeting with our general counsel and then return at the end of the day to gauge progress.

When I left the group in the morning, you could feel the hostility in the room—Performance Materials leaders resented my interference. Later that afternoon, when I returned, I didn't know what I'd find. To my surprise, everyone was smiling. As our Performance Materials people related, they had been pleased to learn more about the technical capabilities that Callidus had at its disposal—they had had no idea. It turned out Callidus equipment would work out great for them. They had agreed to purchase it, and our attorney had confirmed that a purchase would not violate their contract with the outside supplier. This represented tens of millions of dollars of additional sales for Callidus. It also represented a huge teaching moment regarding our culture. Everyone in the room got it: One Honeywell meant something.

It would have been easy for me to walk away from this situation and let Performance Materials make its own decision. If I had, no cultural change would have occurred. It was critically important for us to look out for instances in which we weren't living up to our culture and publicly remedy them. As others learned of these situations, they would change their own behavior to conform to the spirit of One Honeywell. In the aftermath of this issue with Performance Materials and Callidus, I referenced this story again and again to make the point that One Honeywell mattered and that it needed to inform how we all did business.

ONE HONEYWELL—EVERYWHERE

I never stopped calling out decisions or practices inconsistent with our culture. It happened so often that I developed a way of referring to it. "Well, that's not a very One Honeywell approach, is it?" I'd say. Sometimes a phone call or a decision at a meeting was all it took; sometimes a quick comment directing someone to consult another Honeywell leader to help solve a problem they were encountering did the trick. Other times we had to pay sustained attention over months or years.

When I first arrived at Honeywell, our business leaders in Europe were so disconnected from one another that they barely knew one another's names. At one European town hall event, I asked the two hundred people present to raise their hands to indicate which Honeywell business unit they were a part of. As I called out the different business units, a group of five or six people hadn't raised their hands. I asked them, "What business are you with?" They said they worked in our fire products business (part of our Automated and Control Solutions unit, or ACS). "Why didn't you raise your hand when I mentioned ACS?" I asked. They replied that they didn't know they were part of ACS. Think about that for a moment. These people were key employees, and they didn't have the slightest clue how their business fit organizationally into the rest of Honeywell.

As disconnected as our European businesses were from one another, they were even more disconnected from corporate. During my first trip to Europe, out of seventeen European leaders, only ten showed up to a meeting I convened. The seven no-shows never even bothered to explain their absence. I reconvened the meeting again six weeks later, making it clear to my business leaders that I expected everyone to be there. When I asked why some of them hadn't come the first time, they told me directly that they felt they were wasting their time meeting with me—they would be better off using that time to call on customers. Excuse me? I took a deep breath and refrained from yelling and screaming. "That's one way of looking at it," I said. "I'm all in favor of spending time with customers. But all I'm asking is that you spend a few hours with me and our other leaders in Europe so that we can create a One Honeywell culture. I want you guys to help one another out instead of operating in isolation."

Most of the leaders got the message, but we had to let go of certain leaders who just wouldn't warm up to the One Honeywell concept. I also began traveling to Europe twice a year for similar meetings of our European leaders, using this time to receive updates about their businesses and prompt them to engage with one another. In addition to asking for formal presentations from business leaders, I facilitated free-flowing conversations so that everyone could participate and begin to feel more comfortable in one another's presence. I also took the opportunity to go on customer visits with them, which they came to regard as helpful to their businesses. Gradually, the leaders warmed up to these meetings, and about four or five years later a One Honeywell mentality had taken hold to such an extent and leaders had built up so much rapport that they began to hold quarterly meetings on their own.

More generally, my leadership team and I fostered a sense of cultural unity throughout the company by traveling incessantly. My predecessors hadn't traveled very much, but I felt the personal presence of our corporate leadership was necessary if One Honeywell would ever take hold company-wide (it would also prove important to our globalization strategy, covered in chapter 7). Some of our business leaders disagreed, complaining about the hassles of constant travel on commercial jets. To encourage everyone to get out more, I decided to purchase two Gulfstream 550 jets for our leadership. These planes were very nice and designed for intercontinental travel. While some observers might have thought this an extravagance, I saw it as a small price to pay for the cultural benefits we'd reap if our leaders had more frequent contact with far-flung offices, plants, and customers. Our leaders would function as cultural ambassadors, transmitting the Twelve Behaviors far more effectively than a company-wide email would ever do. And that's to say nothing of the business benefits we'd reap thanks to the exposure our leaders would have to conditions on the front lines. It's important for employees everywhere to know that their leaders know what they do is important. The best way leaders can ensure this is by showing up!

With our new planes, our leaders had no excuses—they had to get out there. And get out there they did. Although I don't have hard numbers, I have to think that the time our senior executives spent traveling was ten times more than the time their predecessors had taken. I myself spent between five and six hundred hours a year on the plane—that's about twenty to twenty-five days a year at twenty-four hours a day. Members of my executive team logged about three to four hundred hours each. Was it tiring? Absolutely. But building our culture was *that* important.

DON'T LET YOUR CULTURE LIMIT YOU

In driving for cultural change, it's a mistake to become overly constrained by your desired culture as you've defined it. Are there any other, related behaviors, values, or principles that support high performance than the ones you've formally adopted? If so, don't hesitate to push these as well.

Timeliness wasn't one of our Twelve Behaviors, but an organization in which meetings start late and R&D teams miss deadlines probably isn't going to be that great making and shipping goods to customers on time either. In other organizations I've worked in, late meetings tended to have a ripple effect across the organizations, preventing other meetings from taking place as planned and causing all kinds of operational chaos. People were constantly rescheduling everything—a huge waste of time and energy. Leaders would waste their time showing up at meetings in which other relevant actors weren't present. If nothing else, timeliness is a basic sign of respect, a recognition that other people's time is as important as yours. Just because we didn't include it as a thirteenth behavior didn't mean timeliness wasn't important.

Throughout my tenure, I insisted that deadlines were kept and that meetings started and ended when planned—period. Regarding the latter, if leaders were unsure how long a particular piece of business would take, they were to schedule more time than they needed, then give everyone their time back if they had overestimated. Strict meeting times also produced better meetings. Because leaders knew time was limited, they tended to include executive summaries that got to the essence of the matter at hand. In writing these summaries, leaders were challenged to distill their thinking down to a few key ideas, simplifying them for others in attendance. It became easier to use our precious time to debate questions that really mattered.

Another concept that wasn't reflected in the Twelve Behaviors but that we pushed extraordinarily hard was integrity. To perform well in the short and long term, we needed to build trusting relationships with customers, investors, suppliers, employees, governments, the communities in which we operated—really, with whomever we dealt with. That meant adopting metrics that accurately measured the reality of our performance (chapter 1) and adopting more transparency in our accounting practices, which as we saw in chapter 2 also enhanced our strategic planning. It meant keeping the promises we had made to local communities to clean up and rehabilitate contaminated sites, and also making sure that our operations were environmentally sound and energy efficient so that they lived up to the benefits our energy efficient products purported to deliver (chapter 3). Critically, it also meant complying with the applicable laws in all the countries in which we operated. Every year at our annual senior leadership meeting, I confirmed in no uncertain terms the importance of compliance, pointing out that we would never defend employees, managers, or leaders who broke the law, and that in fact we would actively prosecute them.

When it came time to keep this last promise, I'm happy to say we rose to the occasion. In one instance, a customer in the Middle East flew all the way to Phoenix, Arizona, to tell us in person that one of our sales leaders in the region had been behaving corruptly. We looked into it and found that our customer was right. Some of our senior leaders wanted to deal with this issue discreetly, but I refused. If this one sales leader had been unscrupulous, others in our regional businesses probably knew about it but hadn't said anything. We needed to openly reinforce just how anathema corruption of any kind was to our organization and to our One Honeywell culture.

We wound up prosecuting the Honeywell leader, and we also sent one of our attorneys to the Middle East to hold town hall meetings with our businesses there, inform them of what had happened, and make it clear we wouldn't tolerate similar transgressions. As it turned out, our public handling of this affair didn't tarnish our image, as some leaders had feared— quite the contrary. A couple of months later, while traveling in the region, one of our salesmen told me that more customers now wanted to do business with us because they could trust that we were a "clean" company.

GET REAL ABOUT YOUR CULTURE

Whether you lead a large organization or a small team or business unit, take a closer look at your culture. Most likely you've put words on a page defining the kind of behaviors, attitudes, and general work environment you seek, and you've made at least some effort to spread the culture. But have you really pushed it as hard and consistently as you might? Have you prioritized it and stuck with it? And have you personally acted in accord with your culture?

So much rests on your personal commitment as leader to the culture. Talk about the culture so often that you're sick of repeating the same message—and then talk about it some more. You simply can't repeat it enough. Others in your organization might not get this—if so, educate them. I first introduced our Five Initiatives in March 2002. At the end of that year, our then-global communications leader, Tom Buckmaster, came to me and asked what our initiatives for 2003 would be—he wanted to get a jump on communicating them to the organization. "What do you mean?" I asked.

"Well, we always have initiatives, and I need to get our posters up, and I want to make sure we're ahead of schedule this coming year."

"Let me ask you something," I said. "These five initiatives—do you think we're done with them? Have we completed them?"

His face reddened. "Um, well, I guess not."

"So why change them?"

"I guess we shouldn't."

We never did change them throughout my tenure, nor did we change the Twelve Behaviors. Organizations need consistency. They need predictability. And they need repetition. When I interviewed him, Mark James likened me to a "big annoying bear" who came into the woods demanding cultural change. At first, he said, people just wanted to chase me away and stop me from eating the livestock. When I kept showing up, they realized they had to live with me, so they changed their own behavior. Over time, as they came to see the bear as part of their community, they came to accept the Twelve Behaviors as their own. Cultural change was a gradual process that only happened because I insisted on it, as did members of my leadership team. We were all in—and you need to be too.

As I found, town halls were a great opportunity for socializing the culture. Be straightforward when you speak to groups of employees, and don't just do the usual feel good speeches. When employees at a given plant asked me what future lay in store for their facility, I told them flat out that it depended on them more than me. If they did a great job for customers and stayed so productive that it didn't make economic sense for us to move the facility, then the plant would operate for a long time. On one occasion, a union leader took me to task at a town hall meeting for my compensation. I responded by saying I wouldn't have left my previous company if Honeywell hadn't compensated me as they had, and by the way, I wasn't going to give any of it back. The union leader laughed and said that he wouldn't either, and the audience laughed too. People can handle the truth, and when you give it to them, they become more receptive to what you have to say about the culture.

Of course, going all in as a leader isn't just about talking about the culture.

Devise forcing mechanisms that hold people accountable for embracing it. Peg compensation and promotions to adherence to the culture. And if you uncover practices or decisions inconsistent with your desired culture, demand change and then check back to make sure those changes have really happened. People at all levels need to see that you're permanently focused on culture. As Mark James noted, "You have to hit people in their pocketbook so that it means something to them and forces them to pay attention."[2]

IMPROVE EXISTING PROCESSES AND PRACTICES

When institutionalizing the culture, don't just graft it blithely onto existing processes or practices. Go deeper and question whether those processes or practices themselves need improvement. In 2002, our general counsel asked me to approve an updated version of our code of conduct. Minimal changes had been made, I was told, and I should just sign it so our legal department could get it out to the company. Opting for a less perfunctory approach, I spent four months going through every word to make sure it made sense and wasn't just a high-minded but ultimately meaningless document. We made numerous changes so that the document truly comported with how we wanted people to behave when faced with real-world dilemmas. We put ourselves in the positions our employees would find themselves in during the course of doing business and offered guidance as to the conduct we expected of them.

As an example, we had a zero-tolerance policy in place forbidding employees from receiving anything as a gift, even something as small as a cup of coffee. If one of our buyers visited with a supplier and had a cup of coffee, we expected that buyer to pay for it. Sounds good, but it's not terribly realistic. We were trying to build strong relationships with suppliers, and this policy put buyers in the uncomfortable position of either potentially insulting the supplier by implying that he or she was trying to buy a relationship with Honeywell, or ignoring the code of conduct, implying the code was flexible. The policy also insulted our buyers, suggesting they could be easily influenced in a business deal by something as insignificant as a cup of coffee. The policy put me in a difficult position too, as I frequently had to accept gifts from customers in Asia so as not to insult them. If it was okay for me to accept these gifts because I was the CEO, what kind of message did that send?

Recognizing the limitations of our existing policy, we changed it to a so-called sunshine policy, allowing employees to accept a gift as long as they disclosed it to their boss. The message I wanted to send was that we expected our buyers to use their own judgment and not just adhere mindlessly to a given rule. They needed to be able to understand the difference between accepting dinner in the course of cultivating a business relationship and accepting a new roof on their house so that our suppliers obtained some advantage in a negotiation. We wanted a culture where people thought about the situations in which they found themselves and exercised good judgment. Our new code of conduct had to reflect that. In this instance and in many others, it did.

Another area in which we questioned existing practices or policies so that they accorded better with our culture was in our training programs. We incorporated the Twelve Behaviors into our courses, but we also realized that we needed to revitalize our training in general. That need came home to me one day early in my tenure when I was visiting our training center for a meeting. I popped my head into a class in process, said hello—you know, the friendly new CEO kind of thing—and asked a few questions. Attendees were perplexed by my questions and didn't seem to know who I was. There was a reason for that: they weren't Honeywell employees. Another company was using our space for their training program. Although we had a first-class training center, we were using it so infrequently that our people were renting it out to offset our costs!

We expanded and revamped our course offerings, and our leadership team and I paid close attention to what we taught and who did the teaching. I made a practice of spending at least an hour with many training classes so that students could hear directly from me what we were trying to accomplish. Normally, HR handles this kind of thing, but culture was so important I wanted to ensure it was reflected in everything we taught. Because we were personally involved, we wound up taking our training in house instead of hiring outside experts to design and deliver it. Early on, we sought to create a marketing training program, and we hired a leading academic business program to design a curriculum for us. Before rolling it out to a thousand employees, I wanted to confirm it was teaching the right concepts and practices, so my staff and I went through it ourselves for three days. To our dismay, the curriculum didn't come close to conveying the subject matter the way we wanted it to. So we created a marketing training program ourselves, using our own business and functional leaders as instructors whenever possible. From then on, we never rolled out a training program that my staff and I hadn't first participated in ourselves. Sometimes a program was completely canceled, sometimes just modified, as a result of our participation and evaluation.

Likewise, when we changed our performance appraisals to include measures on the Twelve Behaviors, we also tightened up the appraisal process itself to make it more rigorous. We set up checks in the system to ensure that employees agreed they'd had a robust appraisal discussion. And we instituted a one-over-one appraisal approval (in which a boss's boss had to approve the appraisal before discussion with the employee occurred) to increase the chances an appraisal was accurate and helpful. We also determined to discuss salary changes during the appraisal process. Previously, employees might have received an appraisal and then waited four months to learn whether their salary would increase and by how much. The salary action seemed disconnected from their performance. We wanted compensation decisions to reinforce the message of the appraisal so that people would take the appraisal more seriously and, if necessary, change their behavior. Some HR leaders maintain it is self-defeating to talk salary at an appraisal. In my view, you want the salary action to reinforce the appraisal message (something that, thanks to human nature, doesn't always happen). My stated message to employees was if you get a great appraisal and a low or zero salary action, believe the salary action. That's the way the world works.

TALENT AND CULTURE—FIND THE RIGHT BALANCE

A final piece of advice: make talent decisions in ways that support the culture without acting too aggressively. In organizations, too much change too quickly can leave people reeling. Although I did wind up changing many of our top leaders in an effort to build a high-performance culture, I tried to balance the need for change with the need for stability. You should do the same. Push change as fast as possible, but not so fast that the changes fail to take root. The same reasoning that caused us to proceed slowly with the Honeywell Operating System and to refrain from implementing major cross-company restructuring actions applies here. Go slow to go fast.

It's also important to mobilize hiring as a means of building the culture you want. During my second year as CEO, I wanted our leaders in China to increase their census by 50 percent, hiring five hundred people. Leaders there maintained it would be impossible for them to hire people who behaved consistently with Honeywell values because those values didn't comport in certain respects with Chinese culture. I didn't accept this answer. "How many people are there in China?" I asked them.

The response: 1.3. billion.

"Do all of those people think alike?" I asked.

"No," our leaders said.

"Is there a chance that there are five hundred people among these 1.3 billion who think like we do?"

"Yes," they told me.

"Well, find those people!"

They did, and today we have a thriving business in China with thirteen thousand employees and only seventy-five expats. It's not just possible but necessary to hire for the culture you want, no matter the nature of your business, the size of your workforce, or where in the world you operate.

CULTURE COUNTS

Cultural change was never finished at Honeywell, but we didn't have to wait fifteen years to see change. After just two or three years, people started to put the color wars aside, coming together around the customer and the Five Initiatives and internalizing the Twelve Behaviors. Strolling the hallways at corporate and walking around our plants, we would hear people using "One Honeywell" in conversations: "Oh, that approach is very One Honeywell," they'd say. Decisions our leaders made reflected our desired behaviors more often than they had before. Our people were beginning to collaborate more and help out one another, without my team and me having to force the issue. In any given organization, thousands of decisions get made every day, and leaders can't participate in all of them. With a robust performance culture in place, you stand a much greater chance that people will make decisions the way you wish they would. Culture doesn't merely yield results but helps sustain them.

There did come a moment when I knew for sure One Honeywell had stuck and we had become a profoundly different company. During the spring of 2009, we were in the depths of the Great Recession, and despite having prepared our business for tough times (chapter 9), our leadership team and I had to make some serious cuts. Eager to avoid layoffs except as a last resort, I thought our best option was to reduce our 401(k) match. Nobody around the table wanted to do it, but as I told my team, we had no good options before us. We needed to do what was best for employees and continue to do a great job for customers, but we also had to honor our commitment to investors. "This is the best I've been able to come up with," I said, "but I'm open to other suggestions." I also told them I wouldn't be taking a bonus that year. We were performing well compared with our peers during the recession, and I was working harder than ever, but I felt that if I was asking our people to make sacrifices, they needed to see that their CEO was making them too.

Eager to determine whether my proposed course of action really was best for the company, I broke the team into three groups, and asked each one to go away for a couple of hours, work through our finances, and brainstorm other possible solutions (a great technique, by the way, for avoiding groupthink). They did. When we reconvened, each group independently came to the same solution: we needed to cut our 401(k) match. It really was the best of bad options. And then our leaders said something that brought tears to my eyes—and trust me, I don't tear easily. They told me they had each independently decided that they would volunteer to take a zero bonus too. They believed in our company, they said, and wanted to show solidarity with our people. When I heard that, I knew One Honeywell was real. In the old Honeywell, nobody would have volunteered to take a zero bonus. It just wouldn't have happened. We had succeeded in building an organization that people believed in and would sacrifice for. It wasn't just about "me" anymore. It was about *us*.

Such a change sounds nice enough, but skeptics might wonder how important it truly was from a business standpoint. Did One Honeywell drive our short- and long-term performance to an extent that justified all the time and effort my team and I invested?

To illustrate the impact One Honeywell has had on our business, I'll leave you with a story. In 2008, Honeywell acquired a company called Metrologic, which made scanning technology. Under the terms of our contract, the CEO of Metrologic was required to run the business for a year as a Honeywell employee. After that, he could go on to pursue other jobs or ventures. We liked this leader and wanted him to stay, but we knew that wasn't likely. Having worked previously at General Electric and Ingersoll Rand, he had little desire to work for a massive company again and was annoyed that we had tied him down for a year.

For the first month or so on the job, he essentially phoned it in, doing the bare minimum. After that, he decided to put in more effort—if he had to be there, he might as well contribute. Over the next several months, as he interacted with others at Honeywell, he found he liked the organization more than he ever thought he would. He had expected a hard-edged culture in which everyone was in it for themselves and playing politics, and in which corporate and individual businesses were at odds. What he found was a place where everyone focused on serving our customers and making smart short- and long-term decisions, and where corporate and the businesses worked together with little in the way of politics. As he later told me, "I started to believe that Honeywell was a culture where performance was recognized. It wasn't who you were friends with that counted. It was if you could deliver. A lot of companies say they're about performance and meritocracy, but that's not how things really work. Because they did work that way at Honeywell, I started really enjoying my job."[3]

This leader, Darius Adamczyk, decided to stay, and was soon promoted to bigger jobs on account of his performance. Today he is our very successful, award-winning chairman and CEO.

Culture is notoriously difficult to quantify, but there is no way we would have turned the company around and delivered the short- and long-term performance we did had we not developed and consistently pushed One Honeywell. Sustained performance originates in a strong culture. Ours has allowed us to retain and cultivate the world's best leadership talent, and it continues to make the company a great place to work for our 130,000 employees. Binding the company together, our culture forms the bedrock for our continued growth.

You can build a strong, high-performance culture too, but you need to get past the idea that you're already "doing" culture. Whatever you think you might be doing, redouble your efforts. Drive the culture at every opportunity. Revise your calendar to carve out more time for culture building. Make every decision with your culture in mind. When an opportunity arises to take a stand and make a point about the culture, buckle up and do it, even if it might seem irritating and a waste of time. In short, promote the culture as if your company's future depended on it. Because it does.

QUESTIONS TO ASK YOURSELF

1. How strong is your culture, really? Do employees, managers, and leaders really believe in it, or do they just pay lip service? Are they committed to the organization, or does unmitigated self-interest reign? Is your culture really driving the performance you want?
2. If you have a long-established culture, is it still working for you? Are certain behaviors or attitudes missing in your definition?
3. Ethics must factor into your definition of your culture. Stay alert to any conversations that begin with someone saying, "Look, I can say this because no lawyers are here . . ." Stop the conversation right there. Get the lawyers in and then discuss it.

4. How much time do you personally spend on culture-building activities? Are you driving it home on a daily basis—in meetings, in casual conversations, in your decision-making, and at formal events? Has your own commitment to culture lagged over time? Do you take every opportunity, even if it seems like a waste of time, to reinforce your needed culture?

5. Have you embedded culture as fully as you might in organizational practices such as hiring, firing, performance evaluations, and training?

6. How strong are your underlying "people processes"? Do any of them need revamping in order to better deliver the culture?

7. Are you paying too much attention to external candidates when filling key posts?

8. If you have been doggedly building your culture, are there some additional, supportive values or concepts that you might also emphasize for your workforce?

9. If you lead a larger company, are you and other leaders getting out of headquarters enough to promote the culture on the front lines?

10. Does your code of conduct (or other company documents) reflect the real world in which you and your employees operate? Do you personally comply with everything in these documents, or are they just a bunch of high-minded but ultimately meaningless statements?

11. When deliberating over a tough issue, do you ever break your group into several, smaller groups to avoid groupthink?

CHAPTER SIX

Get and Keep the Right Leaders—
But Not Too Many of Them

One Monday evening in October 2009, about seven years into my tenure, the president of our Aerospace division dropped an unwelcome surprise on me over dinner: he was resigning in two weeks to join a hot, young start-up in the solar panel industry. He loved Honeywell, he said, but he wanted to work at a company that was smaller, nimbler, and more flexible. And that wasn't all. "Oh, you're not going to believe this, Dave," he said, "but on my way over to the restaurant, our CFO told me he's resigning as well and taking a job elsewhere." So there I was, with two top leaders in our biggest business set to depart. What would we do? How would we manage this transition so that it didn't disrupt our operations? And how would we explain it externally so that investors didn't interpret these departures as evidence of a bigger problem rather than the coincidence that it was?

I called our corporate HR head that night and got straight to the point. "Look," I said, "we've got to move. You've got forty-eight hours. I want to be able to announce on Wednesday that these two are leaving and I want to identify their replacements."

"That's impossible," he said. "We can't get the new leaders in that quickly. We've got to interview the internal candidates for these positions, do the same to fill the positions they would be leaving, and so on down the line."

"Make it happen," I said.

We did make it happen. By noon on Wednesday, we had drafted announcements that named the two departing leaders as well as the promotions we were granting to fill positions two levels below them. But we couldn't publicize these announcements yet because our departing president's new company hadn't completed their internal reviews. I called this departing president and asked if he could help get his company to move faster. As I put it to him, "Would you mind telling your new company—the smaller, more nimble guys—that the big, old dinosaur Honeywell is ready to proceed and that they need to get their act together?"

We could move so quickly because we took succession planning seriously. Most companies have succession plans for their leadership ranks, but it devolves into a rote exercise, and the organization lacks a clear sense of who will fill key roles in case of departure. It's another instance of what I call "compliance with words rather than compliance with intent." We put deep thought into our succession planning, identifying who we really would put into a job if its occupant left. As a result, we never required more than a couple of days to name a successor when high-level executives departed. That helped us avoid the period of ambiguity that departures commonly trigger, as well as the resulting disruption. We created an impression of continuity and stability—"The king is dead. Long live the king!"

It's critically important to make leadership transitions rapid and seamless. In the month or two (or longer) it might take to fill a key role, and then the month or longer it takes for a new leader to get settled, organizations typically stagnate. Nobody works all that hard, so short-term goals suffer and long-term initiatives that had been steaming ahead lose momentum. Although leaders often regard such stagnation as inevitable, a fact of life inside organizations, it really isn't. To avoid the hit to performance, prepare far in advance so that you don't miss a beat when someone leaves.

If you want to perform well over both the short and long term, pay close attention to executive leadership in general. As much as you might invest in areas like culture, process transformation, and M&A, you'll only make progress if you have talented senior leaders who are both committed to the company's strategies and capable of executing on them. Having the right *number* of those leaders matters too. Remember the maxim presented in chapter 1: keep fixed costs constant while increasing sales. Just as you're pushing for more efficiency throughout the organization via process change, you can also keep your organization increasingly slender and nimble as you grow by maintaining a leadership corps that is relatively small and stable but that punches far above its weight. Enhance the quality of leaders rather than their sheer quantity, and you'll increase your organization's ability to adapt, compete, and perform over *every* time frame.

TIGHTEN UP TALENT MANAGEMENT

You might think improving leadership quality is pretty simple: just fire all of your weak, underperforming leaders and replace them with better people. You can probably enhance your leadership cadre with this approach, but in the process you'll disrupt the organization by forcing too much change all at once. As I mentioned in the last chapter, we transitioned out several top leaders during my first few years at Honeywell, but it wasn't a radical house-cleaning. We tried to keep as many existing leaders in place as possible to maintain a sense of stability and to allow our organization the time it needed to absorb the effects of these transitions.

Gradual change has always seemed sound to me as a management principle, but it was absolutely essential for us when it came to personnel matters. As you'll recall from the introduction, Honeywell was in disarray when I arrived thanks to our failed merger with General Electric. For about a year, while the two companies awaited regulatory approval for the deal, leaders at General Electric informally ran Honeywell, even though they didn't yet own it. The result was chaos. General Electric told entire parts of our business that they would be eliminated through restructuring once the deal went through. As a result, huge swaths of our middle management and senior leadership corps ran for the exits. Many of those who stayed were biding their time, waiting for the deal to go through so that they could get a big payoff but contributing only lackluster performance. Once the deal failed to materialize, the company remained adrift under the stewardship of a temporary CEO, with no clear strategy. In addition, the company was beset by cultural warfare, as described in chapter 5. In this context, about a quarter of our leadership positions were unfilled when I arrived. My goal was to bring stability as well as change. The last thing we needed was more shocks to our system in the form of a wholesale replacement of our leadership ranks. Many investors didn't see it this way; they wondered why I wasn't bringing in a new leadership team, and suspected that either I didn't have the chops to do my job or that other talented leaders didn't want to work for me. I knew otherwise. We desperately needed to improve the quality of our leadership, but we would do it gradually.

The good news was that improvements in leadership quality didn't require sweeping gestures. As we found, tightening up our people processes so that they actually worked went a long way. I described some of the changes we made to our management resource review (MRR) in the last chapter, including an annual meeting I held with my staff in which we exchanged views on our company's top four hundred leaders. The more fundamental change we made was to enhance the intensity and rigor of MRRs generally. When I arrived, leaders were going through the motions of completing MRRs, but as with our strategic planning and our accounting, it wasn't a meaningful process. If you inquired about the people slotted for particular roles, posing questions like, "Would you really put this person in the job today if so-and-so left?" leaders would shrug and say, "Well, no." Not only didn't we have a deep talent bench—we were fooling ourselves into thinking we did.

We made it clear that such a lackadaisical attitude wouldn't suffice any longer. During the first couple of years, we made leaders redo their MRRs, and then redo them again, until they either had people in place whom they *would* like to see in each position or acknowledged the gap by leaving the form blank. I met with leaders of our individual businesses twice annually to review their MRRs, in addition to our big annual meeting. This greater frequency prompted leaders to pay closer attention throughout the year than they had been to succession planning and leadership development.

When conducting MRRs, we also spent considerable time discussing our strategic plans and the leadership capabilities we needed to execute them, debating which jobs we would give to top performers in order to help them along in their careers. We created personal development plans, assigning these high-prospect leaders, who numbered about two dozen, mentors from my staff, including me. At one point one of my mentees was Darius Adamczyk, my successor as CEO.

MAKE PERFORMANCE REVIEWS MEANINGFUL

We also tightened up the regular performance reviews that fed into our MRR reviews, sending the message that *performance mattered*. Previously, appraisals had been loose and "new agey": the person being evaluated wrote their own appraisal, which their boss then edited and approved. Ridiculous! We mandated that bosses do the actual work of appraising how well their reports were doing. This sparked howls of protest, with leaders claiming they didn't have time to write up thoughtful performance reviews every year—they were too busy meeting with customers and focusing on strategy. I defended our new policy by taking these leaders through the business logic, in a conversation that went like this:

Me: Does having the best people make a difference?
Reluctant Leader: Yes.
Me: How long does it take to do an appraisal?
Reluctant Leader: An hour.
Me: How long does it take to give an appraisal?
Reluctant Leader: An hour.
Me: How many reports do you have?
Reluctant Leader: Ten.

Me: So you don't believe devoting twenty hours a year to ensuring you have the best people performing at high level is a good investment of your time?

Reluctant Leader: Ummmmm.

Exactly.

We made performance reviews more substantive and serious by changing them to include a measure on each of the Twelve Behaviors, and by requiring that each manager secure his or her boss's approval of each appraisal (see chapter 5). This included my one-over-one review of appraisals for my staff's reports—about 125 people in all. I generally rejected about 20 percent of these appraisals on the grounds that, in my view, they were incomplete. We wanted to ensure that people were supporting our culture, and that bosses were taking performance reviews seriously. To that end, as I've explained, we began timing our appraisals so that they occurred in coordination with salary decisions. Our tighter appraisal process might have required more effort on managers' part, but it certainly helped us boost performance at the top of the organization, while also yielding a more accurate picture of leadership quality at any given time.

To Properly Hold People Accountable, Beware Upward Delegation

About twenty years ago, *Harvard Business Review* published a great article about the phenomenon of upward delegation called "Who's Got the Monkey?"[1] Subpar performers love to evade or at least share responsibility for tasks by consulting with their superiors, in the guise of asking for advice. This can take a couple of different forms. In some cases, they'll send you a seemingly innocuous email explaining a problem, or raise this problem in a meeting, asking, "What do you want to do?" In these situations, you must always put the onus back on them to come up with a solution. Ask them to identify various options and explain the logic behind each, and request that they make a recommendation. If you don't do this, they'll think you now bear responsibility for the decision.

Alternately, some reports will ask for your opinion on the thought process they went through in arriving at a decision. This might well be their attempt to get you to co-own the decision, even though you likely don't know all of the relevant information as well as they do. When it comes time for a performance review, they'll then point to this conversation to claim co-ownership to evade responsibility for poor performance. Don't fall for this trick. In such situations, I would offer my opinion, but also put the responsibility squarely back on my reports' shoulders, saying something like, "That sounds right, but just to be clear, the decision is on you, not on me. You are the person on the ground so you have to sort it out, and you're also responsible for the results."

ARE YOU THE "PATRON SAINT OF POOR PERFORMERS"?

Of course, enhanced performance reviews would do little to improve the quality of our leaders if we didn't address subpar performance when we encountered it. For years, the organization had been too soft with under-performers, allowing ineffective or bad leaders to continue in their posts. The reasons varied: bosses cringed at having difficult conversations, they felt bad for the ineffective leaders, and they believed certain leaders were too valuable to let go despite their bad behavior. As we made clear, nobody was indispensable any longer. I myself let go of a couple of key leaders who were delivering their numbers yet failing to support our cultural values. As we told senior executives, if they were afraid or reluctant to let ineffective leaders beneath them go—if they wanted to give them another chance—they needed to consider the lives and careers of the thousands of people working under those leaders, as well as the duty we collectively owed to sharehold-ers and customers to perform well. As a rule, the negative effects of poor performers spread far and wide, because others perceive that the threshold of what an organization will tolerate is lower than they thought. By remov-ing poor performers, we would remind everyone that our standards were high—a lesson I learned when I was an hourly employee. My coworkers and I all knew who the weakest performer in our group was. When that person was let go, we scrambled to make sure we weren't now the weakest!

At Honeywell, leaders at any level, up to and including the CEO and board members, needed to avoid becoming what I called the "Patron Saint of Bad Performers." When we saw leaders who weren't doing their jobs, we had to act. As time passed, it greatly helped that we were now more rigorous about our succession planning. When we had to remove a leader, we didn't hesitate, because we knew we could move his or her replacement right in without disruption.

We found it similarly important to change who bore responsibility for improving poor performance. Conventional wisdom in the HR community held that bosses had to work with underperformers, sitting with them and providing coaching and oversight. As we saw it, that was precisely the *wrong* thing for bosses to do. Helping the single underperformer on a team of ten get back on track sucks up a lot of valuable managerial time. Leaders are much better off working with the other nine to help them notch wins for the organization, while also attending to customers and operational matters. Underperforming leaders (and lower-level managers and employees as well) needed to take responsibility for fixing their own performance. If they didn't change within a fairly quick time period, they'd face the consequences. That might sound cold and uncompromising, but it really isn't—it's honoring and supporting the vast majority of people who *are* working hard and performing. We tried to handle underperformers respectfully and compassionately, and when they deserved a second chance, we gave it to them.[1] But we understood that we needed strong leaders on our team if we were going to succeed over the short and long term. That meant evaluating people rigorously, asking subpar leaders to move on if they couldn't improve, and taking great care of top performers.

---

[1] I am a big believer in providing second chances if someone is truly contrite and willing to change. I benefited quite a few times from second chances when I was younger, once after I had shoplifted a substantial amount, another time after I had fallen asleep in a conference room when I should have been working. In both cases, good-hearted people cut me some slack, giving me the opportunity to mend my ways—which I did.

The trickiest situations occurred when we had strong performers who weren't supporting our values or were even actively undermining them. On three separate occasions, after several softer interventions failed, I got tough, holding what I called a "two-by-four" conversation with offending individuals. In each case, I sat the leader down and told them flat out that I was hitting them with a two-by-four since they had shown themselves impervious to my previous suggestions. I wouldn't argue the facts with them—we were past that. I'd just stipulate that I knew what the facts were, that they had to make a change, and that they had two to three days to decide whether they wanted to do so. I'd add that I was prepared with a backup candidate in case they remained intransigent. After expressing disbelief and demanding where I got my information, these individuals all said they wanted to stay. Rather than accept that decision in that moment, I insisted they take the two or three days to think about it and then get back to me. All three did wind up staying and changing, but I wasn't bluffing—I was prepared for them to bow out.[2] I didn't necessarily change what these individuals believed, but I did change their behavior. To build the right culture, you must be prepared to go to the mat for your values, even letting go of strong performers if they won't play along.

Provide Feedback in a Way Recipients Can Internalize

Too many leaders expect their people to adapt to their particular leadership style. If you want the best performance, look beyond your style and provide feedback tailored to the individual. With some employees, you have to yell

---

2   No matter what kind of transaction you're dealing with, and who is on the other side of the table, it's important never to negotiate with an empty gun. A bluff can work at times, but if you get called on it once, people discover they are dealing with someone they can't always trust or believe. Doing what you say really matters in negotiations. Having backup plans in mind also causes you to behave more confidently and decisively, which in turn affects how your negotiating partners perceive you. This is true whether you're dealing with a union or an employee, and whether you're negotiating a deal to buy or sell a company.

and scream to get their attention. With others, all you need to say is, "You are capable of better work than this." Yelling and screaming at the latter isn't going to help. And treating the former too politely may elicit a grunt but no discernible behavior changes. Know your people well, and adapt your feedback accordingly. Speaking of feedback, experts often advise that leaders should "criticize privately and praise publicly." Criticizing privately might be appropriate in certain, sensitive cases, but in general both criticism and praise should be public. Your people have to understand that certain behaviors or performance are unacceptable. Otherwise they'll wonder why the organization allows it. When leaders share both criticism and praise publicly, team members learn about the high performance culture you're striving to create.

PAY LEADERS WELL

I've always believed that money alone doesn't suffice to motivate talented people, because the vast majority of us also want fulfilling, meaningful work. We want to be able to go home to our families at the end of the day and talk about everything we accomplished. Some business leaders I've encountered take this idea too far, suggesting that meaningful work is *all* that talented people want out of a job. That's not true: money makes a difference. To get the best people, you must pay them extremely well for what they do *and* give them jobs and a workplace environment they love.

The Honeywell Operating System and our cultural transformation helped make working at our company more fulfilling for leaders, as did our constant drive to perform over both the short and long term. As our long-time employees can tell you firsthand, it's a lot more fun to work for a winning, high-performing organization than it is for a losing one. When it came to monetary compensation, we didn't hesitate to pay our leaders above market. We took some flak for that from the compensation rating agencies, and a bit from investors.

The agencies preferred we adopt a more formulaic approach when calculating compensation. Some "experts" believe the best way to determine compensation is to benchmark it directly to a company's stock market performance in a given year. If the stock is the seventy-fifth percentile as compared with its peers, then compensation for leaders should be below the seventy-fifth percentile. That's silly.

First, the stock market isn't a good short-term proxy for performance. Second, you can't chart performance on a proportional scale. A football player who runs the forty-yard-dash in 4.3 seconds is only 2 percent faster than one who runs it in 4.4 seconds—maybe in the 100th percentile versus the 98th. But that one-tenth of a second and two percentile points make all the difference between winning or losing the Super Bowl, between catching the ball or being intercepted. Small differences in performance can have a big impact, in business as well as sports, and we need to acknowledge that in how we compensate leaders.

A similar point holds true for a formula that ties compensation to the achievement of specific numbers, regardless of what happened during the year (industry changes, for instance, or investments required to support an urgent strategy). What you are teaching leaders to do is argue at budget time for a shorter yard stick by which to measure performance—less aggressive goals, a smaller budget. Instead of leaders pushing themselves to perform in the short term while also investing in the long term, they are incented, in effect, to get by in the present and do little if anything to prepare for the future.

Until I left Honeywell, we opted for a compensation formula that prioritized fairness. Human beings must feel they are being treated fairly relative to their performance and to others. I wanted our people to know I would evaluate them based on the totality of their performance, short and long term, and not just if they hit their budget goals. Our approach protected people whose industries wound up faring far worse than expected, while declining to reward people just because their industries happened to be growing more rapidly than expected.

To attract and retain the very best, we also paid the best people what they would command at other companies for a bigger job. Why wait until someone else tried to steal them away before paying them what the market said they were worth? Our corporate compensation consultant felt we were overpaying, and as proof they pointed to the low turnover we were seeing among our senior leaders. I was incredulous: stability in the leadership ranks is a *bad* thing? To achieve strong short- and long-term performance, you want strong performers to stay put, even if they are recruited by other companies (as many of our senior leaders were). Paying them handsomely for their contributions goes a long way. As I explained to that foolish compensation consultant, people did leave Honeywell . . . when I wanted them to!

We also tried to compensate leaders in a way that motivated them to attend to long-term performance, not merely this year's goals. The real problem with pegging compensation to the company's stock price movement is that it encourages short-termism. During my tenure as CEO, short-term compensation for our leaders tended to be about average for our industry—in the fiftieth to seventieth percentile range. Our long-term compensation (consisting of stock options and restricted stock) was in the ninetieth percentile. While the experts complained this was excessive, our leaders aligned behind the long-term growth initiatives described in this book in part because they saw how much they personally stood to benefit if we succeeded. Many of them made a lot of money at Honeywell, not so much from salary and bonuses but from options and restricted stock.

If you're in a turnaround situation like we were, arranging for long-term compensation can prove tricky. The usual means of offering long-term compensation—stock options or restricted stock—don't mean much to people when a company is still very much in the dumps. The prospect of potential gains seems too hypothetical. To help stabilize our leadership corps and boost morale early in my tenure, we developed a special growth plan that paid out cash instead of stock. Over a three-year period, leaders received up to 200 percent of their salary and bonus if they exceeded organic sales and ROI growth metrics for their business and at the company level. If we could drive these metrics, it meant our income and cash flow were growing, and we would eventually see our stock price rise as the market realized we were for real.

To further help us retain strong leaders during this difficult time, we sent out quarterly letters updating them on their current performance, what it meant for their payout, and what they had to do to improve. The plan proved a great success, bringing about a sudden and very welcome increase in retention, and helping a One Honeywell spirit take hold. Leaders were working hard, and for a change, they were seeing both financial rewards and eventually a stock market bump in response.

If a compensation plan pays out well, directors and compensation consultants sometimes assume the plan wasn't rigorous enough. A well-constructed plan, they suggest, would pay out exactly 100 percent of projected compensation; otherwise, the original goals were obviously too easy to meet. How absurd! It's true the original goals might have been too easy, but perhaps the higher payouts reflected exceptional performance relative to a leader's peers. If your compensation plan is always paying out 100 percent of compensation, you risk disappointing your exceptional leaders, who feel they've been outperforming but are not being paid for it. If the performance is there, pay for it! Fairness requires nothing less.

To further boost retention among senior and mid-level leaders, we also changed the way we awarded long-term compensation. We knew our people valued stock options (which only gain value if the company performs well) much less than restricted shares of stock (which have some value even if the company is underperforming) because options were inherently riskier than stock, and we hadn't performed well historically. Conventional wisdom using Black-Scholes math (a pricing model commonly used in the analysis of options) held that four stock options equaled the value of one share of restricted Honeywell stock. Rather than simply assume this rule's validity, we ran a survey and found that our people in fact valued stock options much less—in their minds, ten options equaled one share of restricted stock. This made sense: given our poor performance in recent years, many leaders felt uncertain at best at our future prospects. For lower-level leaders, we increased dramatically the proportion of restricted stock, issuing at the rate of six options to one restricted share instead of the conventional four. As a result, we issued fewer shares than the Black-Scholes math said we should. Leaders liked it, retention improved, and we wound up saving money.

HIRE DELIBERATELY

As important as retention is, you must also hire the right people to begin with—a task that requires considerable thought, effort, and commitment. So often busy leaders compromise on the selection process. When a key job opens up and the organization is scrambling, they throw up their hands and say, "Hiring somebody is better than nobody." That might seem true in the short term, but only because you feel better having someone in the position. In reality, the wrong somebody causes a great deal of pain. It's far better to leave a job open for a few months to get the very best person and deal with the disruption that causes, than to settle for mediocrity.

We invested an extraordinary amount of time to ensure we were hiring top-notch talent. For the approximately two hundred most senior leadership jobs in the company, our HR leader and I personally interviewed the final candidates for each job. Some executives disliked this practice, perceiving that I was micromanaging them, but as I saw it, these interviews were critical. First, they allowed us to exercise quality control. During the first couple of years of my tenure, we probably rejected a quarter of the final candidates we interviewed, finding that our leaders were content to just fill the job rather than hire the very best person. In one memorable instance, one of our business units wanted to hire a leader it had fired just three years earlier. I had hired the same person myself at a different company and had fired him after about six months. Without our HR leader and I exercising veto power, my guess is we'd have had to fire him a third time.

My interviews also imparted a sense to the interviewees of how significant the new job was to the company. When the CEO and global HR leader each take an hour to talk to you about a job you're interviewing for, that says something. Further, these interviews allowed me an opportunity to convey to the new hire what I wanted to see him or her accomplish. I told them I wanted them to build upon what their predecessor had done and not just tear it down.

Sometimes I had to push that point to understand what a candidate would change in the "build" process. When I asked a candidate for the CFO job for one of our businesses what he would change about his predecessor's policies, he replied that there was nothing—his predecessor was "great." I challenged him on this—surely there were ways he could bring needed change. "Nope," the candidate said. I told him that I would step out of the room for fifteen minutes. If he couldn't name three substantive policies he would change when I returned, he wouldn't get the job. Fifteen minutes later, he had come up with eleven significant changes he would make, all of them good. We hired him, and he became a terrific CFO. Further proof of the value of interviews, and of pushing people hard intellectually.

Functional Transformation for human resources also played an important role in making sure we were selecting the right leaders. Consistent with the philosophy of accomplishing two seemingly conflicting things at the same time, we wanted to lower our HR costs while also achieving better service, including hiring people for open positions more quickly. HR had already measured how long it took them to fill an opening, but it wasn't measuring whether we were hiring the right leaders. To remedy that, we implemented a survey of hiring managers at three and twelve months after hiring to see if they were happy with the quality of the person they'd hired. We wanted jobs filled quickly, but not at the expense of quality. By measuring quality, we made everyone in HR much more mindful of making the right hires, and doing so quickly. During the first year, half the scores fell below four on a scale of one to five. Afterward, 90 percent of them were above four. Our survey became a very useful tool, alerting us to hot spots where scores were sliding.

FIND THE TOM BRADY WITHIN

As we saw in the last chapter, we emphasized internal hiring for leadership positions. In part, we aimed to build continuity and entrench One Honeywell in the company, but we also hired internally because we saw it as a way to get the best people. So often organizations overlook the talent right in front of them, stereotyping them because of their credentials or past positions.

When quarterback Tom Brady joined the New England Patriots football team, nobody knew who he was. During his first season with the team, he sat on the bench as the star quarterback led the team to a losing record. Then the star quarterback got injured, and the team turned to this nobody named Brady. The Patriots began to win, and they wound up battling their way to the organization's first-ever Super Bowl victory. Since then, Brady has led the team to eight more Super Bowls, winning five of them, for six total, and emerging as the greatest quarterback in football history. Here was a Hall of Fame player sitting on the bench for a year, his superior talent unrecognized—and this in a business that is exceedingly rigorous in how it evaluates talent.

In business, it's easy to write off people in your organization for big jobs because they don't have experience, or because they never got an MBA, or because they got an MBA from a second-tier state school instead of Harvard, or because they've performed well in a particular job and you have them unfairly stereotyped. As I like to say, in my experience, experience is over-rated. Just a little bit of experience combined with a lot of raw talent is worth far more. In our succession planning, we were always asking ourselves, "Could this person in our ranks be the next Tom Brady?" While we some-times took a chance on people and lived to regret it, in the vast majority of cases our own, homegrown talent rose to the challenge. Just like Tom Brady, they were sitting there the whole time and nobody could see them.

In deciding whom to hire, we also focused on building teams that would work well together, adding people with certain personal qualities that would balance out or complement those of our existing staff. If a given team had a decisive leader, we would seek to put in place people around him or her who were more deliberate by nature, and vice versa. I considered the need to achieve balance in teams when assembling my own staff. I knew I could be defensive and decisive. Although I needed to mitigate my own defensive responses to criticism, it would certainly help if I hired people who would push back at me in ways that were less likely to trigger an emotional response from me. Likewise, I needed more deliberate people on my team. If everyone else was as decisive as I was, we would all go off a cliff together at 150 miles

GET AND KEEP THE RIGHT LEADERS—BUT NOT TOO MANY OF THEM

per hour. When it comes to understanding the personality types of team members, we used the Myers-Briggs test, which in my view is the best tool in the world. I'm generally not a fan of HR stuff, but Myers-Briggs works!

Smart Isn't Enough

Many companies look to hire smart people when filling leadership roles. And yet, being a good leader takes more than just intelligence. Smart leaders get beaten every day by others who have better judgment, less ego, and more common sense; who pay more attention to execution and detail; who possess better interpersonal skills; and who can recover from setbacks better, think more independently, and work harder. Learn how to use all these skills as you lead people and run meetings to arrive at good decisions. And just as importantly, hire people who have those capabilities in addition to being smart. Oh, and be sure to pick people who have something to prove to the world. As the old adage goes, it's easier to take a bit of wind out of someone's sails than to put wind into their sails to begin with.

KEEP FEWER LEADERS

I've discussed how to enhance the quality of leaders, but as good as they might be, it's important not to have too many of them. Too often organizations suffer from a kind of "leadership bloat." They establish new leadership positions in order to lend significance to exciting new business initiatives, but they don't do enough to ensure that their existing leaders are working as efficiently as possible. The result—too many leaders—drags down performance, even if the vast majority of those leaders are high performers. That's because more leaders equals more bureaucracy. Leaders don't just lead—they create work for other people, in the form of meetings, sign-offs, projects, procedures, priorities, and so on, especially if they're good leaders. Others in the organization then spend more of their time responding to these leaders

149

and less time leading or managing their own team members. Each leader has their own staff—adding yet more cost and complexity to the organization. And when you have more leaders, you have more slots you need to fill as people retire or leave the organization.

When I became CEO, we weren't suffering from leadership bloat in investors' eyes—they thought of us as a lean company. Still, as we stabilized the organization over the next few years, I suspected we weren't as lean at the top as we could be. One of our leaders, a manufacturing expert, took all of our top manufacturing leaders on two-week trips every year to far-flung destinations in order to evaluate whether we might build plants in these countries someday, and they also dedicated three days a quarter for staff meetings. That seemed strange to me. Why were we spending so much time on these trips and staff meetings when we desperately needed to work on improving our manufacturing operations and implementing the Honeywell Operating System? I wound up stopping those trips and meetings and eliminating that leader's position.

I still felt that with a bit of effort we could prod our leaders to operate more efficiently. Rather than slash positions indiscriminately, I gave every functional and business leader targets each year for incrementally reducing the number of leaders in their organization as well as financial targets. Whenever one of our top 740 leaders departed, we didn't reflexively hire someone else but instead asked if we really needed that person's position, or whether we could push his or her former responsibilities into another leader's job. Most of the time we really did need the position, but probably two or three times out of ten, we found an opportunity to do more with fewer leaders. We did something similar, by the way, with our workforce as a whole, tracking our employee census by business function and geographic region on a monthly basis to make sure our businesses weren't over-hiring in developed countries. As I'll detail later, we had no hiring constraints in emerging, high-growth regions because we wanted to build capability there. When I saw the census for a developed country's business ticking up, I said something. Keeping tight control over hiring was vital to keeping our costs fixed as our business grew.

In addition to reducing bureaucratic drag, keeping fewer leaders reduces cost, making it easier to compensate richly the leaders you do have, and allowing you to attract and keep the best. Consider the following chart out of our proxy statement, which compares Honeywell's performance in 2003 to that in 2017:

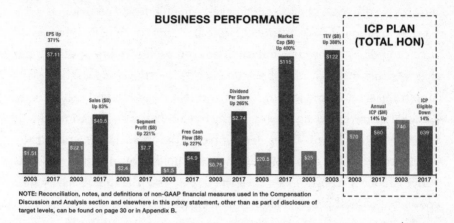

BUSINESS PERFORMANCE

NOTE: Reconciliation, notes, and definitions of non-GAAP financial measures used in the Compensation Discussion and Analysis section and elsewhere in this proxy statement, other than as part of disclosure of target levels, can be found on page 30 or in Appendix B.

As you can see, our sales rose 83 percent during those fourteen years, earnings per share by 371 percent, and total market capitalization by 400 percent. At the same time, the number of senior leaders eligible for our incentive compensation plan (ICP) declined by 14 percent, or 101 people, and the total cost of our bonus pool only rose by 14 percent. That represented a big win for investors—they were getting a great deal of value from their holdings, yet paying only slightly more to our leaders than they had been when our performance had been much weaker (this is true as well if you consider our overall compensation costs, including not merely stock grants and bonuses but also salaries). So much for those analysts who said we paid our leaders too much. When you ask leaders to do more, and they deliver over both the short and long term, leading to wins for shareholders and customers, then those leaders deserve higher than average compensation.

HR IS TOO IMPORTANT TO BE LEFT TO HR PEOPLE

If you haven't thought much about leadership quality, you should—whether you lead a team of ten or an organization of one hundred thousand. In larger organizations, you might be tempted to nod your head at the tactics described in this chapter and then task HR with executing on them. That would be a huge mistake. As the decision-maker in your organization, you must become intimately engaged with leadership development, hiring, and firing.

I've mentioned that my global HR leader and I personally interviewed final candidates for our two hundred senior-most leadership positions. But that was only the beginning. I personally reviewed the compensation plans for our top six hundred leaders to confirm that it was fair and that it corresponded with what we had heard during our annual, cross-functional MRR review, which I also led. To set an example for the organization, I personally developed all of the appraisals for my staff, holding in-depth discussions with each of my reports. I also performed reviews of the appraisals my staff conducted of their people, reading them closely.

In 2006, we created a special restricted stock units (RSUs) award program for about sixty of our key lower-level executives. We would select these sixty people each year to receive awards representing between 50 and 120 percent of their respective salaries. Once a leader received this award, he or she couldn't receive it again for three years, allowing us to touch almost two hundred high-potential, lower-level leaders during that period. Each August I called every recipient to discuss the reward, what they had done to merit it, and what the award represented. That took a fair amount of time, but it was worth it. When these up-and-coming leaders received a call from me, they sometimes thought it was a practical joke. In an organization of over 100,000 people, why was the CEO calling *them*? Personalizing the award left a positive impression, contributing to the significantly higher retention rates we saw among these executives as compared with the rest of their cohort.[3]

When I explained my engagement in personnel matters to my team, I paraphrased French prime minister Georges Clemenceau, who used to say,

---

3   As an aside, I all too often found myself approving severance packages upon a leader's departure and asking our HR folks why we had given this person RSUs a year or so earlier. Performing an analysis, HR found that the RSU recipients most likely to leave were those who had been hired from outside the company less than two years earlier. These individuals had apparently performed well at the start of their tenure, received an RSU award, and then saw our perception of their performance tail off. We implemented a rule that nobody could receive RSUs unless they had been with the company for two years. Lo and behold, this issue of early departures of RSU recipients disappeared.

"War is too important to be left to generals." To the occasional discomfort of our HR folks, I said, "Human resources is too important to be left to human resources people." That is undeniably true. As CEO, I wanted to know the leaders in my organization well, and I wanted to guide them to become the best they could possibly be. Over time I made sure to know personally the top three to five hundred leaders across all of Honeywell. As I remarked in chapter 5, I wanted to make sure they embodied the values we wanted in our culture, and being that familiar with them meant I could help fill positions almost immediately when an executive decided to leave.

Remember, too, that your personal engagement serves as a model for others. Just as we asked leaders throughout Honeywell to perform thoughtful performance reviews of their reports, so we also tasked them with coaching and teaching their reports, eliminating the usual executive coaching and MBA programs that companies offer. That occasioned a fair share of grumbling, but it helped that leaders throughout the organization saw me personally reviewing my own staff's performance, teaching in our training programs, and interviewing candidates for leadership jobs. By becoming more involved, you'll send the message that leadership truly matters to your success, and that you personally value it.

When it comes to compensation, strive for fairness. I've focused on leaders here, but we designed our compensation programs for all Honeywell employees with fairness in mind. When calculating bonuses for an entire business unit, we didn't just consider whether the business had met its goals, but also how its performance compared with the previous year, with the industry as a whole, and with the company's overall performance. We also considered whether leaders had made the right decisions to enable our long-term growth. Sometimes we adjusted an entire business's bonus pool upward if we felt it was warranted, and it also went the other way. We wanted the entire organization to strive to do its absolute best while investing for the future because they knew we were going to recognize them for the actual performance they delivered.

As you develop your leadership talent, be prepared to take some heat. Paying leaders well isn't popular these days—just look at all the controversy about CEO compensation. Many people believe the compensation game is rigged to benefit management because corporate leaders are all friends. In our case, that just wasn't true. What mattered was performance, over both the short and long term. We paid out so well because we actually did well over the long term. When we did the math, we found out that we actually would have paid out more if, as the compensation agencies recommended, we had pegged more of leaders' compensation to our stock price. Hold your ground when it comes to compensating leaders well and in ways that encourage long-term thinking. Much of the business world remains beholden to short-termism. You don't have to be.

LEADERSHIP MATTERS

Despite my arguments in this chapter, you might still wonder whether I'm emphasizing leadership too much. How much of our performance gains really owed to our leadership quality as opposed to the other initiatives described in this book? Is it really worth devoting so much attention and resources to leaders? My answer to the first question is "a lot," and to the second question an unqualified "yes." When I wrote the original draft of this book, I titled it *Leadership Matters*—because it absolutely does. As Mark James, our head of HR, once remarked, many people consider leaders to be like light bulbs. Just replace the bulb, and you get the same amount of light. Nothing could be further from the truth. If we hadn't taken time all along to attract, retain, and develop best-in-class leaders, we wouldn't have generated results worth writing about. Focusing on our growth initiatives, processes, and the general intellectual discourse in our organization was critically important, but without great leadership it wouldn't have amounted to much.

To illustrate the importance of leadership, let me tell you about a man named Carl Johnson. He grew up in the small town of Galion, Ohio, amid very difficult circumstances—his father had been in prison and absent for much of his childhood, and his mother got remarried to a man who was abusive. The trauma of living in the household was so bad that Carl's younger brother eventually died of a heroin overdose. Carl might have met a similar fate had he not developed a passion for athletics. He became the star quarterback at his high school, leading his team to a state championship. His football coach became a father figure to him, encouraging him to leave town and go to college. So that's what Carl did. He won a football scholarship as a quarterback to attend the University of Cincinnati and then went on to earn an MBA from the University of Houston.[4]

In 1998, Carl went to work at Pittway, and in 2000, he became a Honeywell employee when we acquired that company. He rose through the ranks in our fire protection business. In 2006, we put him in charge of our gas detection business, which was then minimally profitable and beset by terrible quality problems—customers would routinely receive defective products. Over the course of a few years, Carl worked hard to implement the Honeywell Operating System. His organization fixed the quality issues, developed some great new products, and focused on pleasing our customers. As a result, the business grew rapidly (over 50 percent organic growth over a three-year period) and achieved operating margins of over 20 percent. Today, it remains highly profitable.

Carl exemplifies the success we had developing and retaining leaders, as well as the tremendous contribution those leaders made toward our success. He was one of those Tom Bradys in our midst, and we never would have found him had we not focused so consistently on our leadership pipeline, with an eye toward developing leaders from within. We also never would have kept him for as long as we did had we not incented him both financially and by providing him with a great work environment in which he could thrive.

Today, our leaders are constantly being recruited for jobs elsewhere, but many of them stick around—and for many years Carl was one of them. "I saw security [in Honeywell]," he recalled. "I saw stability. I saw development. I saw opportunities for growth for me and my family. What I loved about the environment, it was very competitive and a results-oriented business."

---

4   I am indebted to Carl for agreeing to be interviewed for this book, and for sharing a document his daughter composed about his life. This account of his upbringing draws on that document as well as our interview.

He also liked that we were focused on long-term results, that we didn't have a "one-and-done" mentality but one focused on delivering the "right results." Carl did eventually leave the company in 2018, after twenty years of excellent and dedicated service.

To win both today and tomorrow, your business needs more leaders like Carl. It's up to you to find them, nurture them, and create an environment in which they're inspired and empowered to perform. As I think you'll find, doing so creates a virtuous cycle. Put great leaders in the right culture and you'll drive performance, which in turn will give leaders the monetary and emotional incentive they need to take performance even higher. Who knows how much or how fast your business will grow?

QUESTIONS TO ASK YOURSELF

1. How much time do you spend nurturing the leadership pipeline in your team or organization? Does this imperative frequently get lost amid other priorities?
2. Do you perform succession planning with enough rigor and vigor? Is your organization frequently unsettled by departing leaders? If your best people left tomorrow, how long would it take you to lock in replacements? Do you actively seek out the Tom Bradys already in your organization?
3. Are your incentives primarily oriented toward short-term goals? How might you effect more of a balance between rewarding short-term wins and long-term performance?
4. Do you personally interview candidates for important positions?
5. How are leaders in your team or organization trained? Do you play a role in that?
6. Are you paying your best leaders enough? If you want top talent, you have to pay for it! And are you creating the conditions required for them to succeed?
7. Does your organization have too many leaders? When leaders depart,

do you stop to ask whether you really need anyone in that position? Can you combine that position with another one? When a staff member wants a new leadership position in order to focus on an initiative (oftentimes warranted), do you push them to cut a leadership position elsewhere?

8. Are HR practices as rigorous in your team or organization as they might be? Do bosses take performance reviews seriously? Do you time these reviews to align with salary actions? Do you take a hard line with underperformers? Do you amply reward your top performers?

9. Are you careful not to let subordinates delegate upward in either emails or in-person conversations?

PART THREE

INVEST TO GROW

CHAPTER SEVEN

Go Big on Growth

In 1997, when I was running GE's major appliances business, we developed a line of Advantium ovens that cooked at the same speed as a microwave oven but that could brown and crisp food like a conventional oven. Advantium used microwave technology for cooking but supplemented it with a special phase of cooking that used high heat lamps—what we referred to as light wave technology—for browning. When my team first presented the Advantium oven to me, the marketing leader proposed creating an appliance that fit into the existing kitchen space where a microwave goes (an important detail), but that had two doors—one for the microwave and one for the light wave cooker. That seemed ridiculous. A microwave oven isn't big, and consumers would find it odd to have an appliance that size with two separate doors.

I asked the technologists to explain to me in a more detailed way how light wave technology worked. Discovering that it used some microwave technology in addition to the heat lamps, I asked if we might have one cavity in the appliance but allow consumers to toggle between microwave and light wave cooking with the touch of a button. Our technology guy thought for about thirty seconds and said, "Yeah, we can do that." The marketing guy almost jumped at him. "Why the hell didn't you say that months ago when we were first concepting the product?" The technology guy looked over, nonplussed. "You never asked!"

So many companies struggle with R&D because technology and marketing folks don't communicate. This was certainly the case at Honeywell. To address the problem, we mandated that technologists and marketers collaborate closely on R&D projects from the very beginning. We also created a company-wide, annual event, our Tech Symposium, that convened hundreds of technologists and marketing executives from around the world to collaborate and network. These efforts were part of an ongoing push to enhance long-term growth by turbocharging our R&D function. Leaders and shareholders are keenly aware of how important it is to invest today in the technologies you'll sell to customers tomorrow, but putting more dollars behind R&D—which we also did—won't suffice. To perform well over the short and long term, you need to grow your business over time, and that means spending *smartly and thoughtfully* to improve R&D processes, gleaning more benefit from every dollar.

Long-term growth can't just rest on the shoulders of R&D. I've described the planning approach we used to generate flexibility to fund investments in our future: holding fixed costs constant through process improvements and efficiency gains even as we continued to grow sales. It's important to return some of the surplus value you create back to shareholders, and also to retain some to address legacy issues if you have them and improve productivity via process and culture changes. But you should also invest a good portion of that surplus in a portfolio of growth initiatives. In the next chapter I'll describe the aggressive M&A strategy we pursued to expand and improve our company's growth profile. Here, I'll describe how you can mobilize R&D, globalization, and a better customer experience to power your future success. I'll start with customer experience, which truly is the foundation for growth. If you're not pleasing customers today, any progress you make in other growth areas won't have much of an impact. You might be adding new customers, but you'll also be losing many of your existing customers. Be sure you're delivering a really good customer experience, then move on to address areas like R&D, globalization, and M&A. It's a tough and sometimes lonely road, but if you're committed to attaining strong short- and long-term performance, you'll travel it.

DON'T JUST *TALK* ABOUT DELIVERING FOR CUSTOMERS

I first became attuned to the importance of pleasing customers at the age of twelve while working in my dad's garage. I cleaned windshields, kept the bathroom tidy, and helped put the tools in the garage bays back in their place after cleaning them. When I asked Dad why I was doing all of the unpleasant jobs, he told me I had to start at the bottom to understand everything. And he also told me washing windshields was quite important work. People could buy their gas anywhere, so we needed to give them a good reason to come to our shop. A nice, clean windshield was a way for us to set ourselves apart in customers' eyes. Likewise, when customers went to the restroom and found it clean, they felt better about getting their car serviced with us— it was a visual reminder that we took pride in what we did. Dad also insisted we treat customers with courtesy and respect. "Remember," he used to say, "the higher up the flagpole you climb, the more people can see your ass." Colorful, but I got the message. Be nice to everyone—especially customers.

When I arrived at Honeywell, I saw immediately that we weren't treating customers as nicely as we could have. We *talked* about pleasing customers, even "delighting" them. But talk was cheap. In chapter 1, I mentioned an early encounter I had with a customer at an air show—when I asked how he thought we were doing, he informed us that his company was about to sue us for failing to honor a product development contract we had signed with them. I wish I could say this was the only difficult conversation I had with customers, but it wasn't. Customers complained to me about late deliveries, subpar quality, slow introduction of new products, and a number of other issues. But when I asked our business leaders about it, they insisted there was no real problem, because customers weren't complaining to them. They pointed to metrics showing that our performance on quality and delivery were just fine.

I suspected that our metrics were off, so I made them more robust and insisted we audit each plant's performance. As I recounted in chapter 1, we discovered plant leaders were gaming the system; for instance, not counting in their delivery metrics situations in which customers didn't order within previously specified lead times or when salespeople hadn't entered orders correctly. As they saw it, plant managers hadn't been responsible for the problem, so why count it? The metrics looked great—almost perfect delivery and quality performance. But our actual performance as customers experienced it was far worse. Customers didn't care why they received an order late—they were bothered it hadn't arrived when they needed it. We further learned that customers *were* complaining, but that the entire organization had learned over time to ignore or downplay their discontent. Our attitude seemed to be, "This would be a great company . . . if it weren't for those darned customers!" In our drive to make the numbers, we had forgotten a basic reality of business: we only continue to exist if we do such a great job for customers that they place more orders.

Why Metrics Are Trickier Than They Seem

Our initial difficulties with customer experience illustrate an important concept about measurement. Some people say that "what gets measured gets done." Not necessarily true. If you measure something, the metric will improve because people learn to adjust and redefine, "playing" to the metric. As I like to say, if you measure something, the metric will get better. If you announce you want 50 percent of sales to come from products introduced over the previous three years, you'll find people redefining new products or coming out with new model numbers for the same old products with slight modifications, and bingo—you're at 50 percent with no substantive change. In other words, metrics often foster compliance with words rather than with intent. The only fix is to set clear definitions up front and implement some kind of audit process like we put in place for quality and delivery.

We *would* do a great job for customers, if I had anything to say about it. During my first two years, we worked hard to shift the organization's mind-set. In addition to improving our metrics and auditing performance, we focused on serving customers well, including that area as one of our

Twelve Behaviors and as one of the pillars supporting growth in our Five Initiatives, and evaluating leaders on their customer-related metrics. We also created a weekly Chairman's Award for Everyday Heroes, recognizing employees who had done an extraordinary job for customers. At town halls, I put customer experience front and center, framing it as an essential part of the high-performance culture I wanted us to build. As I told people, we could no longer afford to blame someone else for problems with customer orders. We had to identify the root causes of issues and change our processes to fix them.

Improving customer experience didn't take a big infusion of funding, but it did require a great deal of attention on the part of leaders to keep people focused and change this element of our culture. The effort made a difference. Given how bad our performance was at the outset, we saw quick improvement within those first two years, in turn boosting our revenue and sales. We would continue to enhance customer service as our new culture took hold and as we implemented our Honeywell Operating System. We were by no means perfect, and still aren't. But we were and are a whole lot better than we had been initially.

SPEND MORE ON R&D—AND GET MORE

We also wanted to take growth further and develop amazing new products and services that customers wanted. Our R&D function contained some great engineering talent, but on a number of levels, it was subpar. As Tim Mahoney, president and CEO of our Aerospace division, recalled, "We were way under-investing in new products across the board. . . . We were just trying to meet certain numbers, and one of the mechanisms was harvesting your future by not developing new products."[1] Worse, what little we were spending wasn't deployed very efficiently. As I've suggested, our engineers operated in their own silos and were not focused on our businesses and the needs of our customers. Engineering was also highly decentralized, leading to uneven quality and performance among R&D teams. Meanwhile, product development was painfully slow—we couldn't get new ideas turned into viable products and on the market fast enough. Dan Sheflin, chief technology officer and vice president at our Automation and Control Solutions business, remembered that we had fallen into a "downward spiral" whereby we lacked enough new products to drive sales, and our existing product lines were aging, delivering less revenue and hence having less to invest in developing new products.[2]

To boost product development, we consistently upped our spending year over year. Over a fifteen-year period starting in 2002, our self-funded R&D budgets rose from 3.3 percent of our sales to 5.5 percent. Given that our sales doubled from $22 billion to $40 billion during that period, this represents a three-fold increase in total spending. But these numbers only afford a superficial sense of our investment, since they don't reflect the improved *quality* of our R&D function. We took several steps that dramatically improved our efficiency and effectiveness, allowing us to extract much more value from every R&D dollar we spent.

First, we lowered cost by increasing the size of our R&D function in developing countries. Many leaders are afraid to do R&D in places like India, China, Mexico, or Malaysia, fearing that quality in the engineering work will suffer. When I became CEO, we had a facility called Honeywell Technology Solutions (HTS) in India that performed exceptional software engineering work for our markets around the world at much lower cost than in the US and other developed countries. Yet with only about five hundred employees, this facility was fairly small. Sensing an opportunity, I charged our leader of this facility with doubling the size of his workforce. When he protested that he wouldn't have the work to justify hiring so many engineers, I told him to have faith—the work would come.

Our challenge then became convincing business leaders across Honeywell to source their growing R&D needs out of India—and later, similar facilities in China and the Czech Republic—rather than in higher-cost facilities in the United States and Western Europe. As R&D budgets increased, I began meeting with chief technology officers for our businesses every quarter and pushed them to dedicate their new spending to our low-cost, high-quality facilities. In some cases, I required that leaders travel to India and China to see the quality of our R&D facilities for themselves. When they asked for authorization to hire more engineering talent overall, I said they could—but only if they hired them in low-cost countries. Over time, our businesses got the message, and we expanded our R&D in India, China, and the Czech Republic dramatically. Today we have about ten thousand employees at HTS in these countries doing world-class engineering work for teams across Honeywell, at a cost savings of millions of dollars annually. This helped us create a basis for global sales growth, because the R&D footprint we established provided us with much deeper knowledge of local markets.

A second way we improved our R&D function to spur growth was by streamlining how we developed new products. In 2003, as we were beginning to roll out the Honeywell Operating System, we also began an initiative called Velocity Product Development (VPD) that reimagined virtually every part of our development process with the goal of increasing sales. Working with our engineers and marketers, we analyzed the flow of projects through our system, identifying and fixing blockages with an eye toward improving speed. We took apart our development process step by step, improving everything about it—bringing marketing and engineering together from the very beginning, improving how usable our product designs were and how easy they were for our plants to manufacture, implementing rapid prototyping of our designs, and enhancing how we launched new products. We reduced the number of sign-offs new design changes required as they moved through the system, improved software development and testing, and enhanced our use of electronic design tools.

Thanks to this exhaustive work, we managed to reduce engineering time spent on projects considerably. You might think managers would readily prioritize improving the new product development process, but securing their support wasn't easy—they were too engrossed in their day-to-day activities. To make headway, I met quarterly with all of our chief technology officers to discuss how their businesses were progressing with VPD. We started presenting an award at our annual senior leadership meeting to the business

CTO and to business leaders who had most transformed their VPD process cross functionally, and announced at this meeting which of our businesses ranked in the top ten for implementing VPD and which ranked in the bottom ten. I met with business leaders in these bottom ten businesses to hold them personally accountable for improving.[1]

BUILD THE RIGHT TECHNOLOGY COMPETENCY

In addition to tackling R&D overall, we made additional changes to improve our software engineering capacity. During one of my early blue book exercises, I asked my team to run an analysis of engineering talent by discipline. I expected a fairly even breakout between mechanical, electrical, and chemical engineers. To my surprise, we had many software engineers, yet we weren't focusing on software engineering as a discipline. Having worked in the software business while serving as CEO at TRW,[2] I had been impressed with a software development technique called CMMI (Capability Maturity Model Integrated). CMMI ranked how mature software development processes at an organization were on a 1 to 5 scale, with 5 being the best. A level 1 development process was "unpredictable, poorly controlled, and reactive," while a level 5 process was well organized, well understood, and focused on continuous improvement.[3] With a level 5 process, you had a robust, documented development procedure in place that minimized errors and enabled the entire organization to learn from errors so as not to repeat them.

I wanted all of our software engineering worldwide to adopt level 5 processes, but our chief technology officers had little interest in pursuing them. In their eyes, CMMI was too bureaucratic (which it can be) and inhibited innovation. To me, that pushback sounded a lot like what W. Edwards Deming

---

1   Growth Days, described in chapter 1, were a great way of obtaining periodic updates on key projects and initiatives. And it was amazing how often leaders failed to invest sufficiently in high-potential projects. Leaders might feel good because they increased staffing on a project from two to four people, when in fact they needed to dramatically raise their expectations and assign twenty-five people. Just as leaders tend to under-resource problems (chapter 3), they tend to short-shrift opportunities too.

2   I had occupied that post in 2001–2002 before coming to Honeywell.

had encountered during the 1950s when first promoting product quality as a key element of manufacturing that didn't represent a cost to the enterprise. US companies took little interest, so he took it to Japan, where automakers embraced it and became dominant global players. Likewise, CMMI had originated in the US (at Carnegie Mellon University), but the level 5 firms at the time were located primarily in India and Japan. As it turned out, our Honeywell Technology Services facility in India was CMMI level 5 certified and had been for years. Yet another reason it made sense to expand there.

It took years of cajoling on our part, but some of our chief technology officers did become fans of CMMI. In our Automated Control Systems business, Dan Sheflin took several of his CTOs to India for two weeks to investigate in depth how our facility there operated. He came back convinced of the value it would bring to move all of our facilities in his business unit to a level 5. After a six- to-seven-year transition, software engineering throughout Automation and Control Systems became a level 5. As with any initiative, we could have done it better or more efficiently, but it still represented a big step forward for us.

BUILD STRATEGIC R&D

In addition to improving R&D and engineering processes, we pushed hard for our business leaders to treat R&D more strategically. Our individual business units used to decide how much to spend on R&D based on previous budgets and what they thought their proper "share" of available money was, regardless of the impact on current and future projects. We centralized R&D budgeting at the business level, analyzing potential projects and channeling more funds to those we thought would yield the biggest business impact.

In our Aerospace business, we also began choosing new projects in ways that would balance long- and short-term growth. Most new product development had entailed what we called "long-cycle" projects. We'd invest in designing a revolutionary new cockpit design, but it might be six to eight years before the project was finished and sales started coming in. Beginning around 2005, we balanced these kinds of projects with new, "short-cycle" ones—products that customers might purchase within months, not years (incremental enhancements to existing aircraft, for instance, rather than entirely new platforms for new aircrafts). Then we started adding the salespeople to support it, giving it an even bigger boost in 2010. Together, the combination of short- and long-cycle projects would allow us to realize steadier, more predictable growth. Over the years, our shorter-cycle products have grown, and today they are a highly profitable, $1 billion business.

PAY ATTENTION TO THE END USER

Yet another way we improved R&D was by getting our people focused on delivering a better user experience. During the late 1990s, I had a Honeywell thermostat in my home that was blasting the air-conditioning during the summer, to the point where it was too cold. When I tried to adjust the thermostat, I couldn't figure out how to do it. I looked at the instructions printed on the panel and found it confusing, not to mention that the print was minuscule. When I consulted the owner's manual, I couldn't for the life of me figure out how to dial up the temperature setting. Finally, I gave up and put on a sweater.

When I became CEO, we discussed improving the user experience during one of our early strategic planning reviews, but with so many other priorities demanding attention, user experience faded to the background. Then, almost a decade later, while teaching a leadership class at West Point, the U.S. Military Academy (an incredible honor for this small-town boy), I heard a professor talk about how good the school was in teaching "human factors," or the discipline devoted to making everyday objects better suited ergonomically to human users. Here, I thought, was an area that we at Honeywell hadn't yet focused on—and one that represented a potentially important pathway to sales growth. Companies like Apple were great at anticipating important, often unspoken customer needs and incorporating them into product design. If we were to maximize our sales, we couldn't just have more new products rolled out more quickly under VPD. We needed *better* new products that were easier to use, install, and maintain, which in turn meant we had to understand customer needs more deeply. We had to improve the *experience* of the user, installer, and maintainer.

At our next quarterly meeting of chief technology officers, we took action, creating a branded initiative called the "Honeywell User Experience" (HUE). To achieve our stated goal of becoming the "Apple of the industrial sector," we hired consultants to guide us,[3] added people with expertise in user experience, created special design rooms devoted to HUE, initiated a quarterly corporate HUE Award, and began offering a two-day course to expose general managers to HUE (I spoke at each session). Unlike other initiatives I pushed, HUE received a warm initial reception inside the organization. Yet it still took time to stick. Although we had planned to hire two hundred human factor experts across Honeywell within a year, other priorities interceded, and we only managed to hire about fifty. Managers also felt reluctant to send engineers into the field to spend time with customers—they didn't want to use valuable engineering time that they might have dedicated to develop products, totally ignoring the value of insight into customers' needs.

Despite such challenges, HUE has delivered some great successes. An example is the Experian Orion Console developed in our Process Controls business, led at the time by our current CEO, Darius Adamczyk. A control panel inside the control room of an industrial facility functions very much like the cockpit in an aircraft. The industrial control operator receives visual data about the plant's operations and can intervene as necessary when issues arise. Traditionally, these panels were complex and hard to use. Setting out to create "the control room of the future," we embedded a team of Honeywell technologists and HUE experts at customer facilities to observe how operators at refineries, chemical plants, paper mills, and mines were using existing control panels.

Processing feedback from our customers, we found many opportunities to streamline these control panels and make them more like an Apple iPhone—simpler, more intuitive, easier to use. We completely redesigned the industrial

---

3   In general, I resisted hiring consultants because I wanted us to learn how to do the work. In cases where we didn't know anything about a project (like HUE), I would authorize the use of consultants—carefully managed, of course.

control panel, creating a revolutionary, ergonomic panel called the Experion Orion Console. This console contained software that not only revealed operational issues with the plant as they arose but automatically indicated which predefined procedure a plant operator should use to rectify the issue safely and to do so most profitably. The console incorporated digital video and audio communications, and it was also wireless, allowing operations staff to monitor what was happening at the plant at their workstation and also to assist with field operations. Launched in 2013, Experion Orion Consoles have been deployed in hundreds of facilities, not only pleasing users with its unique design, but helping plants achieve greater safety, reliability, and efficiency.

There's a lesson here: even if people acknowledge that an initiative like HUE is a good idea, leaders must still push relentlessly for people to go beyond daily operations and take the initiative seriously. Overall, the enhancements we made to R&D through HUE, VPD, and CMMI helped our growth enormously. Above I mentioned that our overall R&D spending increased three-fold during my tenure. Given our leaner, more efficient, more customer-focused R&D process, the real impact might be closer to a 400 percent increase. New products and services helped us win 75 percent of the aerospace contracts we pursued during my last seven years, and they also helped boost our non-US sales as a percentage of total sales. On the strength of our new technologies, we've taken leadership positions in numerous markets—from small jet engines to commercial cockpit avionics, security systems to barcode scanning, warehouse automation to refinery and petrochemical technologies. And we achieved this growth without having to blow up our quarterly results. You can achieve similar results in your business, but only if you're willing to think critically about how your organization can create new products and services, and how you might do it more swiftly and better.

GO DEEP ON GLOBALIZATION, BUT TAKE IT SLOW

As you tighten up R&D, you'll be in a stronger position to grow sales even more by expanding geographically. When I joined Honeywell, three-quarters of global GDP occurred outside of the United States, but only 40 percent of our sales originated there. That thirty-five-point gap spelled opportunity. A knee-jerk approach might have been to make an all-out global effort, attacking many regions of the world at once and making acquisitions or joint ventures everywhere to establish a broad presence. Having read earlier chapters of this book, you won't be surprised to hear that we favored a more gradual and focused approach, emphasizing large, high-growth regions first; specifically, expansion into China and India. As the chart below indicates, by 2035, 53 percent of global GDP will be in high-growth regions. With over a third of the world's population between them, two high-growth regions in particular—India and China—will see the greatest amount of economic expansion. Rather than spread out our efforts and potentially fail to make much of a dent anywhere, we opted to stake out a beachhead in China and India, and expand from there to other high-growth regions. If we could get our strategy right in these two countries, we'd claim a good part of the globalization prize and be able to replicate our success elsewhere.

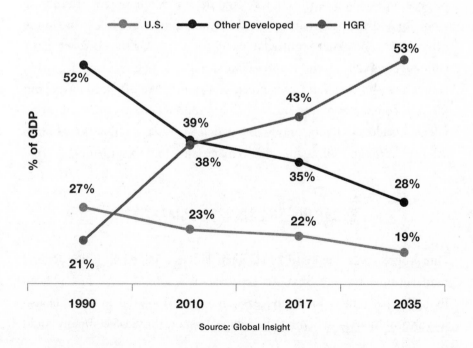

Source: Global Insight

In 2004, our business in China only generated $350 million in revenues each year and was expanding at 4 percent annually. That growth rate sounds okay, but not when you consider that overall GDP in China was growing by over 11 percent and the industrial sector was expanding by 17 percent. As Shane Tedjarati, former head of our business in China and currently president of Global High Growth Regions, remembered, "We were bleeding market share every day and we didn't know that, we actually were . . . defeating ourselves because we didn't know what we should know about the market, the customers, the competitors."[4] Other US-based companies had carved out much more of a presence than we had—a fact analysts didn't hesitate to point out. Restructuring completed before my arrival had significantly reduced our China headcount—we had only about a thousand employees in the country.

Some analysts and staff members urged us to build critical mass quickly in China by acquiring companies or forging joint ventures. We instead opted to grow our existing businesses organically. If we put ourselves through the slow, difficult process of learning how to operate and compete in China, we would develop a capability we could deploy in other areas around the globe. In addition, acquisitions in China were time-consuming due to the extensive due diligence required. Given how unreliable the books of many Chinese companies were, I worried we'd put a lot of effort into acquiring companies and then fail to see much of a return. We did keep an eye out for local companies to buy, but we focused more of our attention on hiring talented leaders in China and hiring people aggressively in anticipation of sales (rather than waiting for sales to materialize and then hiring).

BECOMING THE CHINESE COMPETITOR

Our progress was slow until 2004, when Tedjarati joined us as our general manager in charge of China. An expatriate fluent in Chinese, he had been living in the country for many years and understood the culture. He also had an ambitious goal in mind: he wanted to show that a US company could learn to function as a genuine Chinese company. Most Western companies enter countries like China with little knowledge or insight into local customers, and they compete using the products, practices, and supply chains they created for Western markets. They might win over customers at the very high end of the market in developing countries, but for the vast middle portion of the market in these countries, their products are inappropriate and too costly. Local competitors who do know customers and their needs wind up ripping off these products, manufacturing them more cheaply, and taking the vast majority of the market. No, these copycat products aren't as good as those of the Western companies, but they're good enough—and much cheaper. In many cases, lower cost is much more important to local customers than sophisticated, high-end features, which they might not even require anyway.

Under Tedjarati, we upgraded our leadership talent and went after the middle of the Chinese market as well as the top, retooling our operations to become "insiders" capable of competing with the best of the indigenous competition. As we reasoned, if our Chinese operations couldn't beat their local competitors in China, how would we beat them when these local players eventually matured and expanded to developed markets? We started hiring talented Chinese locals for leadership positions, rather than bringing in expats, and developing more local sourcing for our products. Whereas companies tend to take a big brother approach, with corporate or business headquarters dictating solutions and reserving the right to sign off on projects, we gave our teams in China more autonomy and control as they became more capable. Our strategy of locating R&D facilities in developing countries helped us as well, not just because we could squeeze more value out of our R&D spending, but because we built up local expertise capable of designing products with features and specifications that local consumers wanted and that compared well with the offerings of local competitors.

As our initial effort gained traction, we formalized this approach in an initiative called "Becoming the Chinese Competitor." We wanted everything in our Chinese market to be done locally, including marketing, general management, design authority, manufacturing, sourcing, and staffing—everything—and we were now going to quantitatively gauge our progress. Our leaders had to identify their toughest Chinese competitor and perform a rigorous analysis of how their business stacked up against these competitors, not the Western companies we traditionally considered. I met with the China local leaders, the country leader, and the global business leader twice a year for a full day to discuss how we were doing and what new resources we needed.

This process proved instrumental. As we improved our understanding of our businesses relative to local competitors, our scoring of our businesses across relevant dimensions like sourcing often deteriorated meeting to meeting. We weren't getting worse, but rather we were learning more about our deficiencies, including areas in which our global leaders back in the United States or Europe were retaining too much oversight and control. As these problem areas were exposed, we could take action and improve. (This was, incidentally, a great example of how open, candid meetings can enhance performance. Rather than feel they had to show improvement on each dimension at every meeting, leaders focused more on getting it right and improving, which was exactly what we needed.)

ORGANIZE FOR FLEXIBILITY

In pursuing global expansion, we grappled with the classic question of whether we should organize ourselves as a global business with each of our business units (Aerospace, Performance Materials and Technologies, Automation and Control Solutions, and Transportation Systems) responsible for global sales of its products, or as a series of country-specific units, with the leader of our operations in a given country (the "country leader") solely responsible for all business results within his or her geographical area. Consistent with my philosophy of doing two seemingly conflicting things at the same time, I wanted both: our global businesses needed to retain ultimate ownership of the results, but the country leader had superior knowledge of the market and thus needed a voice in decision-making. The country leader was in an ambiguous position: they both owned and didn't own the business. They were on the ground in the local market influencing business decisions, but they also coordinated with global business unit leaders, who likely worked out of Europe or the United States. To make this arrangement work, we made sure to get clear agreement each year between the country leader and each business on the key priorities we would accomplish in that country. We also hired country leaders very carefully, making sure we had people who inspired trust among both local businesses and global business unit leaders.

This approach afforded us a good amount of flexibility in decision-making. Sometimes, when a global business unit seemed to be ignoring a particular country, we supported the decision-making of the country leader. Other times the pendulum swung the other way. And sometimes we took a different approach entirely. In China, we found that Li Ning, our local business leader for Fire Detection within our Automated Control Systems (ACS) business, was terrific, consistently posting outstanding results. He enjoyed a lot of autonomy due to his outstanding performance, but the leaders of our other China businesses within ACS weren't doing so well and weren't given much autonomy. While it didn't fit our country leader/global business model, we gave Li Ning decision rights over all ACS businesses in China. Annual sales growth almost immediately jumped from 10 percent to 20 percent. If we needed to modify our model to get results like that, we would do it!

Our persistence with China paid off. One of our businesses had lost over a hundred bids in China for hydrogen purification units when it had been designing to Western standards, insisting that we were correct and the Chinese customer was wrong. Chinese standards of quality were as high as Western ones were, but because of the Chinese economy's rapid technological development, Chinese customers didn't require the same longevity. Once our business started designing to Chinese standards, it won over one-third of all projects it bid on. Across our businesses, we built our organic presence in the country slowly but steadily. Beginning in 2005, and continuing for years afterward, we saw explosive growth. Today, China is Honeywell's biggest country for sales, about $3 billion, outside of the United States. We do about $3 billion of very profitable sales and have about 13,000 people working for us, of whom only about 75 are expatriate employees.

Beginning in 2010, we took this same approach and expanded it to other high-growth regions. At the same time, we pushed hard across our businesses to embrace a global mind-set, including assigning salespeople to live in the countries where their customers were located (that might sound like common sense, but all too often common sense is not too common). In the case of one of our businesses, executives protested that spreading people out across the globe would diminish its unique culture. My answer: We could and should both embrace globalization *and* maintain a strong, cohesive culture. Over time the message sank in—and then some. Whereas in 2003 only about 42 percent of our sales originated outside the United States, in 2017 about 55 percent did. Sales from high-growth regions comprised 23 percent of our sales that year, up from only 10 percent in 2003.

PICK YOUR GROWTH PRIORITIES

Although I've described several avenues to growth, companies can't pursue them all with the same level of intensity at any given time. It's important to prioritize. As you start to invest in growth initiatives, take stock of your company and its strengths and weaknesses, identifying your greatest growth opportunities. Perhaps your flow of new products is already great and so is your customer service, but you don't have much of a business in a particular country you think could be big for you. Start there, and as I've suggested, make a targeted effort. Of course, that requires patience. To return to one of my favorite metaphors, you can till the soil and plant seeds, but then you have to water the plants and care for them over a full season and sometimes several seasons as they grow—no shortcuts.

With globalization, you want to really get in there and master the new markets you're entering. With R&D, you want to reimagine processes from the inside out so that engineers, designers, marketers, business leaders, and others change how they work, improve their understanding of the customer, collaborate better, and become more productive. And with customer experience, you want to change attitudes and behaviors on a deep level so that people focus as a matter of habit on delivering for customers rather than on "making the quarter" at all costs.

STAY PERSONALLY ENGAGED

You can't delegate away responsibility for growth and expect to see results. The prospect of growth excites people inside organizations, but as you proceed the changes required will arouse resistance or fall prey to inertia amid the press of daily operations. I've mentioned how reluctant our business leaders were initially to source R&D in developing countries, and how hard our leaders back in headquarters sometimes found it to relinquish control to business leaders in developing countries. But we faced resistance in other areas too. Business leaders chafed when I asked them to increase R&D spending. They claimed they didn't have a big enough pipeline of projects on which to spend it on. My reaction: Go build a pipeline!

Challenges also popped up when we least expected it. Early in my tenure, we conducted an annual salary planning exercise, determining our average pay raise for the coming year. When we had finished our analysis for the United States, the team was ready to pack it in. "What about calculating it for other countries?" I asked. "Nobody does that," leaders around the table told me. "Every country just decides for itself how much of a raise to give." That wasn't a terribly global mind-set—and we had to change it.

On multiple occasions when visiting high-growth countries, I learned that leaders on the ground had been prevented from hiring due to directives from business leaders back home. Each time I had to go back to the senior business leader and raise the issue myself. If you want your organization to globalize, or for that matter to care about customers and reform R&D processes, get out there and make it happen.

While you're at it, make sure the actions people are taking in support of these initiatives really are yielding results. You don't pursue something like Velocity Product Development, globalization, or an improved customer experience for its own sake. You do it to drive sales. And yet it's easy for people in the trenches to conflate all of the hard work they might be doing with actual results. If the initiative is going so well, what does the sales increase look like? Never stop posing such questions to your people. As I said before, the world rewards results, not effort or process.

As engaged as you need to be, you need the right people by your side as well. We never would have succeeded in China if we didn't have Shane Tedjarati serving as a bridge between the local market and our broader company culture. Another leader, Krishna Mikkilineni, proved similarly important in helping us expand our software engineering capacity and capability in India and beyond. Having worked for Honeywell in the United States, he understood our company, but he also understood Indian engineering talent and how to motivate and retain them.

When it came to bringing more of a marketing sensibility to product development, our chief strategy and marketing officer, Rhonda Germany, proved vital. As Tim Mahoney recalled, our Aerospace unit had little sophistication at the beginning of my tenure around marketing—little strategic understanding of which airplane models would succeed in the broader market, and hence where we should channel our R&D efforts. Germany's arrival changed all that, creating "a different level of marketing excellence." Elsewhere in this book I emphasize the importance of building up the quality of your leadership ranks. You might be able to retain some of your existing customers with mediocre leadership talent (and that's a pretty tentative "might"), but you certainly won't be able to grow.

KEEP SCANNING THE HORIZON

As you pursue long-term growth, don't limit yourself to the specific initiatives discussed here. Stay alert for new growth areas. Midway into my tenure, we concluded that a digital revolution would sweep through the industrial economy in coming decades, and that we stood to gain immensely if we could get way ahead of it. In addition to expanding our software engineering in high-growth regions and bringing our engineers across the world to level 5 status, we started to work on new digital business models—like enabling and reselling Wi-Fi time on aircraft, and our Sentience platform for developing new software products—more expeditiously and consistently. Our current CEO, Darius Adamczyk, has built on Sentience and expanded it. Now called Honeywell Forge, the platform is a cloud-based, IoT platform and product development framework within Honeywell for building scalable software. Standardizing the process allows developers to create new software products more expeditiously and consistently than they used to. Honeywell Forge focuses on three key areas for customers, providing end-to-end enterprise performance management for asset reliability; process excellence; and worker safety, competency, and productivity.

We also changed our recruiting practices to improve our digital talent pool. Formerly, we had sought out digital talent from the best, name-brand colleges and universities. Now we focused on attracting members of a small subset of elite programmers who were capable of producing ten times the output of the typical programmer. To attract these premier programmers, or "multipliers" as we called them, we began evaluating potential hires on specific skills related to programming, collaboration, and teamwork, observing their actual behavior rather than just relying on their academic record. We took a similar approach to hiring data scientists as well. Our efforts in this area helped us significantly up our game as we developed software as a business and incorporated it into more of our existing products.

To expand our capability and improve recruiting, we also brought a number of multifunctional teams into a new software center we had built in Atlanta, Georgia. We realized top digital talent wanted to work with other smart people. And although many people assume this talent all wants to be in Silicon Valley, a subset of them wants to live elsewhere, especially if given the opportunity to work on meaningful projects as opposed to just another trendy app. Before I retired, I paid regular visits to Atlanta to help energize the workforce, a practice that Darius Adamczyk also does as part of his important drive to make Honeywell a software-industrial company. This effort has proven essential. Today, almost half of our engineers company-wide are developing software—a massive change from years past.

As you're staying alert to new growth avenues, never lose sight of your older efforts. We thought we had a pretty good handle on our customer experience by about 2004, a couple of years after we began focusing on it. For the next six to seven years, I kept an eye on customer experience, and we continued to make incremental improvement. After that, it fell to the background because we were certain everyone in the company knew what to do. Imagine our surprise, then, when in 2013 we learned we had just ranked at the very bottom among aerospace suppliers in an industry survey put out by the airplane manufacturer Airbus. How could that have happened? I leaned on our business leaders to fix it. After so many years, we had to focus on customers again. It turned out that our metrics had become degraded—we were making so many exceptions in calculating our performance that our measurements no longer reflected the customer's actual experience. We dissected our metrics, identifying and analyzing parts of our operations in which customers were experiencing difficulties, and took corrective action. Thanks to this work, we've moved up dramatically in Airbus's rankings. By 2018, parts of our Aerospace business were among the top quartile of companies.

As we've seen, Honeywell's revenues rose from $22 billion to $40 billion over the fifteen-year period starting in 2002. While $6.5 billion of that revenue growth came from the net impact of acquisitions and divestitures, the remaining $11.5 billion came from organic growth made possible by our customer focus, our pipeline of new products and services, and our globalization strategy. Results like this never would have happened had we not consistently taken a portion of our gains from keeping fixed costs constant while growing sales and invested that money back into longer-term growth projects. We would have given more back to shareholders over the short term had we not invested in growth, but our longer-term performance would have suffered tremendously. If you want to grow, you have to plant seeds. So start planting!

QUESTIONS TO ASK YOURSELF

1. You know you have to invest in growth, but how much attention are you paying to pushing your growth initiatives ahead? Are you resourcing them enough? Do you use Growth Days to drive progress?
2. Are your customers as happy as everyone says they are? How do you know? Have you gotten out there recently to ask them for their candid feedback? How good are your customer-related metrics?
3. Is your culture as customer focused as it could be?
4. How efficient are your new product development processes? Do they encourage constant collaboration across functional areas? Do they engage marketing early on in the product development cycle?
5. Are you doing R&D as efficiently as you might? Have you considered building up your R&D in high-growth geographies to establish a footprint?
6. Are you investing in the right R&D projects, and have you assigned top talent?
7. How much attention do your product development people pay to the actual experience of using your product or service? Are you inside the head of customers as fully as you might be to understand their unspoken needs?
8. Are you as deliberate and strategic around globalization as you might be, or are you trying to operate in too many places at once? In your markets, are you focused on operating as a native company and beating local competitors in the mid-market?
9. Are you getting the most out of your local operators, or are they hamstrung by too much control from corporate? Are your local operators capable of autonomy?
10. If you're just beginning to focus on growth, what are your company's existing strengths and opportunities? Where might you get the most bang for your long-term growth investments?
11. Where can you use the top ten/bottom ten approach to improve overall performance?

CHAPTER EIGHT

Upgrade Your Portfolio

In 2004, Honeywell got into a good, old-fashioned Texas shoot-out with Dow Chemical. For years, the two companies were fifty-fifty owners of a firm called UOP, a world-class developer of process technologies for refineries and petrochemical plants.[1] UOP was performing poorly, having been undermanaged for years since neither partner had paid much attention to it. It had needed to globalize its footprint and pursue more R&D, but when Honeywell had wanted to pump money in, Dow Chemical hadn't, and vice versa. The ownership agreement between Honeywell and Dow had a "Texas Shoot-out" clause stipulating that if one partner bid to buy the other half of the company, the non-bidding partner had the right to sell at that price or buy out the bidding partner at that price. The clause was intended to prevent one partner from seeking to buy out the other at a fire-sale price.

I had always thought UOP was a good business and had wanted to buy out Dow's share, but our Specialty Materials business unit, which would have taken over UOP, was totally against a possible deal. They didn't believe in the business, judging that the challenges it faced overshadowed its potential growth opportunities. In 2004, Dow initiated the Texas Shoot-out by offering us $865 million for our share of UOP,

---

1   These are the chemical processes that transform crude oil into an array of valuable products.

assuming we would sell it. To their surprise, and over the strenuous objections of our business unit, I declined the offer and instead exercised our option to buy out Dow at that price. I was not normally inclined to go against a business leader's recommendations. In fact, this was the only time during my tenure as Honeywell's CEO that I overruled a leader's preference to pass over an acquisition. In this case, I did so because behind the scenes, our acquisitions team had done its homework, and I had come away convinced that our business leaders were wrong. We had diligently analyzed UOP and determined that it enjoyed a great position in a good industry, it had received inadequate investment for years, it possessed superb technology and a highly credentialed workforce, and it would mesh with our own world-class process controls business, giving us capabilities nobody else in the world possessed. We were also getting it at an attractive price: about five times EBITDA (earnings before interest, taxes, depreciation, and amortization). If our calculations were correct, and if we could integrate the business well into Honeywell, we were pretty certain we would see a healthy profit within a few years' time.

Many companies fare poorly with M&A. According to "nearly all studies," one business academic has noted, around 80 percent of deals don't work out as the parties intended.[1] Honeywell knew a thing or two about that. When I took over, we had to take a bunch of write-downs on previous acquisitions that had flopped—notching a $200 million loss, for instance, on a printed circuit board business we had bought for $500 million but was only worth $300 million. The track record was so poor that investors strongly discouraged me from buying other companies and encouraged me to sell our entire chemicals business, even though its portfolio of businesses contained some real winners. I pointed out that there was a good way to do M&A and a bad way. If we did them right, we could improve our growth over the long term. And if we also focused on divesting ourselves of businesses that delivered less growth, we could boost long-term growth even more.

Strategic mergers, acquisitions, and divestitures should be part of every company's efforts to generate impressive long- and short-term results, complementing organic growth initiatives like globalization and R&D described in the last chapter. In the short term, actively managing the company's portfolio of businesses will slice into profits, because buying companies requires amortization expenses and up-front restructuring costs that generally lead to first-year losses, while divestitures result in lost profits from the business unit being sold. Done correctly, however, these deals start bearing fruit a couple of years later, boosting quarterly earnings and cash flow. As profits and cash continue to kick in, companies can use them to fund subsequent deals, setting in motion a virtuous cycle in which short-term results and longer-term growth fuel one another.

The key, similar to what we saw in the last chapter, is to make sure that during the start-up period, when you're first managing your portfolio of companies more actively, you deliver quarterly results that are "good enough" for investors. Don't pursue deals that will totally tank quarterly results and alienate investors. In addition, follow the general business strategy described earlier in the book: growing the business while holding fixed costs constant. If you do that, you can use the profits generated by fiscal discipline to bolster short-term earnings even as you invest in mergers, acquisitions, and divestitures that will yield benefits later on.

IMPROVE HOW DEALS GET DONE

Embracing M&A as a growth strategy requires that you develop an ability to land winning deals consistently. How do you do that? The answer is to approach dealmaking thoughtfully and in a disciplined fashion. You need to put in place a legitimate acquisitions process, and you need to follow that process rigorously.

I first came to understand the importance of process in M&A during the late 1990s. Observers were constantly decrying acquisitions, claiming they didn't pay, but it struck me that the whole business model of private equity firms was based on acquiring companies strategically, taking thoughtful measures to improve them, and then shrewdly selling them off. If private equity firms could add so much value through M&A, why couldn't a big company like Honeywell?

When I became Honeywell's CEO, I knew the company lacked a serious process for doing M&A—our poor track record spoke for itself. But that didn't mean we couldn't introduce such a process. I asked Anne Madden, the new head of our M&A team, to perform a postmortem analysis of deals that Honeywell had completed over the past decade to see what had gone awry and what had worked. On the basis of this knowledge, I hoped to develop a new process that all of our businesses would use when acquiring companies. Anne did a fantastic job. Over the next six months, we discovered the company had been pursuing deals in an ad hoc, opportunistic way, struggling in four key areas: identifying which companies to acquire, performing due diligence on these companies, calculating their value, and integrating acquisitions into our business.

Taking stock of our deficits led us to a powerful, four-step model for pursuing M&A, one that we used and refined during my tenure and that we continue to use today, with a particular focus on not overpaying. At some companies, leaders seem to treat price as independent of strategy, saying to themselves, *Here is my strategy. I must be willing to pay for it.* In reality, price is fundamental to strategy. If you overpay, your investors will never see financial benefit from your strategy. We never minded paying a fair price, but overpaying was anathema to us—and it should be to you.

If your organization has struggled to upgrade its portfolio of companies, I invite you to implement our model, using it to generate long-term growth opportunities without unduly impinging on profits today. Let's take a look at each area individually, noting what Honeywell did to standardize its deal-making and develop new discipline and rigor around it. The chart below, which we used with investors, summarizes well our initial M&A process and what it became.

DISCIPLINED M&A PROCESS

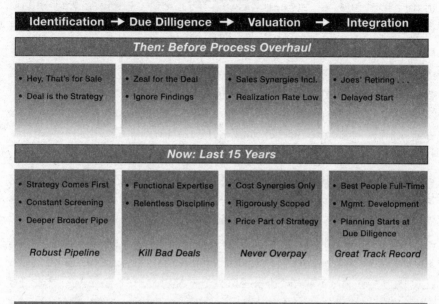

Identification →	Due Dilligence →	Valuation →	Integration
Then: Before Process Overhaul			
• Hey, That's for Sale • Deal is the Strategy	• Zeal for the Deal • Ignore Findings	• Sales Synergies Incl. • Realization Rate Low	• Joes' Retiring . . . • Delayed Start
Now: Last 15 Years			
• Strategy Comes First • Constant Screening • Deeper Broader Pipe	• Functional Expertise • Relentless Discipline	• Cost Synergies Only • Rigorously Scoped • Price Part of Strategy	• Best People Full-Time • Mgmt. Development • Planning Starts at Due Diligence
Robust Pipeline	*Kill Bad Deals*	*Never Overpay*	*Great Track Record*

Smartly Adding to Great Positions in Good Industries

Build a Robust Pipeline (Identification)

To land winning deals, you first have to find them. As Anne learned, we hadn't been proactively and strategically seeking out companies for our existing businesses to acquire and operate. Rather, we'd waited for investment bankers to knock on our door and try to sell potential deals to us, jumping on deals that might have seemed attractive at the time but that had little strategic relevance. During the late 1990s, for instance, Honeywell bought a company called Kaz that manufactured fans and humidifiers for the consumer market. The objective was to build up the Honeywell brand among consumers and give it more of a presence at retail. Honeywell knew nothing about using the retail channel to go to market—we were primarily an aerospace and industrial company. Kaz's leadership team was supposed to contribute expertise, but after a year the entire team grew frustrated at the culture clash between our two companies and abruptly quit. Since nobody inside Honeywell was qualified to run the business, and it seemed there was little interest in trying to turn it around, the business was sold at a loss of several hundred million dollars. The deal closed in June 2002, shortly before I became chairman and could participate in the decision. This was just one of many deals that were strategically dubious from the outset and that plain didn't work.

Under our new M&A process, we began putting strategy first, mobilizing our business units to think hard about their strategic growth goals, aggressively scour the market, and maintain a broad pipeline of desirable targets for acquisition. By "desirable," we meant businesses that occupied great positions—they had good market share or were on a path to getting there via future acquisitions (if, for instance, the competitive landscape was highly fragmented) in good, high-growth, profitable industries.

Michael Porter, the respected Harvard Business School professor, had advanced the concept of industry quality and analysis since the 1980s, spurring its popularity among corporate leaders. While at General Electric, I'd noticed firsthand what a big difference it made to be in a good industry. When I ran General Electric's major appliance business, we had a great position but were in a crummy, highly competitive, low-growth industry. No matter how hard we worked, we stood little chance of excelling—the pressure on prices was just too intense. It was far easier, I found, to make progress with a business that occupied a bad position in a good industry. Our silicones business was struggling when I took it over, but the industry was doing well. In less than three years, we improved the operational issues befuddling the business, doubling revenues and more than doubling profits—a huge success story within General Electric. Of course, it's even better to find businesses in a good industry that don't need so much fixing. Then you're looking at highly attractive growth where the return on investment is likely to be strong. Accordingly, we developed the phrase "great positions in good industries" to summarize the kinds of investments we were seeking to make to grow our portfolio.

To find the best opportunities, our business units at Honeywell sought to identify desirable bolt-on acquisitions for existing businesses of ours (companies that made the kinds of products that our businesses did), and to identify good industries that were closely adjacent to favorable businesses. That way we would have sufficient expertise to run these companies once they were in our fold. Tracking down these companies and developing deals was painstaking work. As longtime Honeywell executive Roger Fradin remembered, "We'd go to trade shows in search of deals. We'd talk to bankers. We'd talk to whomever we could to uncover deals. It was a full-time focus."[2] Leaders stayed focused day-to-day on identifying targets for acquisition, in large part because of the rigorous approach to strategy described in chapter 2. Since leaders were now immersed in strategy every day, they could naturally make an ongoing investigation of acquisition opportunities part of that conversation. This intensive engagement helped us keep our pipeline of deals full, which as Fradin observed allowed us to take a more disciplined stance in negotiations. If a given deal didn't work out, that was no problem—many more were always in the works.

In some cases, our leaders would talk to strategically desirable acquisition targets for years, building relationships with executives and regularly checking in until they were ready to sell. The goodwill we built through such efforts increased our chances of landing a deal, and afterward, made it easier to integrate these acquired companies into Honeywell. On more than one occasion, we managed to acquire a company even though we weren't the highest bidder because we'd taken the time to get to know executives at the acquired company and earn their trust. Of course, for every deal that worked out, there were numerous companies we targeted that we wound up passing on or failing to acquire. Anne used to say that we needed to kiss a hundred frogs in order to find our prince. She was right.

To Build a Robust Pipeline ...

- Don't wait for bankers to knock on your door with potential deals. Instead, scour the market proactively.
- Seek out businesses that have great positions in good, high-growth industries.

- Look for bolt-on acquisitions as well as companies in good industries adjacent to yours.
- Not all perceived adjacencies are the same. If the adjacency is too far removed from your existing business, you will lose your shirt.
- Make identifying targets a day-to-day priority.
- Be patient. Nurture long-term relationships with potential acquisitions.

Kill Bad Deals (Due Diligence)

Once you've identified a potential acquisition and are in negotiations, the next step is to make sure the potential acquisition is everything the seller says it is. When you really dig into a company and its books, do you still want to acquire it, and if so, at what price? Do you want to attach any special conditions to the deal, detailing scenarios in which you'd walk away if outstanding issues aren't addressed? As Anne discovered, Honeywell hadn't put a system in place for performing due diligence on companies rigorously and well every time. All too often, business units eager to get a deal done had passed over red flags and done the deal anyway.

We created a corporate handbook that each business unit had to follow when performing due diligence on a potential acquisition. This handbook contained nothing revolutionary, but it did help us establish consistency in how we assessed financials, growth plans, HR, legal and environmental issues, and so on. Overall, the handbook focused us on trying to disprove our assumptions about a business and thus avoid falling into the trap of confirmation bias. We required that corporate functional experts in areas like law, accounting, or IT weigh in on any issues turned up during due diligence, determining what action, if any, we should take.

For instance, our legal team might conclude that a company we were thinking of acquiring faced potential lawsuits. Analyzing the situation, our team would identify the extent of the risk we faced, whether we could insure against it or secure indemnification, and whether we should walk away from the deal if we couldn't mitigate our risk. Our general counsel would make the call on whether the deal made sense or not.

Finally, we changed our compensation structure, no longer paying bonuses to leaders involved in securing particular acquisitions. Such bonuses incentivize people to make deals, regardless of whether they were good or bad. We wanted people to make *good* deals and kill the bad ones.

To Kill Bad Deals . . .

- Standardize how you perform due diligence.
- Have your functional experts advise you on any potential issues.
- Don't incentivize people for getting deals done, as over time that might lead them to push through potentially questionable deals.

Never Overpay (Valuation)

As Anne's analysis revealed, we lacked a model of our own for valuing companies we acquired, relying instead on the valuations that investment bankers brought to us. If you were buying a piece of real estate, would you take your broker's word for what it was worth? Of course not! You'd do some work on your own, even if it was just reviewing what other, comparable properties in your area had sold for. If we bought a company and four years later the deal didn't work out the way we'd anticipated, we couldn't just tell our investors that the bankers' valuation model had been no good. We needed to create our own model, and then we needed to believe in what our model said and we had to be able to deliver on it. That meant getting in there and actually performing the valuation work ourselves.

As part of our disciplined M&A process, we implemented a standard valuation model that everyone in our company would use, focusing on projected cash flows and earnings impact. We specified that our teams had to rely on our own estimates of the sales and margins acquired companies would deliver rather than the figures these companies might provide to us. We included potential cost synergies acquisitions would enable (efficiencies we could create by combining functional departments such as legal or HR, rationalizing our production capacity, increasing effectiveness by implementing HOS, and so on). Under the old approach, we had included potential sales synergies (sales increases we'd realize because of the ability of our existing businesses to sell to customers of the acquired company, and vice versa). But when Anne and her team analyzed past deals, we realized that although our prior acquisitions had yielded the cost savings we'd expected, and had in fact done a bit better, these deals had only yielded about 10 percent of the anticipated sales synergies. We'd systematically overestimated the value we'd be able to realize from specific acquisitions, leading us to overpay on deals and then fail to obtain the projected results.

We changed our valuation model, basing it entirely on anticipated cost savings. We did calculate potential sales synergies, tracking them during the process of integrating new acquisitions into Honeywell, but we didn't want to count on them to make good on our deals. If these synergies materialized, it would be pure upside for us. In addition, to minimize the short-term hit to earnings and ensure future growth, we required that all deals we did met three specific financial requirements. First, every company we bought had to increase Honeywell's earnings per share with nothing excluded by the second year post-deal (or as finance people say, the deal had to be accretive in the second year). Second, the internal rate of return (IRR) had to be above 10 percent, and third, ROI all in (i.e., with all costs and cash flows considered) during the fifth year had to surpass 10 percent.[2] These were fairly tough metrics. To achieve them we couldn't overpay, and we had to realize great cost synergies. Over time we learned that if we paid eleven to twelve times EBITDA, and if we could reduce the costs of operating the business by 6 to

---

2   Let me say a word about each of these requirements. We knew that companies we acquired would weigh on our earnings at first, and if the acquired company or bankers suggested otherwise, they weren't counting all of the costs associated with the deal. By pushing for accretion after the first year, we could increase the odds that an acquisition would perform financially the way we desired down the road. In effect, short-term performance would be validating our long-term expectations. As far as our IRR target was concerned, many bankers would come to us with deals that were doable in their minds because our cost of capital was down to 8.97 percent or some such. I didn't want our finance people wasting their time performing those calculations, so I picked 10 percent as a reasonable number over time. A deal that doesn't look doable at 10 percent shouldn't become great at 8.97 percent—because it isn't. Finally, ROI of 10 percent all in during the fifth year was the toughest of our three criteria to meet, but if you can get there with growth in sales and earnings, you have a great deal on your hands.

8 percent of sales, we could do very well. With cost synergies factored in, the real cost of acquisitions to us tended to be in the four to six times EBITDA range, which made acquisitions a great growth lever. In our 2013 acquisition of the mobile computing company Intermec, for instance, we paid seventeen times EBITDA for the deal, but were able to realize such great cost savings that the true cost of the company to us was only four times EBITDA.

More fundamentally, we adopted a philosophy of never overpaying. Hailing from New Hampshire, I'd long prided myself on my Yankee thrift, and would rather pass on a potentially good deal if a chance existed that it would underperform. Large companies like ours could afford to make mistakes with small deals, but we had to get the bigger deals right. Applying that philosophy meant valuing acquisitions conservatively and walking away if the deal became too rich. Some leaders don't like to walk away, reasoning that they are pursuing a strategy in buying a company and they have to be willing to pay for it. That's backward: as mentioned earlier, price needs to be a fundamental part of the strategy. If you have a great strategy but overpay for a company, someone else's shareholders will see the benefits of your strategy, not yours.

Of course, it's a lot easier to walk away when negotiating a deal if you're not the leader who put it together in the first place hoping to grow your business. In December 2002, about six months into my tenure, we acquired Baker Electronics, a maker of avionics systems for aircraft cabins. Leaders in our Aerospace division loved the deal and wanted to close it at any price. They foresaw an ability to link Baker's technology for cabins with ours for cockpits, creating an exciting offering for customers. These leaders negotiated the deal themselves, ignoring potential issues raised by our functional experts that suggested a lower valuation, in particular a deterioration in Baker's 2002 sales after a solid performance the previous year. Our experts protested repeatedly, and each time Aerospace insisted that the operational and financial goals it had set for the business—and that justified paying a high price—were realistic. Aerospace leaders also seemed excessively eager and even desperate to do the deal during negotiations, compromising our position with the sellers.

Ultimately, we overpaid for the company. Over the next few years, sales of Baker's products flatlined or even declined. By 2006, Aerospace's leaders were saying they didn't like the business and would sell it if they could. Although other factors contributed to the deal's underperformance, the episode demonstrated how important it was to ask business leaders who are putting together a deal to step back so that other, independent actors could actually negotiate the terms.

In framing our new M&A process, we resolved to maintain a clear separation between our dealmakers and our deal-negotiators. After a business leader had cultivated a company for acquisition, he or she would turn the deal over to our corporate M&A department, which would negotiate the contract based on the results for the acquired company that our business unit would commit to delivering. Sometimes our business units disagreed with how our corporate people were handling a deal—our business leaders just wanted it done, and they had developed personal relationships with the sellers. Our corporate M&A team negotiated more dispassionately, assuring that we really didn't overpay, even if it meant getting tough and walking away. In deal after deal, that made all the difference. Separating dealmakers from negotiators certainly led to some spirited discussions with our business units, but it enabled us to align the price we paid with the performance goals to which our business units were willing to commit.

As the leader, my job was to exercise final oversight over deals that had made it through the process, truly exploring the potential downsides of a deal to determine if it was worth proceeding at the price we'd negotiated. By the time our teams had done their work and the deal was ready for my approval, they believed in the deal and were quite understandably focused on the upside. While that upside might well be the most likely outcome, it was vital that I push one more time to consider what could go wrong, just to be certain we had considered all possible scenarios.

In the Baker fiasco mentioned above, I failed to exercise the proper oversight. I had refused to back a much bigger acquisition a few months earlier in the same space because I didn't care much for that industry. The disgruntled Aerospace team felt I didn't "love" Aerospace or respect their judgment. So this time I succumbed—and wasted about $20 million. That taught me a lesson I didn't forget. Afterward, I did exercise my oversight properly and to good effect (as I've often said, one of the leader's most valuable but least valued contributions is avoiding trouble, not addressing it once it's occurred). On several occasions I prevented us from acquiring companies in industries or countries that were peaking. For example, we avoided acquiring firms dependent on the oil industry when the price of oil was $100 a barrel and everyone was saying it would go higher, an assumption that made these companies more valuable. By pushing us to consider what would happen if oil went to $50, I saved us from doing such oil-related deals. Good thing, since the price of oil did subsequently plunge.

To Never Overpay . . .

- Develop a standardized valuation model of your own.
- Use your own estimates of sales and margins.
- Factor in anticipated cost savings, but not sales synergies.
- Value acquisitions conservatively and walk away if the deal becomes too rich.
- Don't let the dealmakers negotiate the terms.
- Exercise final oversight, exploring the downsides and scuttling the deal if you risk overpaying.
- Maintain a great pipeline of potential deals so that no single deal seems like a must-have.

Great Track Record (Integration)

To obtain attractive cost synergies, you need to integrate acquired companies well with your existing company. Unfortunately, Honeywell had been making serious mistakes in this area. We would do a poor job of planning how to integrate the company and then hesitate to take our anticipated actions once the deal was done, opting to study the situation for a year to be sure we were getting it right. That might sound prudent, but change becomes much more difficult a year into an acquisition because managers and employees in both the acquired and acquiring companies have already become used to conditions as they are—as I say, they've become part of the establishment.

In other instances, our integrations had failed because we hadn't assembled a strong team dedicated to planning and executing the integration, opting instead to make it part of everyone's job. That was a recipe for disorganization and uncertainty—integration is a lot of work, especially when you're acquiring a larger company. You need people dedicated to the task to ensure it's done smoothly and successfully. We also hadn't put our best people on integration teams, tapping instead soon-to-be-retiring company veterans. Finally, we had failed to check in periodically to ensure that acquisitions were on track to perform under our valuation model.

One of the most memorable instances of poor integration on our part concerned our 2000 acquisition of the industrial conglomerate Pittway Corporation. The integration was completely disorganized, leading to any number of poor decisions. In one instance, Honeywell decided that it would close a Pittway factory in Connecticut and move it to Mexico to save $30,000 for each of the plant's 600 workers. It turned out the plant didn't employ 600 people, as Honeywell had believed, but only 220. With that headcount, the decision to move the plant to Mexico didn't make economic sense. On another occasion, corporate announced arbitrarily that it was taking over Pittway's systems for IT, payroll, and other functions, increasing Pittway's costs for no net benefit. Morale among Pittway employees was low, and as we saw in chapter 5, they had no sense of being part of a shared Honeywell culture. "We were headed right down the tubes along with all of the other failed Honeywell deals," remembered Roger Fradin, who was serving as the president of Pittway at the time of our acquisition.[3] The integration was so bad that three years after the deal had concluded, we had to undertake an entirely new, multiyear integration process just to get the business on track.

To tighten up how we performed integrations, we required that each business in Honeywell that was acquiring another business had an approved integration plan in place before the deal closed. This plan had to specify the metrics we were aiming for year after year (including cost synergies, sales synergies, and so on), with the first year broken down into quarterly goals.

The plan also had to cover management changes we anticipated making, changes to pay and benefits, changes to the business's functional systems, and other big moves we planned to make. For any deal over $50 million, I personally reviewed the plan with the team before the deal closed, conducting reviews each month for the first three months after the deal was done and quarterly thereafter for at least a year. As a final check, we required that the leader of a Honeywell business unit that acquired another company report to the board on progress at the one-year point.

We also tightened up executional details related to integration. To reinforce for our newly acquired workforces that change was coming, we put up new signs in their workspaces and handed out new business cards on the very first day. We made it clear that when it came to workforce reductions, we intended to retain the best in both companies (the acquiring division of Honeywell and the acquired company). That was easier said than done, since leaders on our integration teams responsible for staffing decisions tended to favor people from Honeywell, whom they might have known for years, over those at the acquired companies, whom they had known for two hours. We overcame this bias initially by hiring outside consultants to interview employees from both companies. Over time, applying this more objective lens became a cultural norm, and we were able to make the right staffing decisions without going outside the company. As a great example (mentioned earlier), Honeywell's current CEO, Darius Adamczyk, came to Honeywell via our acquisition of Metrologic, the company he ran.

We began putting dedicated, full-time integration teams in place, staffing them with outstanding people. Recognizing that integrations bring to bear all of a business's various functions, we used integrations as an opportunity to give up-and-coming leaders general management experience. We had each business identify in their regular management resource review discussions (covered in chapter 6) whom they would put on an integration team in the event that the business made an acquisition. When deals arose, we knew exactly the people we wanted to run the integration and could assemble a great team swiftly. Critically, we identified our potential integration team in the early stages of putting deals together, since we also used these teams to run due diligence for us. By immersing themselves deeply into the details of acquired companies before purchases were finalized, members of our integration team would be able to move swiftly, decisively, and smartly during the integration phase. They were also more committed to the integration plan and the business goals we targeted because they had helped create that plan in the first place while performing due diligence. We avoided the "hand off" problem whereby one team creates a "great plan" that is made greater because they don't have to actually execute on it!) Since we included leaders from the company being acquired on the integration, they could serve as evangelists within their company, gaining the support of the workforce more easily.

As our teams ran due diligence and helped integrate new acquisitions, they stayed alert to operational elements in these businesses that might be new to Honeywell and able to help us operate better. We never went in and said, "This is the Honeywell way and you will do it." When we discovered innovations we liked, we transferred them over to our existing businesses. Not only did this allow us to improve operations; it also helped win over members of our newly acquired workforces. Instead of feeling dictated to, they felt respected and valued from the very first day.

To Bring Acquisitions into the Fold . . .

- Put integration plans in place before the deal closes, covering management, metrics, and other relevant topics.
- Personally review and approve the plan.
- Tighten up the executional details.
- Put dedicated, full-time integration teams in place, and assemble these teams early.
- Make changes and communicate them immediately to shape the mind-set.
- Stay alert for processes in acquired companies that you like, and introduce them as innovations into your own company.
- Personally perform regular follow-up to ensure that the acquisition really is performing even better than predicted by the valuation model.

Ditch the Losers

A disciplined acquisitions process is only part of what you need to upgrade a portfolio for long-term growth. You also must analyze your current holdings and divest yourself advantageously of undesirable parts of your business. But don't venture into that analysis blindly. In an episode of *The Simpsons*, in response to Homer's complaint about something on television, Marge says, "Homer, it's easy to criticize." "Fun too!" Homer replies. Something similar holds true for portfolio analysis. Bankers, consultants, and your staff will all want to opine on businesses you should shed because doing so is fun . . . and easy too. As I told all of these analyzers, "I already know the strengths and weaknesses of the businesses I'm in. It would be both a lot tougher and a helluva lot more valuable if you could tell me what businesses I should get in and how to do it." Identification of possible acquisitions really is fundamental, which is why it should always be the first step of your new acquisitions process. From there you can go on to figuring out where to divest.

During the first year of my tenure, as we firmed up our acquisitions process, we completed a simple but powerful analysis of our existing business units and their constituent businesses. For each of these businesses, we asked whether it was in a good industry, if it had a great position in that industry, and if it delivered a strong return on investment. Based on the answers we generated, we assigned each business to one of three categories. An "A" rating meant that a business boasted a great position in a good industry with a good ROI. A business received a "B" if it didn't meet the criteria to be in the "A" group, but had the potential to get there. We gave a business a "C" rating if we saw no potential to turn it into a "A" business.

Three Questions to Ask of Each Business in Your Portfolio

1. Is it in a good industry?
2. Does it occupy a great position in that industry?
3. Does it deliver a strong ROI?

About 80 percent of our businesses fell into the "A" or "B" groups—not so bad. I didn't disclose externally how each business rated, and I did so in only a limited way to internal audiences. Over time, we sold off as many as the "C" businesses as possible, continuing to perform our analysis year after year and eventually adding a fourth criteria. After running numerous town halls and business reviews, I realized technology was what got our businesses excited—running a business well wasn't enough. So we began to factor in whether each business in our portfolio possessed exciting, new technology. One business of ours called Consumable Solutions delivered nuts, bolts, and other small items to the Aerospace assembly line. It had a great position in a good industry, and it delivered solid ROI, but its only technology was in its IT systems. Leaders just didn't get excited about it, and the business only seemed to grow if other senior leaders and I paid monthly attention to it. We realized we were dedicating too much of our time to this business, and could invest that time more productively elsewhere, so after spending almost two years developing potential buyers, we sold Consumable Solutions to a company that could operate it better. Since we had taken stock in addition to cash, the deal paid off well for us.

During my initial years, we concentrated on simply getting the best price for our divestitures. We wanted to quickly shed these time-consuming, hard-to-run businesses, freeing up money to make strategic acquisitions. After several years, it dawned on me during a blue book exercise that while I had used the private equity model to develop an acquisitions process, I hadn't done so with divestitures yet, and it was worth a try. Once most big companies conduct a strategic portfolio analysis, they begin a sales process to obtain the best price possible for businesses they are selling. Instead, we started asking ourselves: If we were a private equity firm buying the business today and seeking to turn it around at a profit, what would we do to enhance it, and then how would we sell it?

Working with Anne Madden, our M&A leader, we developed a rigorous process for improving our businesses before sale and selling them off more advantageously (we even wrote an article about this process). Taking more care with divestitures meant that many of them took longer than they would have in the past—sometimes years. We'd work hard to get these businesses ready for sale, investing in new growth areas and developing multiple potential buyers, and over time we'd get much better results for our shareholders.

Our Autolite spark plug business was losing $5 million a year, despite our best efforts to run it. Investors and our business unit leader wanted to sell it quickly to get it off of our books. Instead, we spent the better part of a year enhancing Autolite's manufacturing operations, to the point where the business was turning a $20 million profit. We also knocked on doors trying to find suitable buyers or joint venture partners to develop multiple buyers. That effort translated into a sale price that ran $200 million higher than we otherwise would have received.

CHANGING HOW YOU MANAGE YOUR PORTFOLIO

As helpful as structured processes are, you can't just drop them in place and assume your portfolio management will instantly become much more disciplined, strategic, and productive. There's an important ingredient we haven't yet considered: you and your leaders.

Managing a portfolio of companies for growth requires a great deal of time, attention, and focus on the part of leaders. As CEO, I not only pored over each element of our new acquisitions and divestitures processes; I also kept a close eye on our deal-making activity throughout my tenure. Every six weeks I would conduct reviews of the acquisition pipelines in each business, discussing strategies and potential targets with leaders on an ongoing basis. These meetings were short—only thirty minutes for each of our four business units—but they kept our business leaders on track, preventing them from wasting time and effort on ideas that wouldn't bear fruit. More importantly, these meetings served as a forcing mechanism: knowing we would be following up, leaders made sure to take actions they had mentioned at previous meetings, such as researching specific parts of a pending deal or chasing down particular companies to acquire. These meetings were just one of the venues in which I discussed pending merger and acquisition activity with teams. I also did so when we discussed our annual strategic plan, and during the periodic growth and ops days I've described.

I've said it before: Delegate as a leader, but don't abdicate. Here especially you want to take your oversight role seriously, applying the mind-set of intellectual inquiry described in chapter 1. When people in your team or organization come to you with possible deals to consider, push hard. If you hear that a company is in a good industry, probe into that. Who are the chief competitors? How profitable are they? Is the industry really as attractive as it seems? Regarding a prospective company's position in its industry, think hard about whether you might roll up multiple players in a fragmented industry to create a juggernaut. When we entered the gas detection business, there were no big players, but over an eight-year period we were able to acquire several companies, roll them up into a single Honeywell business, and become number one in the industry. We did the same in other industries, like barcode scanning, safety equipment, and digitally connected aircraft.

When considering potential acquisitions, keep a careful eye on risk as well as the impact on short-term results. Every quarter our businesses would bring me potential "elephants"—really big deals that, if consummated, would double Honeywell's size. I always backed away from these deals, fearful of the impact on our results if the deal didn't succeed as planned, and conscious as well that even if they did succeed, our short-term results would tank for quite a while due to the amortization we'd have to log. Our biggest deal during my tenure was our $5 billion acquisition of the metering company Elster in 2015—large, but not overly so given that our revenues then reached nearly $40 billion. The one exception to my rule was our $90 billion proposed purchase of United Technologies in 2016. In that case, the opportunity seemed too alluring to pass up: United Technologies had many good but mismanaged businesses, and we felt that if we could merge our two companies and spin off certain businesses, we'd wind up with a well-managed, powerhouse company that would make money for everyone. The deal didn't work out, but it was worth pursuing. However, in general, don't bet the farm. You don't need to take extraordinary risks in order to deliver solid long-term growth.

Keeping risk foremost in your mind will also lead you to prioritize diversification. Having read former treasury secretary Robert Rubin's book *In an Uncertain World*, I became more inclined to consider the potential downsides of deals, even if the upside seemed great and far more likely to materialize. Low-probability events sometimes do occur, and you have to prepare, managing your portfolio so that you can stay flexible and respond to changing conditions.

As a leader, you should also ensure that you have the expertise in your organization to do well with mergers, acquisitions, and divestitures. In advancing our more disciplined approach to dealmaking, we had extremely strong functional teams in place—legal, accounting, HR, IT, and so forth. When you do due diligence, you want the financials to be right, and you want to be sure the acquiring business is truly committed to the deal. You want to feel confident that the company you're acquiring has good leadership and a motivated workforce, and that there are no legal or environmental issues. You also want your functional teams to take an objective view on all deals rather than regarding themselves as a damper or cheerleader during dealmaking. Ideally, the business leaders in your organization will look to your functional experts as a resource that helps them land the best results for the company, whether that means proceeding or walking away from a deal. With deals that do pass muster, a strong functional team can help complete the transaction more quickly and smoothly while minimizing risks. Over time you will develop a reputation for reliability in dealmaking, which can give you an advantage in competitive bidding situations.

APPLY M&A LOGIC TO YOUR PRODUCT PORTFOLIOS

My advice in this chapter might seem to apply primarily to senior leaders running large organizations, but smaller companies and nonprofits can pursue a similar approach to deliver short- and long-term results, as can managers of businesses within companies. If you're a product manager, think of your individual products as businesses that you maintain as a portfolio. Many managers tend to make a great number of products available to customers, even if many of those don't sell very well or generate much profit. As new products emerge, managers are loath to jettison the older, inferior ones, reasoning that some customers still want them.

Actively manage the SKUs (stock keeping units) you sell, investing in high-growth, high-profit SKUs, and weeding out the vast majority of underperformers. If you have a thousand low-profit SKUs in your product portfolio, try doubling the price on all of them. You'll probably find that customers will stop ordering nine hundred of these SKUs. Get rid of them. Your revenues will drop, but you'll see little impact on profits, since those revenues have been profitless all along. As for the hundred that customers are still ordering, you now know that these products hold value for customers, and that you've been dramatically underpricing them. Keep these at the higher price and focus on growing sales. For leaders of businesses large and small, active management of your portfolio of assets puts you on the path to better long-term performance. If you're not performing a portfolio analysis such as I've described on an annual basis, you should.

TAKING UOP—AND HONEYWELL—UP

We began work on rebuilding our portfolio management processes in 2002, but it would be a few years before we would be in a position to actually begin acquiring companies. In the fourth quarter of 2004, three deals came together all at once, for a total of $3.5 billion, a big commitment for us at the time. One of these acquisitions, Novar, had been on our radar for a year, but we hadn't contacted the company about a sale since we only liked about 40 percent of the business. When another bidder showed interest in the company, we showed interest ourselves. During the dealmaking process, we could respond at speeds that surprised both Novar and the banks because we'd already prepared. We wound up purchasing Novar and then selling off the pieces of it we didn't want for more than we had initially valued them. We put top people in charge of the integration and held regular meetings consistent with our new process.

One portion of Novar that we had decided to sell was a business that printed checks. Although quite profitable, this business didn't fit well into our existing portfolio of companies, and its industry was in decline thanks to the rise of online banking. We had intended to keep this business for a short period of time, working with its leaders to maximize its value to Honeywell. Unfortunately, the business leader proved arrogant and dictatorial, refused to work well with Honeywell people, and had succeeded in intimidating his subordinates. This situation couldn't last, and it didn't. We recognized that if we didn't act swiftly, this leader would sabotage the business in an effort to cling to power. So we orchestrated a pre-dawn raid.

Identifying ahead of time a new CEO from within this business and a new CFO from Honeywell, we got up early, flew to the business's headquarters, and arrived just as they were opening for the day. I met with the outgoing CEO first to inform him of his immediate removal and to explain why. Our CFO met with the business's CFO to relieve him as well. Our Honeywell HR leader met with the potential new CEO to ensure that he would take the job (he did, but we had a backup plan just in case). I then met with the new CEO to explain what I wanted to see. Our M&A leader, Anne, had coordinated the entire day and had accompanied us to ensure we followed the plan. We sent out an announcement to the workforce, conducted town hall meetings with the new leadership, and then promptly left. Immediately, operations across the entire business improved.

Employees started to speak up, previously impossible ideas became possible, and life for everyone became better. We subsequently sold this business (as well as other parts of Novar) for far more than we had anticipated in our plan.

We never would have pulled off this pre-dawn raid and subsequent improvements to the check printing business had we not had a solid M&A process in place. Overall, the Novar deal paid off handsomely for us, far exceeding our expectations for earnings accretion, IRR, and fifth-year ROI. We integrated the 40 percent of the business that we had wanted more effectively than we anticipated, realizing greater cost synergies than we had planned, and also benefiting from sales synergies we hadn't included when valuing the company.

A second acquisition, Zellweger, was a relatively small deal ($250 million) but an important one, as it was our first step into an adjacent market that we weren't already in (gas detection). The Honeywell business unit that would run Zellweger, Automation and Control Solutions (ACS), liked the deal, but leaders there were also involved in the Novar deal and were concerned they wouldn't have the time to focus on integrating Zellweger well. I pushed for the deal, observing that problems and opportunities choose their own timing, and that we had to jump on the opportunities when they presented themselves. Roger Fradin, who was leading ACS, agreed, and we went for it. We have since added several other acquisitions to the Zellweger business, and the combined entity has over $1 billion in highly profitable sales.

And then there was the third deal of 2004: UOP, which I mentioned earlier. The first inkling that we were right to have made this acquisition came in 2005, shortly after the deal closed. A private equity firm called, saying that they had been negotiating to buy all of UOP from Dow and that they would be happy to buy the entire company from Honeywell for the same $2.2 billion. Now I understood: Dow had offered us $865 million for half the company, planning on turning around and selling it to the private equity firm for $1.1 billion, realizing an immediate gain of $235 million. Good thing we had made our move—we would have looked like complete fools!

In the years ahead, UOP turned into a big success for us. We pumped up what we called "Horizon Three" R&D (projects that would pay off over the very long term) from $4 million to $20 million, and we invested in several capital projects to expand the business's production and technology capabilities. It wasn't long before these investments paid off. In 2006, UOP introduced new technology that created environmentally friendly diesel fuel out of plant material. Other commercially valuable innovations followed over the next decade: a new kind of jet fuel made from renewable sources; a procedure for turning a previously unusable petroleum residue into fuel; and an expansion of our natural gas capabilities.

UOP had been around for a century and already possessed a proud culture of its own, so it would take about a decade before the workforce there truly considered themselves to be part of Honeywell. The toughest part of the integration was getting UOP (which you'll remember develops chemical engineering processes for petroleum) to work closely with our business that produces control systems for these processes. For years, UOP people called Process Controls "Honeywell" and referred to themselves as UOP. Adding to the difficulty, Process Controls was housed in a different business, ACS, giving it more perceived distance from UOP executives. The turning point took place in 2012, when we added Process Controls to the Performance Materials and Technologies (PMT) business unit that included UOP. The new PMT leader we put in charge, Darius Adamczyk, had been running Process Controls, providing us with a unique perspective on how to integrate the two businesses. Since Darius was also a potential successor to me as Honeywell's CEO, these changes allowed us to expand the size of the business he was leading, which meant we could observe how he would do with significantly increased responsibilities (described in chapter 10). Today, UOP and our Process Controls business work very well together, thinking of themselves as part of one company: Honeywell. They develop new products, processes, technologies, and software with advanced capabilities that no other company in the world can match, because no other company has expertise in both the chemical engineering of processes for petroleum and the control systems for these processes. It's a winning combination.

These three successful deals helped convince investors early on that we could handle M&A responsibly and wouldn't blow their money. Still, I couldn't proclaim "mission accomplished" on portfolio management. While our ACS business under Roger's leadership did a great job with M&A early on, identifying companies, reaching out, and building a pipeline, other Honeywell businesses lagged behind. It would take time and leadership changes before the entire company embraced acquisitions as the long-term growth opportunity that it is. We also continued to pore over our portfolio with an eye to upgrading it. In 2007, we again reviewed our acquisition process, assessing its successes and failures, and making minor adjustments.

What we found, and continue to find, is that a disciplined approach really does generate growth. We've had a few failures along the way, but only with very small acquisitions. Our significant acquisitions have all succeeded, some remarkably. During my tenure, we acquired about a hundred companies, increasing our total company sales by $15 billion. We also sold about seventy businesses with a combined $8.5 billion in sales. Overall, that's $23.5 billion in sales transacted on what began as a $22 billion company—quite a bit of activity. As for UOP, we took a small hit to our profits at first, but within a matter of several years we were able to turn that $865 million investment into $5 billion in value. Not bad! That's the power of sound, strategic portfolio management.

QUESTIONS TO ASK YOURSELF

1. How much attention do you pay to managing your portfolio of businesses or products? Have you prioritized it as a pathway to long-term growth? Are people focused on what to get into (the tough part) as well as what to get out of (the easy part)?
2. Perform a postmortem analysis of your previous deals. Do you approach mergers, acquisitions, and divestitures systematically or in an ad hoc fashion? If you do have a system in place, do any weak areas exist?
3. Do you reassess your processes for mergers, acquisitions, and divestitures periodically to ensure that they're working?
4. How well do you identify potential acquisitions? Are you and your teams constantly building a pipeline of potential companies to acquire? Do you vet these opportunities strategically?
5. Do you have a clear process mapped out for performing due diligence? How receptive are you when recognizing or addressing problems with deals as they arise?
6. Have you overpaid in the past? Why or why not? Do you accept the numbers that acquired companies or bankers give you, or do you perform your own valuations of possible acquisitions?
7. How adept are you at performing integrations? Do you have plans in place before the deal closes? Are you taking integration seriously, assigning top people to work on a full-time basis?

8. When considering divestitures, do you rush to get the deal done, or do you spend time and effort readying your businesses for sale and cultivating potential buyers?

9. Do you personally give portfolio management the attention it deserves, or are you prone to abdicating leadership in this area to someone else?

10. If you have a portfolio of products, do you periodically conduct a review of SKU performance to identify low performers? Have you tried doubling or tripling the price to see what happens and allow the market to validate the true worth of these SKUs?

PART FOUR

PROTECT YOUR INVESTMENTS

CHAPTER NINE

Take Control of the Downturns

I n the spring of 2018, I was packing my office in preparation for a move when I came across a letter I wrote back in the summer of 2011. Addressed to unknown future CEOs of Honeywell, this lengthy note (it ran for nine single-spaced pages) offered my personal reflections on how to handle one of the most difficult situations a leader faces: steering an organization or team through bad economic times. I had felt compelled to write this letter because we had emerged from the Great Recession of 2008 in great shape, outpacing our peers and also Honeywell's historical performance during recessions. While the experience was still fresh, I wanted to capture my reflections on how we had done it, in the hopes that my successors would have an easier time dealing with similar situations in the future and wouldn't have to waste time learning what we'd learned.

If you haven't written such postmortem analyses (or white papers, as we called them) for your organization, I strongly suggest it. As we saw in chapter 1, intellectual rigor is vital for organizations seeking to perform well today and tomorrow, and leaders are uniquely positioned to establish and maintain that rigor. By taking a couple of weekends to write up a memo on our handling of the Great Recession, I forced myself to recall key challenges we'd faced and to think carefully through our responses to them. Writing also allowed me to preserve institutional memory about best practices for our organization, and to push readers (in this case, directors and key executives) to think more deeply about recessions. I didn't write these analyses often—only when our organization had navigated a major challenge, learning in the process some lessons I felt it important to pass on.

The specific advice that this particular memo contained is also relevant for any leader seeking to build an organization that delivers both today and tomorrow. Leaders often panic when recessions strike. They go into survival mode, managing quarter-to-quarter and shoring up their numbers by cutting back on the long-term growth projects we've described in previous pages. Such actions might please investors in the moment, but they undo hard-won progress the organization has made. This is a big mistake, and one thankfully we avoided. By looking for creative solutions to the financial challenges we faced during the Great Recession, we maintained our investments while still delivering results that outdid our competitors' performance. Our specific tactics (the ones that had worked, and some others that hadn't), the reactions of staff and the organization to these tactics, and my own responses as a leader were what I conveyed in my memo, and I would now like to share some of them with you.[1]

As unpleasant as recessions are, you can use them to set the stage for future gains against your competition as long as you stay disciplined and maintain a balanced, short- and long-term approach. Two basic strategies become important here. First, prepare for recessions before they hit hard by cutting costs proactively while still keeping the company's long-term growth projects—including process redesigns and culture—intact. Second, even as you are cutting costs during the recession, anticipate what you can do to prepare for the recovery, which does come despite how gloomy conditions might currently look. Managing short-term costs with the future in mind requires more effort on your part, and it requires *independent thinking*. Be quicker than most to prepare for recessions even when bad economic news

---

1   To buttress my memory of events, I also draw extensively throughout this chapter on the concepts and language in a second unpublished, internal white paper entitled "Honeywell: Lessons Learned from the Recession of 2008–2009." This was a separate document that our finance team prepared to retain institutional knowledge about "lessons learned," not to be confused with the one I wrote for my successors.

hasn't yet hit completely. And in the depths of recession, stay calm while everyone else is panicking, remembering that good times will return and that your organization needs to be ready. You'll face passionate resistance from your staff, employees, and investors, but if you can hold your ground and stubbornly continue to manage for both the short and long term, these stakeholders will eventually thank you for it. One day, perhaps, you'll find yourself writing a postmortem of your own.

CONTEMPLATE WHAT *MIGHT* HAPPEN

Recessions don't materialize out of nowhere. The signs and signals are out there, if you're alert to them. To put yourself in a position where you can pursue short- and long-term goals even amid a downturn, you need to try spotting the early signs and take protective measures that others neglect. That's what we did in 2008. The Great Recession officially began in December 2007, triggered by a crisis in subprime mortgage lending that broke out earlier that year. Bankers maintained the subprime problem was limited, and initially it didn't seem to be a big deal because Honeywell's sales, margins, earnings-per-share, cash flow, and orders were all strong. Our M&A machine was working, and we had many new products and services, process initiatives, and geographic expansions in the pipeline.

In the back of my mind, I did harbor some doubts. The Asian financial crisis of the late 1990s had begun with the collapse in value of the Thai currency. Observers had proclaimed then as well that it was no big deal. But the crisis spread to Brazil, and then to Russia. Before you knew it, we had a global crisis on our hands. Would a similar situation come to pass here?

A dinner I had with an investor friend in late 2007 also gave me pause. When I playfully suggested that this person buy Honeywell shares, which were at $65 at the time, he said he would—when they had dropped to $59. "They're not going to drop," I said, but he insisted they would, predicting that a recession was coming. I was so sure that I bet him a future dinner that our share price wouldn't drop to $59 within the next year. Nevertheless, I had a lot of respect for this person, and took a potential recession more seriously after our conversation—especially a few months later, when our stock dropped below $59 (it would eventually fall to about $27 at the recession's low point).

My concern deepened during the first half of 2008. Although our financial performance remained strong, too many people were making dire economic predictions. It would have been easy at this point for us to simply bide our time and not take preventative measures. Investors weren't demanding it, and many leaders in our company looked at our numbers and thought we'd remain insulated from recession. I wound up taking action, in part because of insights I'd gleaned from reading former treasury secretary Bob Rubin's book *In an Uncertain World*. Rubin had argued that many outcomes are possible in a given situation, and you have to anticipate and prepare for eventualities that seem unlikely but that could prove extremely damaging should they materialize. If I had to bet $100, I would have put it on the side of the optimists. But we still needed to prepare for the unlikely (in my mind) scenario that the recession would hit Honeywell hard. As Paul Samuelson famously remarked, the market has predicted nine of the last five recessions, so you don't want to overdo it. That being said, it makes a lot of sense to stay on your economic toes.

TAKE EARLY ACTION

As a preventative measure, we sold our Consumable Solutions business in July 2008 to B/E Aerospace for $1.05 billion. The price was close to the market peak and allowed us to book a $623 million pre-tax gain. Rather than return that money to shareholders, we put about $200 million of it into restructuring (consolidating plants, laying off about three thousand employees, and so on) to prepare for tougher economic times, should they materialize. We had been planning to perform much of this restructuring over time anyway for reasons unrelated to the recession, but now was a good time to do it (it wound up saving us almost $50 million in 2009). During our budgeting process for the 2009 fiscal year, I also asked our leaders to base their plans on the assumption that we would see significant sales declines. That elicited blowback from leaders in our Aerospace division, who claimed their order volume was strong both for short- and long-cycle parts of their business. If sales did start to dry up, they had $120 million of cost reductions they could make. I told them to make those cost reductions now, just in case business got worse.

Good thing, because in October 2008, nearly a full year after the recession's official start, the bottom fell out of our short-cycle businesses. In the fourth quarter of 2008, our sales fell by 8.4 percent, with some areas of our business seeing a 16 percent drop.[1] But because we'd restructured and made conservative assumptions to begin with, our earnings actually *increased* year over year—from 91 to 97 cents a share. We'd been able to take approximately $600 million in costs out of our business—about 60 cents per share. In addition to these positive short-term results, we set ourselves up for better short- and long-term performance down the road. And because we had already begun to pare back our costs, additional cuts we had to make as the recession deepened weren't as drastic as they might have been. We were also better able to continue to fund all the growth initiatives described earlier in the book, and better able to deliver on our promises to customers (more on that in a moment).

Unfortunately for our investors, this advance preparation didn't help our stock price much once the recession hit us. Our shares dropped precipitously, reaching $27 in November 2008 due to fears about our market as well as our reputation as a company that performed poorly during recessions. Our share price wouldn't hit $60 again until the spring of 2011. Once the recession was behind us, however, investors did give us plenty of credit for reacting to the bad economic times long before our competitors did, and for outperforming both during and after the recession. We weren't visionaries, but rather had simply cultivated the foundation of intellectual discipline described in chapter 1. I was reading widely, exposing myself to people and ideas far beyond our industry, and that helped me look beyond our own quarterly numbers to see the broader economic picture and to take reasonable precautions.

Not that our preparations for the recession were perfect. In 2007, after years of pressure from investors for a share buyback, I spent $2 billion to buy our shares back at a price of $55. Although some might argue that returning cash to shareholders wasn't a bad move (especially considering that as of this writing our stock sells at $172), in the depth of the recession that $2 billion in cash would have come in handy. On the whole, though, we had shown caution even when our business still looked strong, and this helped us. I like to think of our efforts cultivating intellectual rigor as an important, albeit intangible long-term investment. It's tough carving out the time to read and think amid the pressures of the day, but that investment does eventually pay off in the form of better decisions. For us, the payoff came when we needed it most: just before and during the Great Recession.

PROTECT CUSTOMERS

Despite our early reaction, our declining sales in 2009 were worse than we'd assumed they would be when we made our plans, forcing us to cut additional costs or pass on steep losses to investors. When it came to cost-cutting, we could pare back a bit what we paid for direct materials (supplies used during manufacturing that we could attribute to a given product), but that wouldn't help much—we had long-term agreements in place with many suppliers that locked in pricing. We could and did reduce our usage of and costs related to indirect materials (materials used in production and other overhead processes that we couldn't attribute to a specific product), but that didn't help us much. So either employees, customers, or investors would have to feel the pain. The question was how best to apportion the pain among these groups.

When cutting costs, our general approach was to avoid taking steps that would unduly compromise Honeywell's ability to perform over the long term. Although times were tough now, better days would return—I firmly believed that despite many views to the contrary—and we had to be ready for the recovery. That meant, first of all, that we wouldn't cut costs in ways detrimental to customers. Once customers flee, they're hard to get back. We would continue to keep the staffing levels and materials on hand we needed to deliver. We would also continue to fund all of our process improvement initiatives, especially the Honeywell Operating System, and the new products and services we had committed to develop for customers. If a given customer slowed the pace at which they were going to introduce their new products (into which ours were incorporated), we would slow our spending. Otherwise, we would keep spending steady. We even continued to fund our annual global technology summit described earlier in the book. After all the emphasis we had placed on investing in R&D, I didn't want to send the message that new products didn't matter during a recession. Our fundamental goal here was to ensure that customers didn't feel any impact from us during the recession, because without strong performance on behalf of customers, both investors and employees would suffer.

MAINTAIN YOUR TALENT BASE

That left investors and employees. Here, we sought to cut costs enough to out-perform our peers financially while also preserving our long-term industrial base. Some leaders feel badly about hurting employees with cost-cutting, so they avoid it, preferring to let investors bear the full brunt of declining sales. Cost-cutting is no doubt unpleasant, but leadership isn't always easy. Many times I would respond to complaints about the pain caused due to our cost-cutting by observing, "That's why they call it a recession, and they don't call it a party." Leaders have no good choices here—they must choose between the bad and the less-bad. The less-bad choices would allow us to outperform for our investors (even though stock prices were still down), keep employee pain to a minimum, and ready ourselves for a recovery.

Essential to our success during the recession was our decision to avoid layoffs unless they were permanent reductions, meaning that we would never rehire for the affected positions. Research shows that layoffs lead to lower levels of innovation, lower morale, poorer performance among remaining employees, diminished corporate reputations, and higher levels of customer defection. One study found that "after layoffs a majority of companies suffered declines in profitability."[2]

Honeywell had itself suffered from layoffs' unintended consequences.

During the 2001 recession, we had let go large numbers of people in our Chinese operations, even though the market in that country was growing by double digits (leaders find it a lot easier to cut employees who are thousands of miles away than they do those in their home country). This proved to be a huge setback for our Chinese businesses, which was why we had to spend so much effort rebuilding them, as described in chapter 7.

For most businesses, avoiding layoffs in a one- or two-year recession is common sense. Leaders need about six months to actually lay off employees once they have decided to do so. They have to identify which jobs they are going to eliminate and attend to all of the legalities. Once employees are gone, it takes six months of operations before you've recovered all of the money you spent on severance and other elements of the layoffs. After that, maybe you'll get another six months of returns before the economic recovery begins. Once it does, you have to hire people back to handle increases in demand. If someone told you that it would take you six months to build a factory, six months to recover your investment, you'll get a return for six months, and then you'll shut it down, you'd never go for it because it would be ridiculous. Yet somehow leaders think it makes sense to do something similar with people.

I felt pretty certain that the recession would not drag on for years and years. While layoffs were a poor option, we couldn't put the entire burden on investors. We had a fiduciary responsibility to protect and grow their investment. If we delivered earnings well below our peers, the investment community would regard us as a cyclical company (one that doesn't perform well in recessions), and our stock would sell at a lower multiple of our earnings, hurting owners of our stock for years into the future. We already were known as a cyclical company thanks to our performance in previous recessions, which was one of the reasons our stock sold at a discount of 10 to 20 percent compared with other industrial companies.

I wanted us to perform better in this recession so that we could improve our reputation and thus secure a higher multiple on our stock. The key, I felt, was to cut costs in ways that would better balance the pain employees and investors would feel, and as I've mentioned, that would allow us to respond well to the recovery by preserving our industrial base. We didn't have to outperform competitors by two to three times—it was enough for us to do slightly better than or in line with our peers. But that meant we had to trim labor costs somehow. I asked members of my team to look into furloughs. It turned out they were more complicated than I had thought—states and countries had different rules governing how companies executed them. But after getting up to speed on the laws, we wound up choosing this option. Employees wouldn't lose their jobs. Instead, they would stay home for periods of time without pay. Although all of our peers were choosing layoffs, we felt it made no sense, as Mark James, senior vice president of HR, Security and Communications, said, to lay off people, "pay [them] a bunch of money, and disrupt their lives to stay home or go find other jobs, and then turn right around and hire them back in the upswing."[3]

STAY FIRM ON FURLOUGHS

We mandated that our businesses execute up to four weeks of furloughs spread out over twelve months, depending on their financial situation (the recession hit our various businesses differently). At first, our people applauded the policy. They knew times were tough, and they appreciated that we were attempting to maintain jobs.

That said, furloughs were challenging both for employees and the company—we had to resort to them multiple times as the depth of the recession became clearer. Imagine, from the employee's perspective, how hard it would be running a household without knowing month to month if your income would dip by 25 percent or more. I began receiving anonymous notes urging me to lay off 10 percent of our people and be done with it. I came to suspect that if we put furloughs to a public vote, the vast majority of employees would vote for them, since they wouldn't want to look heartless in front of their colleagues. But if we put it to an anonymous vote, they would support layoffs, figuring *they* were strong performers and hence not likely to be among the unfortunate 10 percent.

As the months dragged on, furloughs took a toll on our workforce, damaging morale. At one point a business leader called me begging for a reprieve from a fourth round of furloughs. They were confident about their sales forecast and convinced they could make their numbers without asking their people to stay home. The business had missed its numbers for nine months in a row, and when I probed, the business leader admitted they couldn't really be sure they would make their upcoming month's forecast. I had no choice but to impose the fourth round of furloughs for this business (and good thing, because the business missed their forecast for a tenth month).

It was unpleasant but necessary. I stayed firm on furloughs, not only because they allowed people to keep their jobs and because they were less expensive to execute than layoffs (no severance payments required), but because they allowed us to retain our industrial base for the long term. All of the knowledge that our people had would stay inside the organization, and when the recovery came, we would be in a much better position to deliver for customers and to innovate.

LIST OF COMMON COST-CUTTING RESPONSES TO RECESSIONS

To help you think through the pros and cons of various cost-cutting ideas, I've compiled them in the chart below.

COST CATEGORIES	PRO	CONS
Direct Material (material that goes directly into the manufacture of your products)	• If you can get price reductions from suppliers, terrific!	• It's tough to do, as most companies have contracts in place with suppliers. But you should definitely try. • The impact of these cuts are delayed if you have to go through an inventory account.

Indirect Material/ Services (payments to suppliers other than material that goes directly into the product)	• This is a great move to make because by reducing usage, you cut costs immediately.	• As long as these cuts don't impact customers, then they're fair game.
Temporary or Contract Employees	• These cuts lower your costs immediately. They work if you always maintain a small portion (10–20 percent) of your workforce as temporary/ contract while observing applicable state/federal laws regarding classification.	• Make sure it doesn't affect customers. • You have to keep an eye on legal classifications.

Wages/Salaries to Employees

• Layoffs	• These cuts affect only a small percent (10–20 percent) of the workforce.	• The financial returns aren't great. • Your organization will accrue a big expense up front, with the potential for survivor guilt among remaining employees. • Layoffs hurt your industrial base, compromising your ability to respond during the coming recovery.
• Furloughs	• These are a lot less costly in financial terms. • They preserve your industrial base for recovery. • When recovery begins, employees feel better about it.	• Furloughs affect 100 percent of the workforce. • They are more difficult to administer because laws vary in different states and countries.
Benefits	• Employees don't feel the effects of benefits cuts immediately. • The cost savings show up quickly in company financials.	• Employees won't like benefits cuts, but they will recognize that such cuts are better than more furloughs or layoffs.

Depreciation/ Amortization	· As long as it doesn't affect customers, it's much less painful.	· Difficult to impact because most of this is driven by past expenditures.
Bonuses	· Employees see bonus reduction as essential, a sign that "we're all in it together." · Cuts in bonuses have an immediate impact on financials.	· Leaders feel like they're working harder than ever for a lot less. You can minimize resentment by finding a way to help leaders over time (for instance, by issuing bonuses in stock).
Direct Support to Customer (cooperative advertising, etc.)	· Cuts in customer support have an immediate financial impact.	· Customer impact cuts are a really bad idea, as they could cause customers to flee, hurting you over the long term.

A RECESSION REALLY ISN'T A PARTY

Even multiple rounds of furloughs, which saved us $200 million and allowed us to avoid two thousand layoffs,[4] weren't enough to get us through 2009 intact. By the middle of the year, with sales continuing to decline, we found we had to cut our labor costs further to avoid having to revise our earnings estimates downward a second time that year (we had already done so in the first quarter of the year like everyone else). My team and I hashed out this problem on an ongoing basis during 2009, and it was tough going. Team members were divided on the issues, with most arguing, "We can't do that to employees." I had to remind them repeatedly that we were forced to choose between unattractive options. A party it was not.

We avoided mass layoffs and more than four weeks of furloughs by turning to other alternatives, most notably cuts in bonuses and benefits.[2] I had already decided I would recommend that the board award me a zero bonus. As I recounted in chapter 5, I announced this decision to my staff in the course of proposing a reduction in our 401(k) match by 50 percent. Although

---

2   We also froze all hiring, employee reward programs, and salary increases, and managed our supply chain and inventories more closely to cut costs.

team members didn't want to cut benefits, they concluded on their own that this course of action represented the best of bad options, as our employees had already suffered from the initial rounds of furloughs, and this way they wouldn't feel more immediate pain (as they would, for instance, if we instituted mandatory salary cuts, or another two to three weeks of furlough). To my surprise and delight, my team members and the leadership of our Aerospace division all volunteered to take zero bonuses as well. We wound up cutting benefits as I'd proposed, and also cutting the company's entire bonus pool by two-thirds. When bonus time came, we took one-third of the remaining pool and awarded it in the form of restricted stock and options instead of cash. That saved us money and, given that our stock would likely rise once the recession ended, our leaders would be made whole over time.

PLANTING THE SEEDS FOR GROWTH, EVEN DURING A RECESSION

In addition to the $200 million we saved thanks to furloughs, the cuts to our bonus pool saved us another $200 million, benefits cuts another $200 million, and improvements to operations about $900 million. All told, these savings allowed us to perform better than our competitors in 2009, and to improve on our performance during the previous recession (see chart on next page) without having to cut back on our major growth programs. We also continued to invest in our people (training, our technology symposium, our senior leadership meeting, and so on), despite calls from some in our organization to cut those costs. When sales began to bounce back in December 2009, our workforce and leadership corps were intact. Our customer relationships were strong, and we hadn't slid backward on our cultural, process, or M&A strategies. On the contrary, we had intensified M&A, seeking out companies we could buy less expensively. In the middle of the recession, we completed a $1.4 billion acquisition of Sperian, a manufacturer of protective equipment, adding it to our Safety Products portfolio of businesses. We also completed a $720 million acquisition of Metrologic to add to our Barcode Scanning business (and getting my successor, Darius Adamczyk too!).

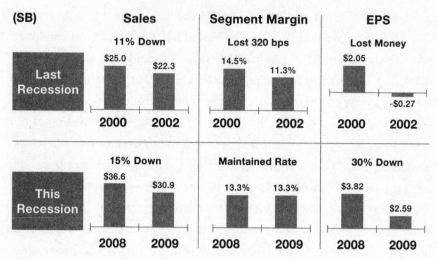

(SB)	Sales	Segment Margin	EPS
Last Recession	**11% Down** $25.0 ▮ $22.3 ▮ 2000 2002	**Lost 320 bps** 14.5% ▮ 11.3% ▮ 2000 2002	**Lost Money** $2.05 ▮ ▬ -$0.27 2000 2002
This Recession	**15% Down** $36.6 ▮ $30.9 ▮ 2008 2009	**Maintained Rate** 13.3% ▮ 13.3% ▮ 2008 2009	**30% Down** $3.82 ▮ $2.59 ▮ 2008 2009

*Last recession shown as originally reported; 2008 and 2009 on proforma basis

"Honeywell: Lessons Learned from the Recession of 2008–2009," Unpublished Honeywell white paper

The pieces were in place for rapid growth. From 2006 to 2012, our earnings per share rose 78 percent, more than doubling the average increase seen by our investor competitors (the other big industrial companies with which we compete for investment dollars). As the chart on the next page shows, our performance continued to dwarf that of the S&P 500 for the next decade. Many of the investments we had been making for years in R&D, the Honeywell Operating System, culture, globalization, and safety training began to bear fruit. Although our employees initially chafed against our cost-cutting measures, a number of them contacted me after the recession ended to thank me for choosing furloughs over restructuring. Employee turnover was only slightly higher in 2009 than in 2008, and the percent of employees who regarded Honeywell favorably only slightly lower.[5] Our leadership corps eventually were made whole in their bonuses, thanks to subsequent rises in our share price. As we grew our business in the years to come, employees benefited too, in the form of higher salaries, more stable jobs, and a company people could believe in. We eventually returned our 401(k) match to about where it had been, although exorbitant medical costs prevented us from reinstating our retiree health benefit.

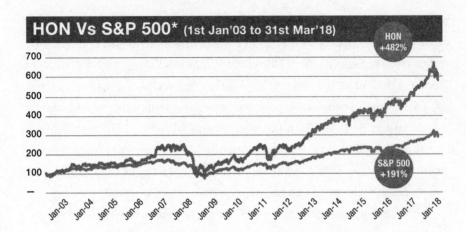

HON Vs S&P 500* (1st Jan'03 to 31st Mar'18)

HON +482%

S&P 500 +191%

Nobody likes recessions, but as our experience proves, they don't have to destroy the foundations for long-term growth you've laid. The key is to stay calm while everyone else is panicking. Remember, as I've said, recessions are temporary. Good times will return eventually. As a leader, you have to think about the recovery and what your organization will need to perform. Don't cut all of your growth investments just to get the best possible shareholder returns. Do everything you can *not* to cut them, delivering returns that are good enough to keep investors reasonably happy. By taking control of the downturn in this way, you can maintain all of the investments you've made in your business up to that point, and keep your ability to perform over the long-term intact.

KEEP SUPPLIER RELATIONSHIPS STRONG

I've focused on labor costs, but our strategy around materials also proved pivotal to our post-recession performance, even if it didn't center around cost-cutting. One of the great difficulties businesses have as they exit recessions is that competitors are also ramping up production, so the supplies required for production become scarce up and down the supply chain. When an airline, say, cuts its flight hours by 7 percent, leaders there reduce their orders for Honeywell spare parts by 25 percent and burn off their existing inventory to conserve cash. On the same logic, we'll reduce our own supply orders by 40 percent, and our suppliers will cut their own orders from vendors by 50 or 60 percent, compounding greatly the effect of a 7 percent decline in the end market. During recoveries, the opposite occurs: spikes in demand grow larger as you go down the supply chain. Yet suppliers one or two rungs down can't meet the demand when their orders double overnight—it takes time for them to rehire laid-off workers and access the materials they need. As a result, our businesses can't grow as rapidly during a recovery as they otherwise might.

I thought a great deal about this problem even as our sales were still declining, and I also anticipated that some of our short-cycle businesses that were seeing the most rapid declines were at risk of struggling the most with supply issues during the recovery. An economist I came across made a very simple prediction that struck me as both intuitive and correct: businesses would leave the recession in the manner they entered it. If you only saw a 2 or 3 percent decline in sales over the course of a year because you were a long-cycle business, you'll only see a 2 or 3 percent increase over a similar period during the recovery. If your short-cycle business tanked as the recession hit, with sales dropping 20 or 30 percent in the space of six months, then you could expect a 20 to 30 percent sales boost at some point as your business came back. By this logic, we could expect that our short-cycle businesses would see demand roaring back over a relatively short period of time. If our businesses couldn't access the supplies they needed, their recoveries would become stalled, and our competitors in these markets would get the upper hand, or we would all struggle equally. I wanted us to have an advantage when the recovery was upon us.

To prepare for this scenario, I asked our business leaders in the depths of the recession to begin working with their suppliers to prepare for the recovery. This seemed impossible to leaders at the time, since many economists and some of my staff were predicting that we'd see an L-shaped recovery—one that was essentially nonexistent. Our sales, according to this view, would never rebound to their prerecession levels. I insisted that recovery would come, just as it always had in the past. And when it did, our short-cycle businesses had to make sure they were first in line for supplies. Our leaders began these conversations, working with suppliers up front to lock in first priority over our competitors when the recovery came. This represented independent thinking on our part—our competitors weren't doing this. We also took the opportunity to negotiate better payment terms, price reductions, and long-term deals, which were all easier to obtain during a recession. As a result of this effort, we got a big lift as the economy improved, outpacing our competitors in our sales growth, to the delight of our investors. Our very profitable Aerospace commercial spare parts business, for example, outgrew its competitors by about 50 percent in 2011–2012 because leaders there had worked with suppliers.

FOUR ADDITIONAL WAYS TO TAKE CONTROL

Aside from preparing for recessions and recoveries when competitors aren't, there are other steps you can take to help your team or organization take control of the downturn. First, if you're a public company, manage investors' expectations. When making earnings estimates, be conservative. You can't know how bad the downturn will be, and you need some wiggle room in case sales come in even lower than you anticipated. You can revise your earnings estimates downward once, but if you do this multiple times, your reputation will suffer. At the same time, you want to commit to—and achieve—performance on par with or better than your peers. Getting this right isn't easy, so you'll have to feel it out. If you find yourself in trouble after lowering earnings expectations once, you might consider making additional cuts. We did that, cutting our bonus pool and benefits. It turned out to be the right move, solidifying our reputation with investors and minimizing the immediate hit to employees, all without compromising our long-term performance.

Second, when making big decisions about cost-cutting and other sensitive issues, work collaboratively with other leaders on your team to make sure they're on board. Faced with actions that hurt employees, some of them will go into denial about the extent of the downturn or insist that shareholders alone feel the pain. You can't dictate a solution and expect everyone's buy-in. Instead, put the conundrum you face, as well as your recommended actions, before your team members and let *them* come to their own conclusions. I like to divide a team into breakout groups for such deliberations, as I find this technique helps teams avoid the phenomenon of groupthink (yet another tool you can use to improve the level of intellectual discourse, as described in chapter 1). Sometimes your team members will generate solutions you didn't think of—and that's great. Other times they'll agree with the cost-cutting measures you propose as the least-bad alternative. Because they had a chance to think through the issues for themselves, they can get behind what might ultimately prove to be a painful decision. In our case, allowing our leadership team to ponder the benefits reductions and other controversial cost-saving measures I was proposing helped them finally buy in. As Mark James remembered, "The whining stopped."[6]

If you lead a large organization with hundreds or even thousands of leaders and managers, get all of them aligned with your cost-cutting strategy, not just your executive team. We saw the difference leadership alignment made when we implemented furloughs in France. Under French law, employees had to volunteer to be furloughed. In some plants, we saw huge differences in the number of employees volunteering—one plant would have 5 percent in favor of furloughs, another 80 percent. When we probed what was happening, we found it all came down to plant managers, how they were portraying the furlough to people and how much trust their people had in them.

Understanding the important role played by leaders, we made sure, as I've noted, to keep our annual senior leadership meeting intact, even as we were cutting labor costs. The event wasn't as nice as in previous years, but we needed it so that we could convey to leaders our general thinking about continuing to serve customers, protecting our talent base, and so on. We also needed to acknowledge how bad the recession was and reinforce that this wasn't permanent—good times would return. We needed to explain to leaders why we were cutting their bonuses, and that we were doing so in a way that would make them whole once the company had recovered. Finally, I needed to let them know *I* wasn't getting a bonus either. Thanks to our senior leadership meeting and other meetings, our leaders got the message and generally supported our response to the recession, despite the grumbling that occurred among the workforce.

A third and critically important way to take control of the downturn is to communicate openly and honestly with the rank and file. People must hear the truth about how the business is doing. If you present an overly rosy picture at the outset, you might have to go back and explain the situation yet again when sales have dried up further. At the same time, don't pretend you know for certain how bad the recession will get—because you don't. Any predictions you make might come back to haunt you. Acknowledge the pain people feel and help them understand why it's necessary. Reassure them that the recession will eventually end, recovery will begin, and all of them will be better positioned to succeed given the difficult actions being taken today. In other words, provide hope—a very powerful human emotion. Whatever you do, let people know you're sacrificing too. Although I knew early on that I would recommend a zero bonus for myself, I didn't make it clear I was doing so until six months into the recession (for governance reasons, I didn't want it to appear that I was preempting the board). This was a mistake, as it allowed some resentment to take root that was entirely unnecessary.

Employees need to understand that the organization will treat people fairly during tough times. But as important as fairness is, please factor in the long-term consequences. It might have been fair, from one point of view, to cut R&D spending, but doing so would have hurt employees over the long term as customers left and our business shrank. It likewise seemed fair during the Great Recession for us to impose furloughs on our Indian software engineering operations, just as we did to employees across Honeywell. And yet the economy in India was strong, and none of our local competitors were furloughing or laying off employees. But because we did so, we saw higher attrition rates among our employees in India, which hurt our business. Just as each business took furloughs based on their markets, it's important to differentiate geographically as well when deploying this tactic. Communicate to your employees that you are all in this together, and do what you can to ensure that you really are—but again not at the expense of your long-term growth.

A fourth way to take control of the downturn is to maximize the cash available to you. Cash is always a good friend to have, especially during the tough times. While I wish I hadn't done the stock buyback right before the recession hit, we were still in a very good cash position at that time, and we did a great job of generating cash during the recession. This in turn afforded us a lot of flexibility, including the ability to make acquisitions. We had no issues with debt, bankers, or creditors because we had been conservative in our cash/debt planning. If you value your ability to get a better night's sleep during a recession, I highly recommend keeping cash on hand.

To Take Control of the Downturns . . .

- Anticipate them as best you can.
- Manage investors' expectations.
- Make sure other leaders are on board as best you can.
- Communicate openly and honestly with employees. You just don't know how bad it can be.
- Maximize your available cash.
- Prepare for recovery!

REAP WHAT YOU SOW

Recessions put leaders' commitment to a balanced, short- and long-term strategy to a profound test. It's far easier to lay the groundwork for future growth when sales are increasing than it is when they're declining. But you can still do it if you remain focused and disciplined on both the short and the long term, and you can build real long-term advantage if your competitors lack that focus. To be sure, attending to both the short and long term during a recession represents one of the hardest challenges a leader faces. As I warned future leaders of Honeywell in my 2011 postmortem, recessions are "an extremely unrewarding time to be the CEO," and by extension, any leader. "It will test all of your leadership capacity. You need to be resolute in your actions (even when you're not sure) and sympathetic in your communications. . . . If there is ever a time when the company needs you the most, this is it."[7]

As hard as it is to stay focused on both the short and long term, it becomes a lot easier if you've been doing that all along. Earlier, I likened cultivating intellectual rigor as a long-term investment that pays off during recessions in the form of better decisions. The truth is that most of your earlier efforts to pursue short- and long-term growth simultaneously also pay back dividends when times get tough. Because we had worked on our culture, our leaders felt moved to voluntarily go without bonuses, and employees suffered through their repeated furloughs without losing faith in our company. Because we had a stronger, higher quality corps of leaders on hand, our leaders were better able to communicate our message to employees, also sustaining morale. Because we had reformed our accounting practices, and in particular done away with distributor loading, we saw smaller sales drops than we otherwise would have. Because we had implemented the Honeywell Operating System, our productivity was higher than it would have been otherwise, which gave us more income to play with, reducing the pressure on us to undertake drastic layoffs.

All the steps you might take to deliver strong short- and long-term performance work together to help you grow in good times, and to shield you from the worst consequences in bad times. In that sense, wise leaders are always preparing for the next recession, even if they don't realize it. Strengthen your company from the inside out, position it for long-term growth while maintaining decent quarterly results, and your organization will weather even the fiercest economic storms. It worked for Honeywell, and it will work for your team or organization too.

QUESTIONS TO ASK YOURSELF

1. Are you paying enough attention to macroeconomic trends, or are you overly focused on the details of your business and industry? Are you talking to enough people outside your industry?
2. Do you heed early signs of bad economic times and take reasonable precautions, or are you content to listen to those who say, "This is no big deal"?
3. If storm clouds appear on the horizon, how might you prepare without dragging down quarterly results too much?
4. When times are tough, are you tempted to make cuts that impact your ability to deliver for customers or that undo the previous growth investments you've made?
5. If you've thought about layoffs, do other alternatives exist? What about furloughs?
6. In the midst of recession, are you planning for the recovery? What accommodations are you making with suppliers to ensure you can quickly ramp up to meet renewed demand?
7. Are you ruling by fiat when it comes to responding to the recession, or are you talking through dilemmas with other leaders and coming to difficult decisions together?
8. Are you setting investors' expectations in ways that give you enough wiggle room in case sales come in even worse than you expected?
9. Are you communicating openly and honestly enough with employees, helping them stay strong even when they're hurting?
10. When you've successfully dealt with hard times, are you taking enough time to reflect on and record what you've learned for posterity?

CHAPTER TEN

Manage the Leadership Transition

No matter how diligent you've been at investing for the future while delivering profits today, your accomplishments always remain fragile, never more so than when it's time for you to step down. Will your successors know how to follow your disciplined approach to management? Will unexpected problems knock your successor off track, despite his or her best intentions? Will tensions or uncertainty arise inside the organization during the succession and transition process, distracting your successor? These are not simply academic questions. Bungled leadership transitions are common in business. In fact, at the time of my retirement, sell-side analysts told me the mere specter of my departure was enough to ring alarm bells in their minds, since the industrial sector hadn't seen a successful CEO transition in twenty years. We were told our stock price was being discounted in anticipation of a failed transition.

These investors needn't have worried. In addition to doing everything I could to smooth the way for Darius, we had undergone an unusually intensive, decade-long process to select our new CEO. Starting with a larger field of potential candidates, we had narrowed down the field over time, settling on several finalists, and eventually selecting Darius. Then we had planned and executed a two-year transition of power. It might sound extreme to start plotting your departure a decade in advance, much less to stretch out the transition over two years, but thanks to this effort we didn't experience the confusion and infighting that so often damage companies during CEO transitions. Everyone in the organization was clear at all times about who was in charge, allowing them to stay focused on what mattered: delivering strong performance. During our transition, Darius and I developed a great working relationship that enabled me to support his efforts to make changes and to pass on valuable guidance and advice, and enabled him to prepare his own agenda in a thoughtful way (a relationship, I might add, that continues to this day). No transition will ever go perfectly, but ours was about as smooth as any we could have hoped for, putting Darius—and Honeywell—in a position to build upon what I had done and to continue to thrive.

If you care about driving long- and short-term performance, plot the hand-off early, deploying the same kind of independent thinking you've mustered all along in other parts of the business. As your retirement nears, devote much more time and attention to shepherding your successor into your role than leaders often do. It's the best way to ensure that all the investments you've made will not only pay off, but they will also benefit the company and its people for years or even decades to come.

IDENTIFY AND TEST CANDIDATES

Many leaders might agree intellectually that it's important to get an early start on succession planning, but when it comes to executing, they let it slide or put in a half-hearted effort, letting short-term challenges take priority. Who really wants to think about retirement anyway? I didn't, but I had seen too many organizations choose the wrong people to lead, and I was determined we would do better. My goal at Honeywell had always been to create a company that would perform well not only while I was there but for long afterward. In fact, I used to say I wanted to leave behind a three-part legacy. First, I wanted everyone associated with Honeywell during my tenure—investors, customers, employees, suppliers—to make a lot of money. Second, I wanted to create a deep bench of all-star leadership talent, leaders who were constantly being recruited for other jobs but who stayed at Honeywell because they loved their jobs and felt proud about the company. And third, I wanted to feel good about holding my Honeywell shares for ten years or more, because the company was thriving without me. This last piece meant that in addition to having the right people, processes, and portfolio in place, I had to be extraordinarily thoughtful and deliberate about choosing a successor.

In 2007, anticipating that I would probably want to retire about ten years later, when I was between the ages of sixty and sixty-five, my team and I started identifying potential internal successors. We looked for executives who were not only top performers and could potentially handle the CEO role, but who would be able to serve for ten or more years. In keeping with our emphasis on performing today *and* tomorrow, we didn't want my successor to leave after just a few years, since that wouldn't be long enough to make a profound difference for the organization. We looked at potential candidates who were about forty years old, bypassing a couple of extremely capable senior leaders who were roughly the same age as me.

Arriving at an initial list of about a dozen candidates, we spent the next several years giving them progressively bigger jobs to see how they performed. We didn't publicize our list of candidates, although we did discuss these promising leaders with our board's Management Development and Compensation Committee (MDCC) and with the full board in its annual review.[1] As time passed, we eliminated some of our initial dozen prospects from our list and added others. We asked one talented young leader to run a $4 billion business located in Switzerland to see how they did with it. Although we suggested that we were grooming this person for something bigger, they declined the job, perceiving it as too risky a career move. We eliminated that leader from our list—if they couldn't handle the risk inherent in that job assignment, they wouldn't succeed as CEO. In other cases, we eliminated people from consideration because they were slow to understand

---

1   Material in this paragraph comes from an internal and unpublished white paper we wrote about transitioning to Darius as CEO entitled "Honeywell's CEO Succession and Transition: Lessons Learned." I draw on the concepts and language in this white paper throughout this chapter to supplement my own memory of events.

their markets or were not aggressive enough in taking action. We also added a candidate who was not on our original list: Darius. As I mentioned, he joined the company in 2008 as part of our acquisition of the barcode scanning company Metrologic. Over the next four years, he had doubled the size of our Scanning and Mobility business, taking it to about $1.5 billion in revenues, and significantly increased profitability. He then did a great job transforming our $3.5 billion Process Solutions business.

CREATE A FORMAL SELECTION PROCESS

While we were watching these potential CEO candidates, I also thought more carefully about how best to run our formal selection process once we'd landed on a few finalists. Reading books and articles on the topic, I found I didn't like the strategies most experts advocated. Although these experts were enamored of the complex selection processes involved, the evidence suggesting that their strategies actually worked was scant. If a new CEO was fired after a couple of years or the company didn't perform well for a decade, how good could the supposedly "magnificent" process have been that selected the new CEO?

Some selection strategies I encountered seemed downright illogical. One school of thought held that leaders needed to contemplate the circumstances their companies would likely face in the future and pick successors accordingly. That seemed wrong, for the simple reason that *nobody* knows what the future holds. According to the literature, before Jack Welch became CEO of GE, McKinsey made four predictions about GE's future, and on that basis, Jack was selected. He performed well over a twenty-year stint, even though three out of four of those predictions never came to pass (and the fourth, the notion that technology would change faster than ever, was obvious to anyone with a heartbeat). What Welch's example suggested, I thought, was that being able to foretell the future mattered much less than the ability to develop and implement successful strategies as the future unfolded—the ability to figure it out regardless of what the future held. Since I had become

CEO of a Honeywell that was very different from what I had been told it was, that ability struck me as quite important indeed.

My research left me convinced that we at Honeywell had to design our own process for selecting a future leader. One book recommended by one of our directors that stuck with me was Joseph L. Bower's *The CEO Within*, which argued for choosing leaders inside the company to serve as CEO. According to Bower, you wanted a special kind of insider: someone who intimately understood the company and its operations, but who could also maintain a sense of distance and understand what about the company needed to change—an outsider's perspective from someone on the inside. That seemed exactly right. Although some on our board sought to consider external candidates in addition to the dozen we'd selected, I demurred. The way I saw it, we had invested a lot of effort developing leadership talent internally and would find it hard to find better candidates outside the organization.

To further help us design a strong succession process, I interviewed half a dozen or so prominent sitting or former CEOs, some who had engineered successful transitions for their successors and others who hadn't. From these conversations, I learned it was important to time the selection process carefully once we'd landed on a few finalists. We needed a process that was long enough that it allowed us to evaluate the finalists' performance but that was short enough to keep these candidates interested in the job—three years seemed about right. I also came away thinking that while a candidate's performance in his or her current job mattered, we needed to consider intangible qualities related to their character, intellect, and personalities. But what intangibles should we look for? Aside from raw problem-solving ability, I wasn't quite sure.

In 2013, Mark James, our head of Human Resources, and I drew up a list of possible leadership attributes we should seek in my successor and solicited input from Honeywell's board. The resulting list included about forty-five items and stretched out to a page and a half, single-spaced. We all felt good about it, but one night, while performing a blue book exercise, I realized we had gone too far. I could imagine us evaluating candidates on each element using a 5-point scale, with 5 the highest, and averaging their scores to arrive at a final rating. Since nobody would score perfectly on each element, we would wind up with final ratings that roughly fell in the same range. How insightful would it really be to find that out of three contenders, one had managed a 4.5 total rating out of a possible 5.0, while the other two had scored 4.4 and 4.2, respectively? This wasn't an Olympic figure-skating competition. We needed a way of analyzing candidates that allowed us to tease out clear, meaningful differences.

We decided to boil our list down to just a few key criteria around which we could easily evaluate candidates. We settled on six:

- **An intense desire to win:** We didn't want a new CEO who was adept at explaining why something didn't happen, but rather someone who could figure out how to win even if unanticipated problems cropped up.
- **Intelligence:** We wanted someone smart and analytical who could avoid problems before they arose.
- **The ability to think independently:** Fad surfers need not apply.
- **Courage:** My successor had to be capable of making bold decisions, while also checking afterward to verify that these decisions were correct.
- **Curiosity:** We needed a CEO who could stay fresh over time by exposing him or herself to novel ideas—someone who was self-aware and dedicated to learning.
- **An ability to motivate and build a strong culture:** Our next CEO had to be able to mobilize the company behind the strategy, hiring great people and motivating them.

VET YOUR FINALISTS

Applying these criteria, we arrived by 2014 at a list of finalists for the CEO job, including Darius. We never announced these leaders as our finalists but simply gave each of them a big "leap" job to see how they reacted. Giving them so much responsibility represented a risk on my part, but I wanted to see what they would do and how they would think, and that required giving them more rope in their decision-making. I mentored them all, meeting on a quarterly basis with them to gauge their decision-making ability. I remained steadfastly neutral and closed-mouth about our upcoming CEO succession, mindful that if I talked about the selection process in any way, shape, or form, others inside the organization would too, and the process would become a distraction or even devolve into hostility and backbiting between the candidates. When one of the finalists did a great job at something, I told them so, and when they didn't, they also heard about it. In general, I posed open-ended questions during our sessions, trying to understand how they were thinking about various elements of their businesses.

Darius became president and CEO of our $11 billion Performance Materials and Technologies (PMT) business—a big jump up given the size and complexity of the business he'd been running. From the beginning, he impressed me not merely by his hard work but by his ability to deal with unforeseen difficulties. Many of PMT's customers were in the oil and gas industry, which shortly after he took over was sunk into a severe recession, spurred by low oil prices, that was much worse than what the industry had seen during the Great Recession. Darius responded by cutting labor costs via furloughs and layoffs, running the business more efficiently, and performing well in other parts of his business not affected by the recession. He took cost-cutting and efficiency measures even though many managers and employees resisted. And ultimately, he made his numbers.

If our "leap" assignments were challenging, the finalists (who by this point knew they were being considered to succeed me, although I'd never said so directly) had no idea what they were in for. In late 2015, we asked each to prepare a strategic plan for the company and present it formally to our board in early February, with me present as well. We debated as a board if I should be there for it. I had planned not to attend so as not to influence the discussion, but as one director said, "If we can't count on them to say what they think with you there, what hope will we have that they will tell us what they think after you've left." Good point! If the candidates were trying to kiss up to me now, they would likely do the same with the board later. We

243

wanted a CEO confident and conscientious enough to say what they truly felt was best for the company.

Each finalist would have a financial analyst at their disposal to help research their plan, and each would have a vice chairman of ours advising them. The assignment was completely open-ended: the candidates could decide for themselves what topics they wanted to cover. I made it very clear to all the candidates that I would provide no input or direction, nor would I review a draft version of their plans in advance. As one board member, former US ambassador to the World Trade Organization Linnet Deily, said, "We wanted to see how their minds worked. How bold would they be? How reasonable would their ideas be?"[1] This assignment meant that our finalists would be working feverishly over the Christmas holiday to research and write their strategic plans. As Darius later recalled, he spent about fifty hours per week over a two-month period preparing for the presentation, in addition to doing his job, creating a 240-page document, as he understood how weighty it would be in the board's final decision. (He also recognized that he would never make it through 240 pages, so he also created a brief executive summary, which worked out great.)

All the presentations were terrific, but when we considered them in conjunction with our six criteria, Darius was the clear choice. In preparing for the presentation, a different candidate asked me multiple times for advice on how to proceed, eager for any insight into what other board members or I would find compelling. Not Darius: once I told him that he could shape his strategic plan in any way he wanted, he prepared on his own, a decision that suggested independent thinking on his part. He was also perceived inside the company as a hard-driving boss, which caused a fair amount of consternation, but I liked it and took it as an indication of his desire to be the "CEO within." He also had a unique perspective as a small-company veteran of Metrologic who thrived at Honeywell and mastered its big-company culture once his company was acquired.

During his "leap" assignment and beforehand, he had consistently shown courage and a drive to win. In one instance, he had recommended that Honeywell sell one of the businesses he was running—not typically what a high-potential leader does when gunning for a big job (they usually seek out more financial responsibility, not less). I had decided against the sale because we wouldn't get a great price, and we'd also see a lot of tax leakage. But Darius persisted, prompting me to think about the idea more seriously. We wound up spinning this business to shareholders so that there were no tax consequences. There was no hit to Honeywell's stock price, in effect creating $1.5 billion of value out of nothing. What we learned here helped a lot when under Darius's leadership Honeywell came to restructure its portfolio.

In the aftermath of these presentations, the board held two-hour interviews with each finalist. Then it came down to a vote, and the board unanimously selected Darius as our next CEO. To test whether we were making the right choice, we had engaged two consulting firms to give us their own independent recommendations as to whom we should select. During the run-up to the presentations, the firms had performed 360-degree assessments for the candidates and put them through intensive psychological testing. "I underwent extensive testing over six weekends," Darius recalled, "four weekends of personality testing, two weekends of cognitive testing. All of this testing was in addition to the intense preparations required for the business plan presentation. . . . It was one of the toughest periods of my life."

Companies should use external consultants sparingly if you wish to build a foundation of intellectual rigor; you want leaders inside the organization to learn how to handle big management tasks themselves. In this instance, we engaged consultants not to do our work for us but simply to provide validation that our own analysis was correct. Despite numerous requests, we provided the consultants with no input as to what we thought about the candidates. It turned out that we had chosen wisely: the consulting firms both came back arguing that we should appoint Darius our next CEO.[2]

---

2   When I told Darius we had selected him, he was shocked and said, "Remind me to never play poker with you. I had no idea." It was a testament to our ability to stay neutral during the process.

MANAGE THE TRANSITION

Now that we had selected our next CEO, we had to transition power to him in a way that would cause a minimum of disruption inside the organization and that would position him to thrive in the years ahead. Many companies and leaders favor quick transitions, and in situations where a company has been struggling, that approach might well prove best—you want to make a clean break with the past, and you don't want the old leader hanging around very long and getting in the way. But if a company has been successful, like we had, then a protracted transition has advantages. It gives the organization time to adapt to the new leader, and it reassures investors who might worry about a performance dip. A longer transition can also allow the incoming CEO to learn from the outgoing one. Of course, this will only happen if the outgoing leader is willing to let go and can sustain a healthy, helping relationship with his or her successor. The successor, meanwhile, must also feel secure enough to work collaboratively with the outgoing CEO. Both individuals must be able to set aside their own egos for the company's sake.

We settled on a two-year transition that I would help manage. During the first year, Darius came on as my COO and we ran the company together as a united front, operating out of adjacent offices. I bore responsibility for making our numbers, and he spent the first six months meeting with leaders across the company and learning about their businesses in greater depth than he had while writing the strategic plan (and yes, remembering my own experience, I gave him full access to all of our numbers). He also focused on assessing Honeywell's portfolio of business. I'd been able to take Honeywell from about $20 billion to about $120 billion in market capitalization over sixteen years, but for him to generate comparable results, he'd have to take the company from $120 billion to $600 billion. Thanks to the law of large numbers, that would prove a much more challenging and unlikely task. To achieve the best possible growth, he would have to be extremely shrewd in deciding which of our businesses he wanted to grow with and which would be better off spinning. During those first six months, Darius spent a great deal of time analyzing our business and soliciting my thinking (along with that of others) on a possible strategy.

During the second six months, Darius began to lead a range of formal meetings, including strategy reviews, operating plan reviews, growth days, operating days, and financial planning. Whereas during the first six months I had sat at the head of the conference table with Darius to one side, now we sat together at the head, and I made sure we came to decisions together and agreed on them. I wanted everyone in the organization to understand that he and I were working together, and that Darius was going to run Honeywell—I wouldn't make any decisions on my own, and he wouldn't make any decisions either without checking with me first. I stopped attending our strategic reviews and operating plan discussions entirely, although Darius and I did debrief and discuss after each presentation. I wanted leaders to have no doubt that they were making commitments to Darius, the incoming CEO, not to me. Otherwise they might have an excuse to backpedal later if they didn't meet their goals.

Darius also traveled with me to meetings with customers, to plant visits, and to meetings with political leaders. By "feathering in" Darius's responsibilities as CEO over the first year in this way, we allowed him to establish himself gradually as a leader, with me providing daily mentorship and support behind the scenes. We talked every day about his observations, proposed decisions, interactions with others—everything. I enjoyed these conversations immensely, feeling increasingly more certain that we had made the right decision in choosing Darius.

During the second year, Darius became CEO, and I remained on in a limited capacity as executive chairman. I continued to offer my thinking to Darius when he wanted it, while publicly and unconditionally affirming that he was in charge. I made it clear to our senior leaders that I wouldn't be reaching out to them as much, and that I would provide any input I had to Darius directly. I emptied my office, moving to the smaller one that Darius had previously occupied as COO—a symbolic statement about who was in charge. I told people that while I felt very proud of what we had accomplished under my tenure, our company wasn't perfect, and Honeywell had to continue to evolve under his leadership. In my final speech at our annual Strategic Leadership Meeting, I told leaders I didn't want anything at the company named after me because we had to keep the company looking forward, not backward.

THINK ABOUT THE COMPANY, NOT YOUR EGO

Initially, Darius felt uncertain about a two-year transition. He didn't need handholding—he had been a CEO before and had been highly successful running large businesses. Also, he wasn't quite sure how a partnership with me would work. "One of my concerns," he remembered, "was if Dave was really going to want to take a half a step back and let me do some things. Was he really going to take time to explain things to me, let me make decisions, and empower me enough to have some influence over the company during the transition? The last thing I wanted to be was a puppet head, with Dave calling all the shots."[2]

Our arrangement did work because both of us approached the transition with the right mind-set. I was open to having him as a partner—I was ready to depart, as I've said, and was happy to transfer decision-making over to him and to work with him as a partner as opposed to a boss-subordinate relationship. I *expected* Darius to make his own decisions, because I was aware that he had a different perspective and would spot opportunities and threats I had missed or elements of the business that just needed to change.

Observing our great track record, some wanted everything at Honeywell to stay the same, but as I told anyone who would listen (investors, employees, staff, directors), I wasn't leaving Darius a perfect company. By every measure, Honeywell was a lot better than I'd found it, but it could also be a lot better than how I was leaving it. If the company was to thrive, we needed to continue to change and move forward, and Darius had to make it happen, not me. On a personal level, I also felt deeply invested in his success, and I was eager to share any knowledge or insight I had that might help him.

For his part, Darius was eager to learn, even as he began to lay out his own agenda and assert his authority. He never felt threatened by asking for or accepting my help—never felt like he had to do it all himself. Ultimately, we both were able to put our egos aside for the company's sake, which allowed us to function well as a team and build trust over the course of the transition. Others in the organization saw that we were united, and as a result experienced the transition as a process that unfolded naturally, rather than as an abrupt and worrisome shift.

LEAVE THE PLACE CLEAN

A final strategy to deploy to shepherd your organization smoothly through a leadership transition is to put your house in order, so to speak, during your final months so that your successor won't face unpleasant surprises upon taking over. Part of doing this entails dealing promptly with new problems that emerge so that your successor doesn't have to. In 2016, when I was preparing to step down as CEO, we spotted a problem with our company's popular work-at-home policies. We were planning to develop new office space, and our real estate team was calculating how many employees required offices at specific sites around our company. It turned out we didn't need as many offices at some of our locations as we thought given the number of employees. Darius, who was then serving as our COO, suspected this owed to a proportion of our employees working remotely. We asked the team to perform an analysis and discovered that about 5,000 of our 135,000 employees at the time were working from home.

That number might not sound excessive, but Darius and I felt it was. We had always intended our work-at-home policy to be a way to help employees grapple with temporary hardships, like a sick parent or child. In general, we felt it was important for employees to interact with one another in person, and like many companies, we had redesigned our offices to facilitate spontaneous encounters. I asked our team to identify every employee working from home and evaluate whether he or she truly needed to do so. We discovered that about 80 percent of the employees who worked from home did so in violation of our policy's spirit. Too many managers had acquiesced to employee requests to work from home, in some cases because they didn't feel they could or should say no.

Some of our senior leaders were okay with a good chunk of our people working remotely. Younger generations of employees liked it, they argued, and if we tightened up our policy, we would look old-fashioned. Darius and I disagreed. Employees who worked remotely were less productive, and over time their 130,000 colleagues who did bother to trek into the office each day would come to resent those who didn't. Darius and I decided we needed to make a change.

I could have pushed action off into the future, leaving it to Darius to crack down on the issue after my retirement. I would have come off looking great to employees, and he would have been the bad guy. But as outgoing CEO, I wanted Darius to get off to a good start in the top job, focusing his energies on growth and other vital issues rather than managing employee discontent. I also believed that since the problem had occurred on my watch, I needed to fix it. So, in October 2016, I announced changes in our policies that would drastically reduce the number of employees eligible to work remotely, explaining why we felt it was so important for employees to come into the office. From now on, I said, every new request to work remotely would require the approval of our global head of HR. Employees who had worked from home disliked these changes, but at least Darius wouldn't face an unpleasant reaction during his first months on the job. Interestingly, contrary to what some senior leaders thought, we experienced minimal attrition and no discernible impact on hiring as a result of the change.

Aside from changing our work-at-home policy, we timed Darius's transition so that he would show strong financial results right away. According to our five-year plan, we were due to take a $500 million expense hit (about 50 cents per share) in 2016, thanks to concessions we'd paid in order to land big contracts in our Aerospace business. Consistent with our conservative accounting practices, none of this expense would go on the balance sheet. Afterward, profits were projected to soar as we reaped the fruits of investments made years earlier. Instead of timing Darius's transition to CEO so that he got hit with the $500 million charge, I stayed on through 2016, taking the hit myself and priming him to perform well during his first full year on the job.

During my final year or so at Honeywell, I also took some added financial hits with an eye toward leaving Darius in a better place when he took over in 2017. In 2015 and 2016, our businesses had felt the impact of a recession in the industrial sector. The third quarter of 2016 was especially difficult for us. I could have pushed the businesses hard to make our numbers but instead missed consensus by 2 cents on $1.60 in earnings per share to position Darius better in subsequent years (although we did fall to the bottom end of the range and recorded 25 cents in additional restructuring). I didn't want to shortchange restructuring efforts, for instance, that would bolster our future performance. In the fourth quarter of 2016, I refinanced a bunch of Honeywell debt, taking a big expense. That made me look bad to investors, but since I had already built up a strong record with investors I knew it wouldn't damage my reputation very much. Meanwhile, it would gave Darius an easier time of it, as it would lower our interest expense in 2017, 2018, and beyond. If Darius came in and had to deal with financial issues right away, investors would question whether the new guy could really perform, or if the company was in rough shape, indicating a weak transition. Better for me to take the hit.

I knew what it felt like to encounter big, unexpected messes when first becoming CEO—it wasn't fun. After what I'd experienced upon joining Honeywell, I had promised myself that whatever happened, I wouldn't leave my successor in a similar position. By leaving my company in a "clean" state, I'd enable him or her to focus on long-term growth from the very first day rather than on putting out fires. He or she would have a far greater chance of generating outstanding short- and long-term performance. Of course, I am not suggesting that Darius didn't have to do much to achieve outstanding financial results. Clearly, he has worked hard and accomplished a lot. But at least he didn't have to deal with the kinds of time bombs that had greeted me upon first becoming CEO.

SUCCESSION: A VITAL PART OF STRATEGY

As tempting as it might be to procrastinate when it comes to succession, don't do it. The more you look at your business from both the short- and long-term perspectives, the more you realize that arranging for your successor isn't something outside the daily work of running your business—it's a vital part of your strategy and an outgrowth of the efforts you should be making all along to cultivate a strong leadership corps (chapter 6). If you don't plan successions well throughout your team or organization, chances are you won't do it well at the top level either.

As Darius told me in late 2018, less than two years into his tenure, he was already beginning to identify and develop potential leaders who could one day succeed him. "It's always your job [as a leader] to do that," he said. "If I don't have anybody to replace me, then I'm not doing a great job." Look closely at your slate of potential successors. How might you test them to learn their true capabilities? Keep the whole process as low-key as possible, recognizing that the more you talk about it, the more others will too. If you don't have many good candidates from which to choose, then look outside the organization, but also review your leadership corps and the succession-planning process you deploy. Maybe they're not as strong as you think. Don't string out the selection process for too long either, or you'll risk losing your top prospects. As Darius recalled, he was prepared to go elsewhere if the process didn't resolve in a timely way. "I've always wanted a top job, and if this would have dragged on for years, I probably would not have waited."[3]

BUILD A WINNING RELATIONSHIP WITH YOUR SUCCESSOR

No matter what you decide, hold ongoing conversations with your successor about elements of the business that need to change and elements that can stay the same. In mentoring leaders, I've found there is a tendency to focus on what's wrong with the existing business, but that's not the most thoughtful way of looking at it. In any business, there are almost always ways to build on what your predecessor built, even as you recognize the importance of change. As an outgoing leader, sharing your objective and frank assessment of the business can help your successor devise smart, thoughtful strategies (and be sure to listen, too, to what your successor thinks needs to change).

If you're stepping into a leadership role, seek out such conversations. Even if you're taking over a failing team or organization, there's nothing wrong with reaching out to a predecessor to get his or her rough impressions of the organization and its challenges. If your predecessor was successful, then you'll want to devote much more time to gleaning his or her views. If you don't have the luxury of a two-year transition, try to engage with your predecessor informally as a potential mentor.

As you embark on a longer transition with a successor, lay the ground rules for open and honest communication early. Darius and I both agreed that we would tell the other of any important conversations each of us had with board members or others, and that we would come to one another if we didn't understand something the other of us was purported to have said or done. This open line of communication served us well, allowing us on a couple of occasions to avoid misunderstandings and the tensions that might have otherwise arisen. We also jointly established that it was okay for the two of us to disagree—it wouldn't break our relationship. "Neither of us got emotional," Darius recalled, "because the other might have a different point of view. We just decided that two reasonable people can disagree from time to time, and that's normal."[4] Of course, it's vital to keep any disagreements between you private. Otherwise, you open the way for others to pit you against each other in an attempt to work the system. In any case, I always made it clear that the decisions now were Darius's to make, not mine.

Despite laying the groundwork for a strong relationship, you might find that you and your successor still aren't working very well together. Consider how you're behaving to make sure you're not the source of the problem. If you ask your successor to keep you apprised of any conversations he or she is having with board members or other leaders, but you fail to do the same, then no wonder the relationship is breaking down. On the other hand, if after an honest evaluation you believe your successor is causing the problem, then the two of you must have a frank conversation about how to improve your working relationship. If despite your best efforts you still can't make it work, then you should question whether the organization has really selected the right person to succeed you. Perhaps it hasn't.

BRING THE BOARD INTO IT

Throughout the lengthy process of selecting and transitioning to a new leader, involve your board. During the selection phase, help board members get to know prospective candidates (my entire staff attended all board meetings), and give them the opportunity to see the finalists in action, as we did in board meetings with our strategic plan presentations. The board clearly has to make the decision, but it would be a mistake for any CEO (assuming they have been successful) to feel that they are just another vote in that decision. Directors only get to see the candidates eight or nine times a year. The CEO deals with them every day, so he or she is critical to the selection process. That said, don't take too heavy a hand in ensuring that your favorite gets picked as your successor. After our finalists gave their presentations, our board spent time deliberating. When a fellow member asked my opinion, I didn't hesitate to tell them I wanted Darius. But I also insisted on holding a director-by-director vote instead of a group vote. I wanted us to come to what I perceived to be the right decision, but I also wanted to feel sure that board members owned the decision and didn't feel imposed upon by me. As it turned out, as I mentioned, they all independently came to same conclusion that our external consultants and I did: Darius was our guy.

During the transition itself, the incoming leader will usually have to start from scratch and build credibility with the board. But board members need to give incoming leaders the freedom to do that. Sometimes board members regard leadership transitions as opportunities to push forward pet strategies of theirs that the outgoing leader hadn't pursued. Board members become overly assertive, telling the new leader how to do his or her job. New leaders start second-guessing themselves, looking over their shoulders and worrying excessively about what board members think. Leaders and board members alike must be thoughtful about their role and keep the organization's best interests in mind so as not to overreach.

To ensure that you're handing over the best possible team or organization to your successor, sit down with your blue book and brainstorm unpleasant tasks your successor might have to handle. Consider how many of these problems you might be able to solve before you leave. If you find yourself shrinking back from this work, unhappy with how it might make you look as a leader, then you need to check yourself and your priorities. A great leader puts the organization first.

A VALENTINE'S DAY SURPRISE

On February 14, 2017, about six weeks before I was set to retire as CEO, an activist investor, the hedge fund Third Point Management, sent Darius a letter advising him to spin off our entire Aerospace business. At many companies, such a move would set off alarm bells, triggering fears of conflict to come and perhaps an impending takeover. We saw it differently: if this investor had a good idea for increasing value, we were eager to hear it. After all, we had the same goal as Third Point: to increase Honeywell's stock price.

We met with Third Point and heard out the team's thinking about why spinning off Aerospace would be a good idea. The discussion wasn't acrimonious: they respected the performance we'd achieved in recent years, and we respected their business acumen. But because Darius had done so much work analyzing our portfolio, we had well-developed ideas of our own. We weren't going to spin off Aerospace, but instead we decided to spin out part of our Homes and Buildings Technologies business as well as our Turbocharger business. As Darius explained, we had invested a great deal in our Aerospace business and expected it to grow quite well for us. Meanwhile, divesting ourselves of these other two businesses would allow them to grow more quickly than if we operated them as a combined business. We had run financial analyses, spoken to leaders of these businesses, and consulted with investment bankers. Although I had been involved all along, Darius had taken the lead.

His logic won over the community of Honeywell investors, who supported our plan over Third Point's. Good thing, because our plan succeeded, sending our share price soaring 32 percent in the twelve months beginning January 1, 2017 (shortly before the Third Point episode). By comparison, the S&P 500 notched only a 19 percent gain during that period. Everyone won, including Third Point. Meanwhile, the presence of an activist drew other investors to take a closer look at our stock, pushing our price even higher than it would otherwise have been. Investors saw how capable Darius was and that this would not be another industrial transition that misfired. The episode was a turning point for us, the moment when it became clear to our organization that our transition was over and Darius was firmly in charge. He showed strong leadership, never wilting under pressure from Third Point. He wasn't too proud to consult with me and involve me in meetings, and as a result could draw on my knowledge and experience to supplement his own. All told, it became clear to me and to everyone that we had definitely picked the right person.

Darius has continued to do an excellent job leading Honeywell, showing himself to be every bit as smart, disciplined, decisive, and independent-minded as we'd supposed. During his first two years as CEO, Honeywell's stock has provided a total shareholder return of 55 percent, as compared with 32 percent for the S&P 500.[5] All the time and effort we put into selecting him and then getting him off to a strong start has been worth it.

During my last investor day meeting in 2017, after explaining the process by which we had chosen Darius and saying farewell, the audience of about 150 people gave me a standing ovation. This response was highly unusual—nobody present could remember it ever happening before at such a meeting. The truth is, we never would have selected Darius had we not opened ourselves up to such a lengthy and rigorous selection process. As I've mentioned, he wasn't on our initial list of contenders. Once we added him to the list, he was by no means the favorite from among our finalists. Yet we'd given ourselves enough time to really test our finalists and see what they could do. In the end, Darius distinguished himself as the clear choice. Once we'd selected him, we gave him the time, space, and mentoring he needed to lead strong growth at Honeywell right from the beginning. Further, we gave the organization and investors sufficient time to get used to the new CEO and embrace him.

If it sounds like I'm pretty proud of our process, well, I am. And I'm proud of Darius too. A native of Poland, he came to the United States at age eleven knowing no English and wound up receiving degrees in electrical and computer engineering from Michigan State University, a degree in computer engineering from Syracuse University, and an MBA from Harvard. Having led a small company (Metrologic), he understands how both large and small companies operate, and will thus help us operate with small-company speed and big-company efficiency. Most of all he's an independent thinker who not only understands how Honeywell works but how it *ought* to work. In every sense of the word, he truly is the "CEO within."

I didn't do everything right at Honeywell, but when it comes to Darius and how the company has fared after my exit, I must say I feel pretty damn good. Will I agree with every decision Darius makes? Probably not. But will I feel excited about holding Honeywell stock for the next decade or longer under his leadership? Absolutely.

QUESTIONS TO ASK YOURSELF

1. Are you thinking about who will succeed you, or have you pushed this analysis off to some nebulous future time?
2. If you're early in your tenure, have you compiled a lengthier list of potential successors to watch and develop? How will your organization run its selection process when you get closer to retirement?
3. Are you considering internal candidates carefully enough, or looking exclusively to candidates from outside?
4. Is succession planning through the organization truly good, or is it just a bunch of forms and processes driven by HR?

5. Are you thinking independently about the selection process, or simply assuming that a consultant or the board will take care of it?

6. What key qualities should your team or organization's next leader have?

7. Have you thought about giving "leap" assignments to potential successors to see how they perform? Are you giving them sufficient latitude to make decisions so that you can see how they really think?

8. How are you engaging your board in the selection process?

9. Given your team or organization's current performance, would a shorter or longer transition to the successor make sense? How might you organize it to obtain the best results?

10. What outstanding problems or issues might you handle before turning over power to your successor?

Epilogue

I've told many stories about Honeywell in this book, but there's a relevant one from my personal life I haven't yet shared. When I graduated from high school in 1970, I was lazy, immature, and directionless—anxious to get going in life, whatever that meant, but lacking any idea where. I was admitted to the University of New Hampshire, but initially declined to go, opting instead to work at my father's garage and afterward with my uncle in Michigan as a carpenter. None of that worked out, so the following year I enrolled at the university, having begged the administrators to let me back in without reapplying. I showed my gratitude by spending most of my time over the next couple of years drinking, smoking, and playing cards instead of going to class. At the end of my sophomore year, the assistant dean of students hauled me into her office to explain that they wouldn't allow me to live on campus any longer. It wasn't any particular thing I'd done wrong. Rather, she said, I was a general troublemaker. Wherever I went, trouble followed.

The next year, as I continued with my studies, I took a night job running a punch press at the General Electric plant in Hooksett, New Hampshire. A friend and I also bought a thirty-three foot, seventeen-year-old fishing boat, intending to start our own business as commercial fishermen in York Harbor, Maine. It was a lot to handle, and something had to give. Guess what it was? During the second semester of my junior year, I stopped attending classes entirely and earned a 1.8 grade point average. I quit a second time, determined to become filthy rich as a fisherman while working nights at General Electric. Fishing was a lot more fun than sitting in class. My buddy's dad said we had more empty beer cans in our boat than any other boat in the harbor. What we couldn't do very well was actually catch fish. So six months later, when my buddy got married, his wife asked him, "You're not going to keep fishing with that idiot friend of yours, are you?" He wasn't.

After we sold the boat, I wasn't sure what to do. Marrying my girlfriend seemed as good an idea as any. It was April of 1975, and we were living in a third-floor, unheated, uninsulated apartment, taking it a day at a time with no plans for the future. We both had jobs, so supporting ourselves seemed no problem. And then, a month after our wedding, my wife told me that she was pregnant, despite being on the pill. A couple of months after that, she told me she couldn't work any longer because of the pregnancy. It was on me to provide for the three of us.

I was terrified. We had only $100 in the bank. When I sat down and did the math, I learned that we were spending $2 more each week than my job paid. In less than a year, assuming we stuck to a bare-bones budget, we would go broke, if we didn't freeze first. If you've never been to New Hampshire in the winter, it's cold. In our apartment, the only heat came in from the units below us and a blower off the gas stove. I lay awake at night tossing and turning, fearing that my kid, who would be born the following February, would die because I was a screw-off and couldn't provide for my family.

I had to get serious about my life—our survival depended on it. I needed a better paying job, and that meant I would have to finish college and get my degree. So I did that, attending college during the day while continuing to work nights at General Electric. Overnight my entire life changed. I quit smoking cigarettes and started exercising. I became more diligent as an employee. I stopped wasting my suddenly scarce time. If I was going to succeed, I had to focus. At the beginning of every semester, I mapped out my schedule in advance, determining precisely which days and hours of the day I would study and write papers. Whereas previously I had been late with my assignments, I began getting them done early—sometimes six weeks before the due date. Previously, I had a 3.1 grade point average, including that one semester when I'd earned a 1.8. Now I was getting straight As.

My son, Ryan, was born on February 24, 1976. I still remember sealing the window cracks with masking tape to reduce the draft, looking at him bundled up against the cold in his crib, and fearing I'd never be able to take care of him. It was all the motivation I needed to continue working my butt off. I graduated college in May 1976. About six weeks later, I applied for and received my first salaried job, as an internal auditor at the General Electric Aircraft Engines business in Lynn, Massachusetts. I was on my way, and I've been working my butt off ever since.

As we've seen, winning today and tomorrow requires extraordinary effort and commitment on the part of leaders, teams, and organizations. I share my story of how I got my life together to illustrate a simple but under-appreciated fact: individuals and groups can push themselves much further than they think. So many teams and organizations produce disappointing short- or long-term results because they don't know how to operate differently than they have, but also because they don't think they *can* operate differently. You have it in you as a leader to push your people to do two seemingly conflicting things at the same time, and your people have it in them to deliver, so long as you provide diligent encouragement, guidance, and oversight along the way, while also making sure you have the right people in the right positions. When providing guidance, try to do more than just saying, "Do better." Provide some thought starters or suggestions that can mobilize your people to think differently about the issues at hand.

DO THE SEEMINGLY IMPOSSIBLE

Again and again I've seen what people and organizations can do when pushed. When I took over GE's silicones business in 1994 (chapter 3), I inherited a business that had consistently underperformed over the prior decade. Three out of the previous four general managers had been fired. Sales were stuck at about $500 million in an industry that was growing at

5 percent annually, and the business was routinely missing its financial commitments. The physical plant was a complete mess—essentially, a hazardous waste dump site. When my boss introduced me to the team there, he casually asked the environmental leader how the fire at the site's underground landfill was going. The environmental leader responded that it was fine. I asked how long the fire had been raging, and he said about four months. I thought it was a joke. It wasn't. It would take us four more months to put that fire out.

A few weeks into my tenure, at the end of a two-day group meeting of about two hundred people, I delivered a passionate, stem-winder of a speech proclaiming that our performance totally sucked and that we could only fix it if we owned up to it. I did so because at the end of the first day a union leader had approached me and said, "Dave, I don't know why you're saying there's an issue here. It sounds like everything is great." He was right. In an attempt to sound motivational, every speaker so far had talked about how well the business was running. We hadn't dealt with reality at all. In my speech, I made clear what kind of performance I expected, and that we would fire anyone who didn't want to contribute. Although my staff panicked, a couple dozen lower-level employees came up to me afterward and thanked me for intervening. "We know there's a problem here," they said, "and we want to have jobs well into the future. We have to fix this. We want to help." I hadn't expected that, and it taught me a valuable lesson: often it isn't frontline staff who impede great performance; it's the leaders.

In fact, at that same meeting, our manufacturing leader came up to me to say that we'd have to shut down production of a chemical called siloxane because of a problem with an air permit. That was devastating. Siloxane was required for all of the chemical processes in the plant, and without it we'd have to shut down our production entirely. I was furious. Acting on impulse, I told this leader flat-out that I wouldn't accept shutting down production. He would have to convene with the environmental leader and the technology leader, and I wanted a different answer by 5:00 P.M. the next day as to how we would handle this problem.

The next morning as I drove in, I was in a foul mood, grousing about how I'd have to tell my boss about our production shutdown. Arriving at

7:30 A.M., I was promptly met by the manufacturing leader, who seemed in good spirits. He told me that he and the others had met for a couple of hours the previous evening and figured out a way to resolve the permit issue, keep siloxane production going, and save $100,000 per year. I was shocked and delighted. "Why didn't you do that in the first place?" I asked.

"Well," he said, "nobody ever asked us to before."

I kept pushing like this, refusing to accept the usual solutions and excuses. Over the next few years, we improved our new product pipeline, developed a high-performance mentality among the workforce, expanded globally, and upgraded our talent pool at all levels. Sales doubled, and profits more than doubled. We became a huge success story within GE—all because we had expanded our sense of our own potential and were pushing ourselves relentlessly to reach it.

BE RELENTLESS

At Honeywell, rather than throw up our hands, make excuses, and assume that the way we've always done it is the only or best way, we challenged ourselves to remake our organization and our culture top to bottom so that we could accomplish two conflicting things at the same time. We followed through relentlessly to make sure we actually executed, giving teams the tools they needed to succeed. Our turnaround wasn't easy. Think back to our Three Principles of Short- and Long-term Performance—scrub accounting and business practices to what's real; invest in the future but not at the expense of acceptable short-term returns; and grow while keeping fixed costs constant to generate flexibility. Think, too, of the many specific changes we made:

- Requiring managers to perform substantive appraisals of employees and no longer delegate that task to employees themselves.
- Changing compensation policies so that they're fairer and better tied to actual performance and long-term support.

- Developing robust succession plans.
- Making strategic planning real.
- Developing rigorous metrics company-wide related to customer delivery and quality.
- Scrubbing the financials to eliminate all bookkeeping gains, one-time "specials," and distributor loading.
- Changing our acquisition and divestiture policies and realigning our portfolio.
- Driving a One Honeywell culture.
- Implementing numerous process improvements, especially the Honeywell Operating System.
- Creating and pursuing a range of growth initiatives.
- Addressing legacy issues strategically and in a financially sound way.
- Responding to the recession with an eye toward the subsequent recovery.
- Implementing a highly successful CEO transition.

Advancing the three principles and making these specific changes aroused considerable resistance within our organization. Even if some people liked a new idea or direction, they still wondered how they could pull it off while continuing to perform their existing jobs. My staff and I had to meet that resistance head-on, pushing the organization and ourselves beyond what we thought was possible. Only when leaders push like that do we really make progress and win both today and tomorrow. Of course, it's possible to take performance expectations too far. You don't need to be a twit in articulating these expectations, and you shouldn't ask people to do the truly impossible. But you do need to request the *seemingly* impossible, putting it to them in a kindly way and even with a sense of humor. It is possible to overdo it, as I have on occasion. On balance, though, organizations, people, and leaders would do well to be much more demanding of themselves than they are. Whatever you do, stay hungry. Investors often asked us what would cause us to miss our numbers, thinking I would name some industry or economic issue, but I always gave the same answer: "If we ever lose our hunger." That hunger starts with the leader.

Toward the end of my Honeywell career, investors also asked me why we were performing so well versus our peers. As I always told them, it wasn't because of what we were doing then, but rather because of the seed planting we had done five years earlier. Create that virtuous cycle in which you generate short-term actions sufficient to satisfy investors while still supporting long-term investments. If you do, you'll find that over time the short-term results will begin to take care of themselves. You'll also find that the company will do a lot of good for everyone, not just investors. Employees and communities have benefitted immensely from the approach we've taken at Honeywell. Not only have we created 2,500 401(k) millionaires, but we have contributed billions to our pension plan to ensure that employees' futures will be secure. We have also invested $3.5 billion to remediate all of our environmental issues and retooled the company to operate much more sustainably.

Scan back through the chapters in this book and determine some high-priority areas on which to focus. Dedicate resources to obtaining the results you need. Measure performance in these areas rigorously and objectively. Attend at all times to the quality of discourse in your team or organization, running meetings to get a full hearing of facts and opinions.

Work, too, on the quality of your own thinking. Carve out the time you need for blue book sessions, and make use of the other techniques I've described. Challenge yourself to reflect on your business or organization. And challenge yourself to think independently. Remember, smart leaders abound, but leaders who can think independently are rare. Ignore people around you who demand that you devote all of your energy and resources to "making the quarter" and who advise pushing concern for the future off to another day. Ignore, too, those who, in their zeal to escape from short-termism, argue the opposite: that you have to sacrifice short-term results to invest in the future and perform well over the long term. You really don't. It's entirely possible, and in fact necessary, to achieve two seemingly conflicting things at the same time. Be that kind of leader. It all starts with you.

Acknowledgments

I've often been asked who my primary source was for leadership lessons, and my response has always been the same, my mom and dad. While they only had eighth grade educations—my mom did eventually receive her high school diploma by going to night school once I was in college—they also had a wealth of knowledge about the values their kids should live by.

There were eight of us in a small six-room house . . . with one bathroom. I was the first to graduate from high school. Throughout my youth and young adult years, my parents strongly reinforced the importance of working hard, taking care of your family, and thinking for yourself. Thinking independently is much rarer than being smart, and they both constantly talked about the need to work hard to be a leader and not a follower. My Dad used to say that if every man just took care of his own family, the world would be a much better place.

I was blessed to have been raised in a good family that focused on the values necessary for a rewarding life. We had our faults and mistakes, all families do, but the good far outweighed any issues. My own family has been a tremendous source of focus and joy for me. Yes, I have made my own share of mistakes, but somehow it mostly worked out.

Two sons, eight grandchildren, and my wife, Maureen, continue to be a source of inspiration.

During the course of my life, I've been fortunate to have some really good friends and relationships. This book likely wouldn't have happened without the encouragement I received from Hank Paulson and Barack Obama. The fact they both felt I had something worth writing about make a big difference.

There also would be no story to support this book without the magnificent performance of all the people of Honeywell. Several are mentioned by name, and there are tens of thousands more who did the right things every day to support our customers and investors. All our performance on our Five Initiatives—Growth, Productivity, Cash, People, and the Enablers—happened because they made it happen. Leadership creates the right environment and direction for excellence to flourish, but it doesn't actually happen unless the people working there engage and make it happen. I can't thank the people of Honeywell enough for what they did to make the story possible. A very special mention goes to my successor, Darius Adamczyk, who continues leading the magnificent performance that customers and investors have come to expect from Honeywell.

I wrote a version of this book myself first and submitted it to my agent, Jim Levine, for consideration. Jim kindly said it had great content but would never sell because it was a memoir and I wasn't famous enough. It needed to be repackaged. I agreed with him on his fame assessment, but it was about what we did at Honeywell, not what I did in sixth grade. Jim said that's still a memoir. After several failed attempts to address his point, I finally asked for a ghost writer recommendation, and he introduced me to Seth Schulman. What a difference Seth made! It was still a lot of work, but Seth just thought differently about things. We spent long hours on the phone, going back and forth as Seth quizzed me about what points I wanted to get across, what I thought the theme should be, what were the anecdotes that supported a particular point, etc. And that was all before the writing even began! Then it was review after review, chapter by chapter, and then for the book in total. He made me work hard, and all that effort was worth it, because I'm really proud of the book and believe it will be as helpful twenty years from now as it is today. For sure, this book wouldn't be anywhere near as good if it hadn't been for Seth. Thank you, Jim, for all your guidance, and thank you, Seth, for all your hard work. It's a much better book than the first one I wrote because of the both of you.

ACKNOWLEDGMENTS

The team required to pull a book together, I've learned, makes a huge difference to its success. Jim and Seth made a big difference. It also wouldn't have happened without the wonderful support and guidance of Harper Collins Leadership, especially Sara Kendrick and Sicily Axton. I can't thank them enough for being with me very early on, helping with my innumerable questions about the publishing process. Our publicist, Mark Fortier, and our speaking engagements leader, David Lavin, provided great support to get the story out there. Mary Ellen Keating was a big help early on to point me in the right direction and introduce me to Jim.

Writing and publishing a book was not the most pleasant process. However, the result has been incredibly rewarding. It caused me to think more deeply about how much family, friends, and good business associates have made a difference in my life.

I hope you like the book and that it helps you in your own careers.

Enjoy!

Notes

Introduction

1. "Measuring the Economic Impact of Short-Termism," McKinsey Global Institute (February 2017): 1, 2, 4, https://www.mckinsey.com/~/media /mckinsey/featured%20insights/Long%20term%20Capitalism/Where %20companies%20with%20a%20long%20term%20view%20outperform %20their%20peers/MGI-Measuring-the-economic-impact-of-short -termism.ashx.
2. Dennis Carey et al., "Why CEOs Should Push Back Against Short-Termism," *Harvard Business Review*, May 31, 2018, https://hbr.org/2018/05 /why-ceos-should-push-back-against-short-termism.

Chapter 1: Banish Intellectual Laziness

1. Tim Mahoney (senior vice president of enterprise transformation at Honeywell), interview with author, November 12, 2018.
2. The quote originally appeared in his *Lettres Provinciales*; Tania Lombrozo, "This Could Have Been Shorter," National Public Radio, February 3, 2014, https://www.npr.org/sections/13.7/2014/02/03/270680304/this-could-have -been-shorter.
3. Kate Adams (senior vice president and general counsel at Apple), interview with author, November 16, 2018.

Chapter 2: Plan for Today *and* Tomorrow

1. Roger Fradin (former Pittway president and longtime Honeywell executive), interview with author, October 24, 2018.

Chapter 3: Resolve Serious Threats to the Business

1. "Honeywell: Downgrading on Environmental Uncertainty," analyst report, JP Morgan, North America Equity Research, April 27, 2006.

2. Quoted in Maria Newman, "Court Orders Honeywell to Clean Up 34-Acre Site," *New York Times*, May 17, 2003, https://www.nytimes.com/2003/05/17/nyregion/court-orders-honeywell-to-clean-up-34-acre-site.html.

3. "Lakeside Toxic Tombs," *Post-Standard* [Syracuse, NY], November 26, 2003; Amanda J. Crawford, "Honeywell Sued on Toxic Fuel Test Facility Releases at Issue for Arizona," *Arizona Republic*, July 10, 2004.

4. Victoria Streitfeld, "Former Honeywell Manufacturing Site Becomes National Brownfield Model," *Honeywell*, March 18, 2015, https://www.honeywell.com/en-us/newsroom/news/2015/03/former-honeywell-manufacturing-site-becomes-national-brownfield-model

5. Timothy B. Wheeler and the *Baltimore Sun*, "Dundalk Port Cleanup Plan Set," *Baltimore Sun*, September 23, 2012, https://www.baltimoresun.com/news/environment/bs-gr-port-chromium-cleanup-20120923-story.html.

6. Honeywell promotional video, untitled and unpublished.

7. "Honeywell: Upgrading to Neutral," JP Morgan, North American Equity Research, January 11, 2008.

8. Evan van Hook (vice president of Health, Safety, Environment, Product Stewardship & Sustainability at Honeywell), interview with author, October 26, 2018.

9. For more on this time, please see Donald H. Thompson, *The Golden Age of Onondaga Lake Resorts* (Fleischmanns, New York: Purple Mountain Press, 2002).

10. Rick Moriarty, "When Onondaga Lake Crackled with Dancing and Rides: A Search for Our Lost Resorts," Syracuse.com, updated March 22, 2019, https://www.syracuse.com/empire/2015/07/a_search_for_the_lost_resorts_of_onondaga_lake.html.

11. Catie O'Toole, "Onondaga Lake Cleanup Continues; Next Up: Dredging, Capping Contaminated Lake Bottom," Syracuse.com, updated March 22, 2019, https://www.syracuse.com/news/index.ssf/2012/03/onondaga_lake_cleanup_continue.html.

12. "Onondaga Lake Superfund Site," Atlantic States Legal Foundation, accessed October 10, 2019, http://onondagalake.org/Sitedescription/OnondagaLakeBottomSediments/docs/Onondagalake_asFS1Aand%201B_ver%203.pdf.

13. S. W. Effler and R. D. Hennigan, "Onondaga Lake, New York: Legacy of Pollution," *Lake and Reservoir Management* 12, no. 1 (1996), DOI: 10.1080/07438149609353992.

14. Matthew Liptak, "A Bunch of People Just Went Swimming in One of the US' Most Polluted Lakes for the First Time in 75 Years," *Business Insider*, July 23, 2015, https://www.businessinsider.com/r-swimmers-take-dip-in-long

-polluted-new-york-lake-to-hail-cleanup-2015–7; David Chanatry, "America's 'Most Polluted' Lake Finally Comes Clean," National Public Radio, July 31, 2012, https://www.npr.org/2012/07/31/157413747/americas-most-polluted -lake-finally-comes-clean.

15. Liptak, "A Bunch of People"; Chanatry, "America's Most Polluted."
16. "Superfund Site: Onondaga Lake Syracuse, NY," United States Environmental Protection Agency, accessed October 6, 2019, https://cumulis.epa.gov/super cpad/SiteProfiles/index.cfm?fuseaction=second.cleanup&id=0203382.
17. William Kates, "Honeywell Agrees on $451 Million Plan to Onondaga Lake in Syracuse," *Post Star*, October 12, 2006, https://poststar.com/news /honeywell-agrees-on-million-plan-to-onondaga-lake-in-syracuse/article _7213adc9–3965–5d44-a8aa-5a8d29b2f700.html; consultation with current and former Honeywell executives.
18. "Onondaga Lake," *New York State*, accessed October 9, 2019, https://www.dec .ny.gov/lands/72771.html#Revitalizing; Liliana Pearson, "Onondaga Lake Sees the Return of Threatened Bird Species," *NCC News*, July 28, 2017, https://nccnews.expressions.syr.edu/2017/07/28/onondaga-lake-sees-the -return-of-threatened-bird-species/; "Onondaga Lake Cleanup Progress," New York Department of Environmental Conservation, October 2017, https://content.govdelivery.com/attachments/NYSDEC/2017/10/23/file _attachments/901196/OL%2BProgress%2BFact%2BSheet%2B10.23.17 %2BFINAL.pdf.
19. Honeywell promotional video, untitled and unpublished.
20. Honeywell promotional video, untitled and unpublished.
21. Glenn Coin, "Onondaga Lake Cleanup, Decades in the Making, Will Be Done This Month," Syracuse.com, updated January 4, 2019, https://www .syracuse.com/news/index.ssf/2017/11/onondaga_lake_cleanup_decades_in _the_making_will_end_this_fall.html.
22. Glenn Coin, "Survey Asks: Would You Swim at an Onondaga Lake Beach?," Syracuse.com, updated January 15, 2019, https://www.syracuse.com/news /2019/01/survey-asks-would-you-swim-at-an-onondaga-lake-beach.html.

Chapter 4: Focus on Process

1. "From Bitter to Sweet," *Economist*, April 14, 2012, https://www.economist.com /business/2012/04/14/from-bitter-to-sweet.
2. "From Bitter to Sweet."
3. Shawn Tully, "How Dave Cote Got Honeywell's Groove Back," *Fortune*, May 14, 2012, http://fortune.com/2012/05/14/how-dave-cote-got-honeywells-groove-back/.

4. Joe DeSarla (manufacturing head of Honeywell's Automation and Control Solutions business unit), interview with author, November 5, 2018.

5. "Toyota Production System," *Toyota*, accessed October 8, 2019, https://www .toyota-global.com/company/vision_philosophy/toyota_production_system /origin_of_the_toyota_production_system.html.

6. Joe DeSarla, interview with the author, November 5, 2018.

7. "Honeywell Performance," *Annual Report* (2006): 10.

8. Joe DeSarla, interview with the author, November 5, 2018.

9. "Honeywell Performance," 17.

Chapter 5: Build a High-Performance Culture

1. Mark James, senior vice president of Human Resources, Security, and Communications at Honeywell, interview with the author, March 18, 2018.

2. Mark James, interview with the author, March 18, 2018.

3. Darius Adamczyk (CEO of Honeywell), interview with author, March 18, 2018.

Chapter 6: Get and Keep the Right Leaders—But Not Too Many of Them

1. William Oncken Jr. and Donald L. Wass, "Management Time: Who's Got the Monkey?" *Harvard Business Review*, November-December 1999 (reprint), https://hbr.org/1999/11/management-time-whos-got-the-monkey.

Chapter 7: Go Big on Growth

1. Tim Mahoney (president and CEO of Honeywell's Aerospace division), interview with author, November 12, 2018.

2. Dan Sheflin (chief technology officer and vice president of Honeywell's Automation and Control Solutions business), interview with author, March 12, 2019.

3. "CMMI Maturity Levels," *Tutorials Point*, accessed October 8, 2019, http://www.tutorialspoint.com/cmmi/cmmi-maturity-levels.htm.

4. "How Honeywell Found Success in China," interview with Shane Tedjarati, *Edward Tse* blog, March 10, 2016, http://www.edwardtseblog.com/view /gao-feng-viewpoint-how-honeywell-found-success-in-china/.

Chapter 8: Upgrade Your Portfolio

1. Roger L. Martin, "M&A: The One Thing You Need to Get Right," *Harvard Business Review*, June 2016, https://hbr.org/2016/06/ma-the-one-thing-you -need-to-get-right.

2. Roger Fradin, former vice chairman at Honeywell and president and CEO of its Automation and Controls Solutions business, interview with the author, February 25, 2019.
3. Roger Fradin, former vice chairman at Honeywell and president and CEO of its Automation and Controls Solutions business, interview with author, February 25, 2019, and October 24, 2018.

Chapter 9: Take Control of the Downturns

1. Jamie Dlugosch, "Recession Proof? Honeywell Runs a Tight Ship," *Investor Place*, February 2, 2009, https://investorplace.com/2009/02/recession-proof -stock-honeywell-runs-tight-ship/.
2. Sandra J. Sucher and Shalene Gupta, "Layoffs That Don't Break Your Company," *Harvard Business Review*, May–June 2018, https://hbr.org/2018 /05/layoffs-that-dont-break-your-company.
3. Mark James (senior vice president of Human Resources, Security, and Communications at Honeywell), interview with author, March 18, 2019.
4. "Lessons Learned from the Recession of 2008–2009," Honeywell internal white paper, November 2011.
5. Prior to the recession, 80 percent of employees viewed the company favorably, as compared with 78 percent in 2009: "Lessons Learned from the Recession of 2008–2009," Honeywell internal white paper, November 2011.
6. Mark James (Honeywell's head of Human Resources), interview with author, March 18, 2019.
7. Unpublished personal letter to future Honeywell CEOs concerning the Great Recession, July 13, 2011.

Chapter 10: Manage the Leadership Transition

1. "Honeywell's CEO Succession and Transition: Lessons Learned," unpublished white paper.
2. Darius Adamczyk (COO and CEO at Honeywell), interview with author, March 18, 2019.
3. Darius Adamczyk (COO and CEO at Honeywell), interview with author, November 2, 2018.
4. Darius Adamczyk (COO and CEO at Honeywell), interview with author, March 18, 2019.
5. Total shareholder return and market capitalization numbers are for the period between March 31, 2017, to July 2, 2019.

About the Author

David M. Cote is Executive Chairman of Vertiv Holdings Co, a global data center products and services provider, a member of the Aspen Economic Strategy Group, and on the Boards of the Council on Foreign Relations and the Conference of Montreal. Previously, as Chairman and CEO of the industrial giant Honeywell for 16 years, he grew the company's market capitalization from around $20 billion to nearly $120 billion, delivering returns of 800 percent and beating the S&P by nearly two and a half times.

In 2010, Cote was appointed by President Obama to serve on the bipartisan National Commission on Fiscal Responsibility and Reform, also known as the Simpson-Bowles Commission. In 2014, he was selected for the prestigious Horatio Alger Award, which recognizes dedicated community leaders who have accomplished remarkable achievements through honesty, hard work, self-reliance, and perseverance over adversity. And he has been recognized as one of the World's Best CEOs by *Barron's* for five straight years—2013-2017.

Drawing from his remarkable turnaround case study at Honeywell, *Winning Now, Winning Later* shows how to run any organization, division, or team, whether a non-profit or for profit, with a new kind of rigor and balance.